Best *of the* Best
from
America
Cookbook

★ ★ ★ ★ ★

*Preserving Our Nation's Food Heritage
One State at a Time*

In their trusty van, amidst clothes and clubs, coolers and cookers, books and music, and a whole lot of other "necessities," Barbara and Gwen have traveled fifty states in search of the best cookbooks and the best recipes in America.

Best *of the* Best *from* America Cookbook

★ ★ ★ ★ ★

*Preserving Our Nation's Food Heritage
One State at a Time*

EDITED BY
Gwen McKee
AND
Barbara Moseley

Illustrated by Tupper England

QUAIL RIDGE PRESS

Library of Congress Cataloging-in-Publication Data

Best of the best from America : preserving our nation's food her-
itage one state at a time : featuring "we did it!" The Story of How
Two Ladies Collected America's Best Recipes / edited by Gwen
McKee and Barbara Moseley.
      p. cm.
Includes index.
ISBN 1-893062-71-6
1. Cookery, American. I. McKee, Gwen. II. Moseley, Barbara.

TX715.B48563544 2005
641.5973—dc22   2004020321

Manufactured in the United States of America.
Book design by Cynthia Clark.
Cover photos by Greg Campbell. Inside photos courtesy of Gwen McKee.

On the cover: Seafood Chowder, page 119; Iowa Chops, page 85;
Oklahoma Pecan Pie, page 201.

QUAIL RIDGE PRESS
P. O. Box 123 • Brandon, MS 39043
info@quailridge.com • www.quailridge.com

Contents

PHOTO BY GREG CAMPBELL

Gwen and Barbara admit this is posed. "We're not nearly this neat when we're cooking. In fact, the flour is usually flying as fast as we are. But we truly love to cook, and you can usually find us in the kitchen . . . the heart of our homes."

Preface

Best of the Best from America Cookbook is a state-by-state sampling of the best recipes from the best cookbooks in the country. In this cookbook, we have chosen recipes from our BEST OF THE BEST STATE COOKBOOK SERIES that we felt represented each of the fifty states of our nation.

More than two decades ago, we set out on a journey to find out what people across America like to cook. Since the two of us have favorite recipes that are quite different—and we're from neighboring states (Louisiana and Mississippi)—we wondered, what are the favorite recipes and how are they different in Michigan and Arizona and Pennsylvania? We wanted to know what dishes are served for family meals, made for parties and tailgates, brought to church socials, etc. The pursuit of this goal proved to be an adventure of a lifetime. Not only did we discover extraordinary recipes, we met wonderful people and got a chance to visit a great portion of our beautiful country.

Best of the Best from America Cookbook includes a full color "We Did It!" section that tells the story of how we accomplished the task of finding the best recipes in each state. Included in this section are some personal reminiscences of our experiences related to developing the BEST OF THE BEST STATE COOKBOOKS. We have included travel stories that give accounts of some of our adventures along the way, things we found interesting or amusing to share about each state.

Everywhere we traveled, we asked about local fare and did our best to find it and taste it. Local cookbooks revealed best what people in that area cook, and often their stories attached to the recipes told us why. The authors and editors and chairwomen of these marvelous community cookbooks graciously gave us permission to share them. In exchange, we listed their cookbooks in a special "Catalog of Contributing Cookbooks" section in each of the BEST OF THE BEST STATE COOKBOOKS so that others could purchase a copy of their book.

Though we had a systematic approach to searching out cookbooks, we often "moved with the spirit," making unscheduled stops to check out local restaurants, libraries, and stores, always meeting people—our favorite part—who seemed happy to share their food or recipe or cookbook knowledge. We liked traveling the back roads. To catch a farmers' market open or a seasonal fruit stand meant we may be able to "taste the land." A handful of peaches from nearby orchards, a bag of sunflower seeds from surrounding sunflower fields, a jar of huckleberry jam, a stem of grapes, a basket of straw-berries . . . these were treats for us that came from the soil we traveled over—what a delight!

The short introduction on each state's page is meant to bring you into that state by giving just a little of its "personality." We also added tidbits of interest—historical facts, famous people, and sometimes just things we found humorous, and hope you will, too.

Though we are the compilers and editors of every book in the SERIES, it is the people all over the country—thousands of them—who are the creators of these hometown recipes. They wanted to share recipes that brought them pleasure, so that other people could enjoy them, too. It's like telling someone about a great book you read or a movie you've seen . . . it's so much more fun when others experience your joy.

We particularly wish to thank all the cookbook authors, committees, publishers, tourist agencies, chambers of commerce, shop managers, and wonderful people all over the country who helped us. Our talented artist Tupper England has illustrated every one of our BEST OF THE BEST STATE COOKBOOKS, and with her drawings has taken us visually into each state. Cyndi Clark brings our recipes to life with her lovely designs. Terresa Ray, our assistant, helps us bring it all together. The rest of our staff, Sheila Simmons, Annette Goode, Christy Campbell, Keena Grissom, Leona Tennison, Trey Moseley, and Melinda Burnham are our support team who continually work to make it all happen. Especially we are grateful to our families, who have encouraged us and are always there for us. Thank you all . . . sincerely.

Since 1982, we have endeavored to "preserve America's food heritage" in all fifty states. We have finally reached our goal. On behalf of all those who helped us all over America, we are so proud to say, "We did it!"

Gwen McKee and Barbara Moseley

Alabama

CAPITAL: *Montgomery*

NICKNAME: *The Heart of Dixie*

*S*outhern belles and antebellum houses, football and fishing, boiled peanuts and southern fried chicken.... You can embrace the past at the Shakespeare Festival in Montgomery and look into the future at Huntsville's Space and Rocket Center. Helen Keller was born in Tuscumbia. Dr. Martin Luther King began preaching in Montgomery. Baseball greats Hank Aaron and Willie Mays as well as Willie McCovey and Satchel Page were all from Alabama. And some of the best music you'll ever hear comes from one of our favorite bands, "Alabama." Among Alabama's many festivals, Gulf Shores hosts the Annual National Shrimp Festival in October, and Russellville has a watermelon festival in August. "Sweet Home, Alabama."

Southern Fried Chicken

Mama used to have the kids run down a chicken. She would chop or wring his neck off. The next step was to dip him in hot water, and then dress him for the frying pan. A chicken could be in the yard one hour, and on the table the next hour. As soon as "Thanks" was offered, everyone grabbed for the chicken plate to try and be lucky enough to get the breast or pulley bone. If company happened to be present, only the chicken gravy was left for the little folks. Fried chicken was a favorite dish for breakfast in those days.

½ cup all-purpose flour
1 teaspoon salt
¼ teaspoon pepper

2½–3 pound broiler-fryer
   chicken, cut up
Vegetable oil

Mix flour, salt, and pepper. Coat chicken with flour mixture. Heat oil (¼-inch in 12-inch skillet) over medium-high heat until hot. Cook chicken in oil until light brown on all sides for about 10 minutes; reduce heat. Cover tightly and simmer, turning once or twice, until thickest pieces are done, or about 35 minutes longer. (If skillet cannot be covered tightly, add 1–2 tablespoons water.) Remove cover during last 5 minutes of cooking to crisp chicken. Makes 6 servings.

Kum' Ona' Granny's Table

Belle Fontaine Crab Dip

2 (3-ounce) packages cream
  cheese, softened
1 very small onion, grated fine
Few dashes Worcestershire

1–2 dashes hot sauce
Salt and pepper to taste
4 tablespoons mayonnaise
1 pound crabmeat

Mix cream cheese and seasonings. Add crabmeat. Serve as hors d'oeuvre with crackers or vegetables, or stuff into tomatoes.

Recipe Jubilee!

Alabama Eggplant

1 large eggplant
¼ cup chopped onion
2 tablespoons parsley
1 (10¾-ounce) can cream of
  mushroom soup

1 teaspoon Worcestershire
½ teaspoon salt
⅛ teaspoon pepper
1 cup cracker crumbs, divided
2 tablespoons butter

Remove stem end of eggplant and cut in half lengthwise. Cut and remove inside pulp, being careful to leave ¼ inch inside the shell. Cook pulp about 10 minutes. Drain. Mix pulp with remaining ingredients, except butter, using enough cracker crumbs to make filling of stuffing consistency. Return eggplant to shells. Cover with remaining cracker crumbs. Dot with butter and put in baking dish with ½ inch boiling water. Bake at 375° for 30–35 minutes until set. Yields 6–8 servings.

Huntsville Entertains

Hot Fruit Compote

This is a very good accompaniment to ham or turkey.

1 cup (heaping) dried prunes, pitted
2 cups dried apricots
1½ cups pineapple chunks, undrained

1 (21-ounce) can cherry pie filling
½ cup sherry
1½ cups water

Combine prunes, apricots, and pineapple, and put in buttered baking dish. Combine cherry pie filling, sherry, and water, and pour over fruit. Cook at least one hour at 350°. Serve hot.

Treasured Alabama Recipes

Jeweled Buffet Ham

1 (8-ounce) can whole-berry cranberry sauce
1 (8-ounce) can jellied cranberry sauce
1 (8¼-ounce) can crushed pineapple, drained
1 (11-ounce) can Mandarin orange segments, drained

½ cup orange juice
1 teaspoon seasoned salt
½ teaspoon garlic powder
2–4 dashes Tabasco
1 (5- to 6-pound) fully cooked ham

Combine all ingredients except ham in a medium saucepan. Cook over low heat 15–20 minutes, stirring occasionally. May be refrigerated several days and reheated.

Have butcher slice ham into ¼-inch slices and tie in original shape. Preheat oven to 350°. Place ham in a shallow roasting pan. Bake one hour. Remove from oven. Pour off juices. Spoon enough fruit mixture over ham to coat well, mounding fruit generously on the top. Return ham to oven. Bake uncovered 30 minutes; baste occasionally with remaining fruit mixture. Place ham on serving platter. Cut and carefully remove strings. Serve any remaining fruit mixture with ham slices, if desired. Makes 10–12 servings.

Anniversary Collection of Delectable Dishes

French Onion Casserole

5 medium onions, sliced
5 tablespoons butter or
  margarine, divided
2 tablespoons all-purpose flour
Pepper to taste
1 cup beef bouillon

¼ cup dry sherry
1½ cups plain croutons
¼ cup shredded Swiss cheese
2 tablespoons grated Parmesan
  cheese

Cook onions in 3 tablespoons butter till tender. Blend in flour and dash of pepper. Add bouillon and sherry; cook and stir till thick and bubbly. Turn into 1-quart casserole; cover and chill. Toss croutons with remaining 2 tablespoons butter, melted. Bake casserole, covered, in 350° oven for 30 minutes. Sprinkle with buttered croutons, then cheeses. Bake uncovered, 5–10 minutes more. Serves 6.

Try Me

Fried Shrimp

Fresh shrimp
Lemon juice
Cayenne pepper
Flour seasoned with salt
  and pepper

Beaten egg
Cracker meal

Peel and devein shrimp and put in a bowl. Squeeze lemon juice over all and sprinkle with cayenne. Let sit for a half-hour. Dredge in seasoned flour. Let sit another half-hour. Dip in beaten egg and dredge in cracker meal. Fry in hot fat until golden brown, 3–5 minutes depending on size of shrimp. Drain on paper towels and serve with horseradish dressing, ketchup, or tartar sauce.

Recipe Jubilee!

The battleship *USS Alabama* survived many major World War II battles without sustaining damage by enemy fire. It is now a National Historic Landmark, and is open to the public at Battleship Memorial Park on Mobile Bay.

Coca Cola Cake

2 cups unsifted flour
2 cups sugar
2 sticks margarine
2 tablespoons cocoa
1 cup Coca Cola
½ cup buttermilk

2 unbeaten eggs
1 teaspoon baking soda
1 teaspoon vanilla
1½ cups miniature
   marshmallows

Combine sugar and flour in a bowl. Heat margarine, cocoa, and Coca Cola to boiling; pour over sugar and flour mixture. Mix well, then add buttermilk, eggs, baking soda, and vanilla. Mix well and add marshmallows floating on top. Bake in 9x13-inch pan for 35 minutes at 350°.

ICING:
1 stick butter
2 tablespoons cocoa
6 tablespoons Coca Cola

1 pound powdered sugar
1 cup chopped nuts

Combine butter, cocoa, and Coca Cola, and bring to a boil. Pour over powdered sugar. After beating well, add nuts and pour over hot cake.

More Fiddling with Food

Santa's Christmas Trifle

We aren't sure just why this is named Santa's Christmas Trifle, but it may be because making this is like a gift. Keep these ingredients on hand and you can whip up a great trifle in a very few minutes. Looks impressive, too!

1 frozen pound cake
¼ cup orange juice
1 (20-ounce) can apple pie filling
4 tablespoons raspberry jelly
  (or seedless preserves)

2 cups prepared vanilla
  pudding
1 (8-ounce) container Cool
  Whip
Toasted coconut for garnish

The bowl you choose for the trifle is very important because the effect is gained by seeing the layers of the trifle through glass. You could make an individual trifle serving by using a clear parfait or sherbet glass, but it is a lot more trouble. Arrange in layers. Cut ½ of cake into cubes. Sprinkle on orange juice, then ½ of pie filling, dot with all the jelly, and top with ½ the pudding. Repeat all these layers except jelly, which has all been used. Top with Cool Whip and garnish with toasted coconut.

Gazebo I Christmas Cookbook

Alaska

CAPITAL: *Juneau*

NICKNAME: *The Last Frontier*

*A*laska is our wild and wonderful frontier. So unspoiled, it is a land where nature's majestic beauty is everywhere. And it is huge—2½ times larger than Texas. It even has its own time zone. Did you know that it is farther from the Lower 48 than Hawaii, but only 55 miles from Russia? We bought it from Russia in 1867 for $7.2 million, which breaks down to about 2 cents an acre. Since there aren't that many roads for this huge territory, roughly one in every 58 Alaskans has a license to fly. The hunting and fishing and adventure is unequaled. More than 55% of the nation's total catch of fish and shellfish come from Alaska.

King Crab and Artichoke Dip

During one fishing season in Kodiak, we canned king crab legs, thinking that we would have the summer's abundance for winter feasting. Our family's over-indulgence of fresh crab had spoiled our enthusiasm for canned crab. Our very happy yellow Labrador dogs gobbled up the crab without complaint. Their beautiful, sleek coats at the end of the summer were testaments of the nutrients and value of the crabmeat. Two cans of crab legs ended up in our winter fish supply, and on Superbowl Sunday, I made this recipe. Everyone wished we had every can of crabmeat back!

1 (8-ounce) package low-fat
  cream cheese, softened
1 cup low-fat mayonnaise
1 cup crabmeat
⅓ cup chopped green onions

1 (13¾-ounce) can artichoke
  hearts, drained and chopped
½ cup shredded Parmesan
  cheese

Preheat oven to 375°. Blend cream cheese and mayonnaise in a bowl. Stir in all remaining ingredients. Spread evenly into an oven-proof baking dish. Bake uncovered for 15 minutes, until heated through and golden brown on top. Serve with sliced baguettes and cut vegetables such as carrots, celery, red bell peppers, and cucumbers.

Wild Alaska Seafood—Twice a Week

Bear Tracks

¾ cup peanut butter
¼ cup brown sugar
1 teaspoon vanilla
1 (14-ounce) can sweetened
  condensed milk

2 cups all-purpose baking mix
1 (4-ounce) package slivered
  almonds

Preheat oven to 350°. In a large bowl, combine peanut butter, brown sugar, vanilla, and condensed milk. Stir in baking mix. Shape dough into 1½-inch balls, and insert 5 almond slivers on the side of each cookie (claws). Place on ungreased cookie sheet and bake for 8–10 minutes. Makes about 2 dozen.

Moose Racks, Bear Tracks, and Other Alaska Kidsnacks

Vosie's Famous Iditarod Bean Stew

1 good ham bone for broth
6 cups water (more, if needed)
2 cups dried pinto beans
1 pound hamburger meat
1 cup ham pieces
1 or 2 hot sausages, sliced
1 green pepper, sliced
2 cloves garlic, chopped
1 cup chopped celery

1 medium onion, chopped
2 (14½ ounce) cans Italian-style
  stewed tomatoes, crushed
1 teaspoon smoke flavor
2 teaspoons sugar
1 teaspoon salt
1 teaspoon dried oregano
⅓ cup peanut butter

Boil ham bone in 6 cups water and prepare the beans (sort, wash, and soak). Brown hamburger, ham, and sausage in pan and remove from pan when done. Sauté green pepper, garlic, celery, and onion in the same pan and stir for 5 minutes.

  In a large pan with a heavy bottom (if it's not heavy, the bottom will burn), combine ham broth and beans and cook for 1 hour. Add meat, vegetables, crushed tomatoes, smoke flavor, sugar, salt, oregano, and additional water, if needed, to cover. Cook for 2 or more hours for thickness. About 15 minutes before done, add peanut butter. Cool slowly and stir often.

Simply the Best Recipes

Eskimo Ice Cream

Grate reindeer tallow into small pieces. Add seal oil slowly while beating with hand. After some seal oil has been used, then add a little water while whipping. Continue adding seal oil and water until white and fluffy. Any berries can be added to it.

Eskimo Cookbook

Editor's Note: The recipes from this cookbook are somewhat impractical to prepare, but are fascinating to read.

Grilled Cedar Planked King Salmon

Southeast Alaskan natives long ago discovered the wonderful flavors that result when smoking and cooking seafood with wood. Cedar or alder are traditional favorites.

Grilling plank	½ teaspoon each, salt and
2 king salmon steaks	pepper
1 tablespoon olive oil	Juice of 1 fresh lemon

Soak plank in water for at least 30 minutes. Lightly coat salmon with olive oil. Sprinkle both sides with salt and pepper. Place salmon on grilling plank and set on grill over indirect heat. Grill for approximately 20 minutes, or until internal temperature reaches 145°.

Tip: Cover salmon with the grill lid or make a foil lid which will trap in and surround the salmon with more smoke.

Wild Alaska Seafood—Twice a Week

 A 97-pound, 4-ounce giant king salmon caught in the Kenai River was the largest ever caught in Alaska. The giant king salmon is the Alaska state fish.

Sea Otter Biscuits

1 (18¼-ounce) box chocolate
  cake mix
½ cup oil

2 eggs
1 cup chocolate chips

Preheat oven to 375°. In a large bowl, combine cake mix, oil, and eggs, stirring until blended. Stir in chocolate chips. Drop by tea-spoonfuls onto ungreased cookie sheets. Bake 8–10 minutes. Cool completely before removing from cookie sheet. Makes 3 dozen.

Moose Racks, Bear Tracks, and Other Alaska Kidsnacks

Individual Baked Alaska

1 sponge cake or pound cake

Vanilla or strawberry ice cream

Cut cake into 4- or 5-inch rounds ½ inch thick. Place cut cake on wooden plank or foil-lined cookie sheet. Top each round with a scoop of ice cream, centering so a ½-inch rim of cake remains. Cover light-ly with wax paper and place in freezer until needed (up to 3 days) and Meringue is made.

MERINGUE:
3 egg whites
¼ teaspoon cream of tartar

⅓ cup superfine sugar

Whip egg whites and cream of tartar until stiff; gradually adding sugar, continue to beat until very stiff peaks form. Heat oven to 450°. Remove cakes from freezer and quickly frost completely with Meringue. Bake in hot oven about 5 minutes, or until light brown all over. With spatula, remove to serving dishes. Drizzle with Raspberry Topping. Also good with strawberry, blueberry, or rhubarb sauce.

RASPBERRY TOPPING:
1½ cups raspberries, fresh or
  thawed
¼ cup sugar

¼ cup orange liqueur or juice
1 tablespoon cornstarch

Place in small saucepan. Cook over low heat until thickened. Cool.

A Cook's Tour of Alaska

Editor's Extra: If using a frozen pound cake, slice in thirds lengthwise. Using the bottom of a coffee or nut can as a guide, cut circle shapes in cake with a serrated knife to make six rounds.

Wood Stove Stew

Put all the ingredients in a Dutch oven in the order given; put the lid on, put it on your wood stove and go chop wood or work in your garden—that's more fun!

1 (10-ounce) can beef broth
1 (28-ounce) can whole or
  stewed tomatoes
1½ pounds trimmed moose
  roast, cut in 1-inch chunks
  (well, beef will do!)
1 onion, chopped
4 carrots, peeled and cut in
  large chunks
1 medium potato, cut in
  bite-size pieces

2 ribs celery, cut in bite-size
  pieces
1 tablespoon Worcestershire
2 tablespoons parsley
1 bay leaf
1 teaspoon garlic salt
¼ teaspoon pepper
2 tablespoons quick-cooking
  tapioca to thicken (or you can
  stir 2 tablespoons flour into
  the beef broth)

Put lid on and set on hottest part of stove and let simmer for 6 hours or until you get the wood chopped or the garden weeded. Serve with homemade bread, real butter, and dill pickles.

Note: If you don't have beef broth, you can use water or even, in a pinch, steal a can of your husband's beer.

Grannie Annie's Cookin' on the Wood Stove

FROM GWEN'S ROAD DIARY:
Barbara and I made separate trips to Alaska with our husbands. Barney and I were fortunate to catch the State Fair in Palmer. We were aghast at the vegetables that grew so huge in the long summer sun. We were told that the zucchini grows so well and fast you might find a bushel of it on your doorstep, usually as a joke from your neighbor who can't get rid of his either! While there, I chatted with a young TV reporter asking his opinion about Alaskan foods, fairs, etc., and I was soon on the air with my request for community cookbooks. When Barbara and her husband, Lonnie, returned the next summer, she was so tickled to be asked to sign books for happy customers all along the way. Alaska is so beautiful . . . so far away, but still in the good ole U.S.A.

Custard Igloo or Lemon Snow

2 tablespoons unflavored
  gelatin (2 envelopes)
½ cup cold water
2 cups very hot water
2 cups sugar

½ cup lemon juice
6 egg whites, beaten stiff
  (reserve 4 yolks for Custard
  Sauce)
1 tablespoon grated lemon rind

In a large mixing bowl, soften gelatin in cold water; dissolve in hot water. Add sugar and stir until completely dissolved. Add lemon juice. Chill until partially set, or consistency of unbeaten egg whites (usually about 2 hours).

Beat until frothy (about 2 minutes), then fold in beaten egg whites. Beat until gelatin will hold its shape (another 2 minutes); fold in lemon rind. Pour into mold and chill until firm. For "Custard Igloo" use round bowl for mold. When set, invert pudding to serving plate (use thin knife around edge, if necessary to loosen) which is several inches larger than bowl. Make ice block lines with thick Custard Sauce or pour sauce over. Serve with extra sauce.

CUSTARD SAUCE:
4 slightly beaten egg yolks
Dash of salt
5 tablespoons sugar

2 cups scalded milk
1 teaspoon vanilla

In top of double boiler, combine egg yolks, salt, and sugar. Gradually stir in scalded milk. Cook over gently boiling water until mixture coats spoon, stirring constantly (usually 2–3 minutes). Remove from heat, and stir in vanilla. Chill thoroughly.

A Cook's Tour of Alaska

Editor's Extra: This makes four igloos, so half a recipe is plenty for an average dessert.

Barney and Gwen are amazed at the size of Alaska's king crabs.

Arizona

CAPITAL: *Phoenix*

NICKNAME: *The Grand Canyon State*

*A*rizona's strongest economic support came from the four C's: cotton, copper, cattle, and citrus. In recent years, a fifth—climate—has been added. Rolling mountain ranges, sparkling rivers, and lush grasslands . . . yes, we're talking about Arizona! The Grand Canyon State is fertile ground for beef and dairy products, as well as a variety of fruits and vegetables. Of course, there are countless cactuses (is that a sixth C?) and many miles of arid deserts. Arizona, among all the states, has the largest percentage of its land set aside and designated as Indian lands. And there are ghost towns; Tombstone, Ruby, Gillette, and Gunsight are among the ones scattered throughout the state. The indescribable grandeur of the spectacular Grand Canyon is something the whole world comes to see. And Arizona has the original London Bridge! It was shipped stone-by-stone and reconstructed in Lake Havasu City. Guess what the official state neckwear is . . . the bola tie, of course.

Loaded Nachos

1 (8-ounce) bag tortilla chips
1 (15-ounce) can black beans
1 (4-ounce) can chopped green
  chiles, or 2 tablespoons
  chopped jalapeños

1 small tomato, chopped
½ pound pepper Jack or
  Sonoma Jack cheese,
  shredded
1 cup sour cream (optional)

Preheat broiler. Layer chips onto 2 (10x15-inch) jellyroll pans. Sprinkle with drained beans, chiles, and chopped tomato. Cover evenly with cheese. Place under broiler for 3–5 minutes. Remove from oven and serve immediately with a dab of sour cream on top of each loaded chip, if desired. Makes 3 or 4 dinner-size servings, or several more servings as a snack.

Chips, Dip, & Salsas

Green Chile Cornbread

1 (16-ounce) can creamed corn
1 egg, beaten
1/2 cup cornmeal
1/2 teaspoon garlic salt
1/4 cup salad oil

1/4 teaspoon baking powder
1 (4-ounce) can diced green
  chiles
1/3 pound grated longhorn
  cheese, divided

Mix all ingredients together, except for 2 handfuls of cheese. Pour into greased casserole dish (the flatter, the better). Sprinkle remaining cheese on top. Bake at 350° for 40 minutes or so. Recipe can easily be doubled, tripled, etc. But, if using a deep dish, allow extra baking time. Serves 4.

Padre Kino's Favorite Meatloaf

Breakfast Chimichangas

2 2/3 cups ricotta cheese
3 (8-ounce) packages cream
  cheese, softened
2 egg yolks
3/4 cup sugar
2 teaspoons grated lemon rind

1 teaspoon cinnamon
1 tablespoon vanilla
16 (8-inch) flour tortillas
Melted butter
Fresh strawberries, peaches,
  or blueberries for topping

Combine cheeses, egg yolks, sugar, rind, cinnamon, and vanilla. Mix well. Soften tortillas and place 1/16 amount of filling on each tortilla. Fold 2 sides in and over to enclose filling. Brush top with melted butter. Bake on cooking sheet at 350° for about 20 minutes until light brown. Serve topped with fresh fruit. These can be prepared ahead and frozen. Makes 16 servings.

What's Cooking Inn Arizona

Gazpacho

5 small cans Snap-E-Tom Tomato
  Juice Cocktail, divided
1 tablespoon sugar
¼ cup fresh lemon juice
¼ cup olive oil
4 or 5 cloves garlic, crushed
1 teaspoon salt
⅛ teaspoon white pepper

Tabasco to taste
1 medium-size tomato,
  chopped
3 tablespoons chopped
  Bermuda onion
½ medium cucumber, coarsely
  chopped

Put 2 cans of the juice and the other ingredients in blender or food processor, and liquefy. Add remaining juice and blend. Refrigerate 24 hours. Offer garnishes of diced tomato (squeeze out pulp), Bermuda onion, green pepper, cucumber, and croutons to pass. Makes 12 first-course portions.

Coronado's Favorite Trail Mix

Jicama Strawberry Salad

1 pound fresh spinach
1 head Bibb lettuce, torn
1 pint fresh strawberries, sliced

¼ cup chopped, toasted pecans
1 medium jicama, peeled and
  cut in julienne slices

Combine salad ingredients. May add papaya, mango, and kiwi, if desired.

DRESSING:
⅓ cup raspberry vinegar
⅓ cup sugar
1 tablespoon poppy seeds

2 teaspoons finely minced
  onion
¼ cup canola oil

Mix Dressing. Add to salad ingredients. Mix together. Serves 8.

Vistoso Vittles II

How big is the Grand Canyon? Counted in river miles, it is 277 miles long. The width is as much as 18 miles and the deepest point is 6,000 vertical feet from rim to river. A trip to the bottom of the Canyon and back (on foot or by mule) is a two-day journey. Rim-to-rim hikers generally take three days one-way to get from the North Rim to the South Rim. A trip through the Grand Canyon by raft can take two weeks or longer.

Calabacitas
(Sautéed Squash)

1 pound zucchini squash (or
  combined zucchini and summer
  squash), sliced lengthwise
  and cut into ½-inch pieces
½ onion, chopped
1 tablespoon olive oil

2 large tomatoes, diced
6 ounces green chiles
1 cup corn
Salt to taste
1 cup grated Cheddar cheese

Sauté squash and onion in oil, then add tomatoes, chiles, and corn. Salt to taste. When squash is tender, add cheese and continue cooking until cheese melts. Serves 6–8.

Corazón Contento

Pat's Arizona Chocolate Turtle Cheesecake

3 cups chocolate cookie crumbs
5 tablespoons melted margarine
14 ounces caramels
  (approximately 51)
5 ounces evaporated milk
½ cup chopped, toasted
  Arizona nuts (walnuts)

2 (8-ounce) packages cream
  cheese, softened
½ cup sugar
1 teaspoon vanilla
2 large eggs
½ cup semisweet chocolate
  pieces, melted

Combine crumbs and margarine. Press into sides and bottom of 9-inch springform pan. Bake 10 minutes at 350°.

In heavy pan, melt caramels with milk over low heat. Stir frequently until smooth. It takes a while. (They scorch easily; don't get on the phone.) Pour over crust and top with nuts. Combine cream cheese, sugar, and vanilla. Mix at medium speed on electric mixer until well blended. Add eggs, one at a time, mixing well. Blend in chocolate. Pour over nut-topped crust. Bake 40 minutes at 350°. When done, the top will crack gently at the outside edge. Take out of the oven. Do not overbake. Loosen cake from rim of pan. Chill. Garnish with whipped cream, if desired. Serves 8–12.

Outdoor Cooking

Nanaimo Bars

½ cup butter
¼ cup sugar
1 square unsweetened chocolate
1 teaspoon vanilla
1 egg, beaten
2 cups graham cracker crumbs
½ cup chopped walnuts or
  almonds
1 cup flaked coconut

½ cup butter, softened
2 tablespoons instant vanilla
  pudding
3 tablespoons milk
2 cups powdered sugar
1 tablespoon butter
4 squares semisweet chocolate
⅔ cup chocolate chips

Melt first 4 ingredients together in a double boiler. To this mixture, add egg. Cook 5 minutes, then mix in graham cracker crumbs, nuts, and coconut. Press into 8x8-inch pan. Chill 15 minutes.

Cream together ½ cup butter, vanilla pudding, milk, and powdered sugar. Spread over graham cracker mixture and chill 15 minutes. In double boiler, melt last 3 ingredients and spread over entire mixture. Chill until easy to cut.

Red, White & Blue Favorites

FROM GWEN'S ROAD DIARY:
In the early days before email, cell phones, calling cards, and fax machines, it was sometimes a bit scary out there so far from home. We rarely made reservations . . . we just struck out! One of us called home each night to let our families know where we were. One call sent us home immediately—Barbara's house caught on fire! (Just smoke damage, thank goodness.) We always left cooked meals with taped instructions, and depended on Dad taking care of kids . . . and kids taking care of Dad. "I think they like us to go . . . at least for a while. It makes them more independent. Thank goodness they are always as happy to see us come home as we are to get there!"

Arkansas

CAPITAL: *Little Rock*

NICKNAME: *The Natural State*

The Ozark National Forest covers more than one million beautiful acres. Arkansas contains six national park sites, and six national scenic byways. America's only national park located in a city, Hot Springs is famous for its healing waters from thermal springs. Forty-seven hot springs flow from the southwestern slope of Hot Springs Mountain, at an average temperature of 143 degrees. Preserving the pioneer way of life, Mountain View is called the Folk Music Capital of America. It is one of the largest producers of handmade dulcimers in the world. The Great Passion Play is America's #1 attended outdoor drama, and is performed on a multi-level staging area from April to October in Eureka Springs. Though cotton was once king, the flat, fertile land was perfect for growing soybeans and rice. Now more rice is grown in Arkansas than in any other state. And talk about world-record watermelons—one weighed in at 260 pounds!

Company's Comin' Cornbread

2 tablespoons shortening
1 cup buttermilk or sweet milk
2 eggs
2 tablespoons honey
½ cup chopped onions
1 (2-ounce) jar pimentos, drained
1 (16-ounce) can whole-kernel
  corn, drained
1 (4-ounce) can chopped green
  chile peppers, or about ½ cup
  pickled peppers, chopped
1 cup yellow cornmeal
1 cup white flour
1 teaspoon salt
1 teaspoon baking soda
1 cup grated cheese

Place shortening in a 10- or 12-inch cast-iron (or heavy-weight) skillet and place in oven while preheating oven to 350°. Stir together liquid ingredients and combine with dry, reserving cheese to fold in as the last step. When oven is preheated and skillet sizzling hot, pour mixture in and bake for 1 hour.

Arkansas Celebration Cookbook

Mousse au Chocolate

Incredible!

¼ pound butter
4 bars German sweet chocolate
6 eggs, separated
6 tablespoons white corn syrup

1 cup sugar
¼ cup water
2 cups whipped cream
Shaved chocolate for garnish

Place butter and chocolate in a double boiler and melt slowly. Set aside and cool. Beat egg yolks until thick and creamy. In saucepan, heat corn syrup, sugar, and water until it spins 8-inch thread, or 232°–234° on a candy thermometer. Pour (slowly) hot syrup into egg yolks, beating constantly with electric mixer. Add melted chocolate and butter. Fold in stiffly beaten egg whites. Chill for 2 hours.

Beat furiously. Fold in whipped cream. Chill for at least 4 hours before serving. Serve in parfait glasses with shaved chocolate for garnish.

Nibbles Ooo La La

Chicken and Dumplings

Delicious!

1 large fryer or 4 breasts
1 tablespoon salt

3 tablespoons butter

Boil chicken in 2 quarts of water, to which salt and butter have been added, until tender. Remove chicken; strain, and reserve broth. Remove skin of chicken and bone. Cut meat into large pieces.

DUMPLINGS:

1 egg, slightly beaten
¼ teaspoon salt
2 tablespoons butter

1 cup chicken broth (cooled)
2 cups flour

Mix egg, salt, butter, and broth together. Add flour, mixing with a fork, a small amount at a time. Knead in flour until a stiff dough is formed. Roll out very thin. Cut in strips. Bring chicken broth to a boil. Pull apart and stretch strips of dough as you drop into broth. Reduce heat and cook about 10 minutes (covered), stirring occasionally. Add cut-up chicken to dumplings and enjoy! Serves 8–10.

A Great Taste of Arkansas

Fresh Raspberry and Peach Shortcake Supreme

Light, pretty, and refreshing summer dessert.

1 (9x5-inch) loaf angel food cake, cut in half lengthwise
⅓ cup naturally sweet fruit spread
3 fresh peaches, skinned, sliced thin, and soaked in ½ cup orange juice

1 pint fresh red raspberries
1 (8-ounce) carton whipped topping

Place bottom piece of cake on serving platter. Spread with fruit spread. Drain peach slices from orange juice and pat dry using paper towels. Reserve orange juice for another use. Layer half the peach slices over fruit spread. Place half the raspberries over peach slices. Spread ⅓ cup whipped topping over fruit. Set second (top) layer of cake over fruit, with cut-side-down. Ice entire assembled cake with whipped topping. Arrange remaining peach slices and raspberries in a row on the top. Serve within 15 minutes of assembling. Cut at the table, so this presentation can be enjoyed. Serves 4–6.

A Kaleidoscope of Creative Healthy Cooking

In Hot Springs, Gwen and Barbara take a break from research to see what the hot baths are all about. When in Rome . . .

Oven-Poached Rainbow Trout with Cucumber-Dill Cloud

Rainbow trout is one of our guests' all-time favorite entrées. Partly this is because we serve it only when we can get it really fresh-fresh. There are those who still like their trout dipped in milk, rolled in cornmeal, and pan-fried, a classic Ozark treatment, but we prefer the sweet and delicate flavor of this oven-poached trout. With white wine for a poaching liquid and a grated cucumber and fresh dill garnish, this recipe fairly sparkles.

CUCUMBER-DILL CLOUD:

½ cup sour cream
¼ cup plain yogurt
1 teaspoon soy sauce

1 tablespoon minced fresh dill,
  or 1 teaspoon dried
¼ cup finely grated cucumber

Blend together well, preferably several hours in advance so flavors have a chance to marry.

4 small rainbow trout, about
  10 ounces each
½ cup white wine

1 cup water
Juice of 2 lemons
Paprika

Preheat oven to 325°. Wash and pat dry the rainbow trout; place them in a buttered baking dish and pour over them the wine and water; sprinkle with lemon juice and paprika.

Bake for 35–40 minutes, or until fish is firm to the touch and flakes easily with a fork.

Gently spoon Cucumber-Dill Cloud over each trout and serve, garnished with a large sprig of fresh parsley. A tomato provençal and a heap of tiny steamed and buttered new potatoes works very well with this, as with so many fish dishes. Serves 4.

The Dairy Hollow House Cookbook

Eureka Springs, named for the 63 springs found there, is a charming village etched into the mountainside. It has been called Little Switzerland of America, the Stairstep Town, and the Town That Water Built. A real getaway from the hustle and bustle—there are no traffic lights. "Eureka" means "I have found it."

Franke's of Little Rock
Egg Custard Pie

2 tablespoons butter, softened
1 cup less 3 tablespoons sugar
Dash of salt

6 eggs, divided
1 pint and 2 tablespoons milk
1 unbaked pie shell

Cream butter, sugar, and salt by using medium speed on electric mixer. Add 3 eggs; beat one minute; change to high speed and add remaining 3 eggs. Beat 3 minutes. Remove from mixer and add milk. Pour into uncooked crust and cook 10 minutes at 450°. Turn heat down to 325° and bake 25 minutes longer or until set. If desired, sprinkle top with nutmeg just before baking.

Crossett Cook Book

Marinated Duck Breasts

4 boneless duck breasts
½ cup Italian dressing
1 tablespoon Worcestershire
Juice of 1 lemon

¼ teaspoon garlic powder
¼ teaspoon ground cloves
Bacon slices

Soak duck in salt water for 3 hours. Remove from water and drain on paper towels; pat dry and place in shallow pan. Combine Worcestershire, lemon juice, garlic powder, and cloves; pour over duck breasts and marinate for 4 hours. Wrap each breast in bacon and secure with toothpick. Cook on grill over a slow fire 7 minutes per side, or until bacon is done.

The Farmers Daughters

California

CAPITAL: *Sacramento*

NICKNAME: *The Golden State*

California is the Golden State . . . the beautiful land of golden opportunities. Maybe that's why over 35 million people live there—more than in any other state. There is so much bounty there that it can be said it is the fruit plate, the salad bowl, the fish net, the wine glass . . . perhaps the dinner plate of the world. California is fascinating: Did you know that the giant Hollywood sign originally said Hollywoodland? And the Golden Gate Bridge has enough concrete poured into its piers and anchorages to pave a five-foot sidewalk from New York to San Francisco? Or that Marilyn Monroe was the Artichoke Queen in 1947? From the newest in high tech to the latest in entertainment, California is forever fascinating.

California Tri-Tip

Tri-tip is California's own cut of beef and a common name for the triangle tip, part of the bottom sirloin. Barbecued whole is a popular way to serve tri-tip, which is smaller than most roasts we're accustomed to seeing in markets.

2 whole beef tri-tips (2 pounds each)
1¼ cups beef broth
⅔ cup lime juice
½ cup olive oil

2 tablespoons dried cumin
2 tablespoons dried coriander
5 garlic cloves, minced
Vegetable oil
Salt and freshly ground pepper

Remove all fat from tri-tips. Make marinade by whisking broth with lime juice, olive oil, cumin, coriander, and garlic until well blended. Place tri-tips in glass baking dish. Pour marinade over beef and cover. Refrigerate at least 6 hours, no longer than 24.

Remove tri-tips from marinade. Barbecue over medium-hot coals, turning occasionally, about 1 hour for medium-rare or until desired doneness. Use a meat thermometer or instant-read thermometer to be certain meat is cooked the way you want it. Brush meat with oil frequently while barbecuing. To serve, cut across the grain into thin slices; season with salt and pepper. Yields 12 servings.

Jan Townsend Going Home

Hollywood Black Mint Cheesecake

This luscious cheesecake, laced with subtle chocolate mint flavor, is a real show-stopper at the end of an elegant dinner party.

CRUST:

8½ ounces chocolate wafers

⅓ cup unsalted butter, melted and cooled

Generously butter a 9-inch springform pan. Break chocolate wafers into a food processor and pulse until fine crumbs form. Add melted butter and pulse until just blended. Press crumb mixture onto bottom and 2 inches up sides of the prepared pan. Refrigerate. (Can be prepared a day ahead.)

CHOCOLATE:

1½ cups mint chocolate chips, divided

3 tablespoons water

1 tablespoon crème de menthe

Preheat oven to 325° and position oven rack in lower third of oven. Place 1¼ cups mint chocolate chips together with water in microwave-safe bowl; microwave on MEDIUM setting until melted, approximately 1½ minutes in 30-second increments. Blend in crème de menthe. Spoon chocolate mixture over bottom of Crust, using back of a spoon to spread evenly. Set aside.

FILLING:

1½ pounds cream cheese, room temperature

1¼ cups sugar

4 large eggs

2 teaspoons vanilla extract

2 cups sour cream

Place cream cheese in large bowl. Using a mixer, mix for 30 seconds until smooth and creamy. Add sugar in a steady stream, mixing for about 1½ minutes. Mixing on low speed, add eggs, vanilla, and sour cream, blending well. Pour the Filling over the Chocolate, starting around the sides and then filling in the middle. Bake for 50 minutes. At end of 50 minutes, turn oven off and leave cake in oven for an additional hour without opening oven door. Remove from oven.

Chop remaining ¼ cup chocolate mint chips and sprinkle evenly on surface of warm cake. Cool on rack for 3 hours, then refrigerate for at least 24 hours before serving. To serve, run a thin knife around edge of pan and carefully remove the rim. Serve in wedges. Serves 10–12.

California Sizzles

Almond Roca

2 cups butter
4 cups superfine sugar
2 cups whole almonds
4 cups semisweet chocolate
  chips, divided

2 cups finely ground walnuts,
  divided

Melt butter in heavy saucepan over medium heat. Add sugar, stirring vigorously. Cook until caramel in color (or to 270° on candy thermometer), stirring constantly. Add almonds. Cook until medium brown in color (or to 290° on candy thermometer), stirring constantly. Pour onto buttered baking sheet. Top with 2 cups chocolate chips, spreading evenly. Sprinkle half the walnuts on top. Chill until set.

Turn candy over. Melt 2 cups chocolate chips; spread over candy. Sprinkle with remaining walnuts. Let stand until set. Break into pieces. Yields 32 pieces.

California Gold

Italian Frangelico Pie

PIE CRUST:
1½ packages Pepperidge Farm
  hazelnut cookies

½ stick sweet butter, softened

Crush cookies in a blender or by hand. Mix in butter with hands until mixture is uniform in texture. Press into 12-inch pie plate with spoon.

FILLING:
16 ounces white chocolate chips
  (dark will do nicely, but
  changes the color)
2 (15-ounce) packages ricotta
  cheese

4 ounces Frangelico liqueur
  (hazelnut flavored)
Chopped nuts for garnish
Chocolate curls for garnish

Melt white chocolate chips in double boiler. Put ricotta cheese and liqueur in blender. Blend, adding melted chocolate to cheese mixture as it is blending. Pour into pie shell. Chill. Top with chopped nuts and shaved chocolate curls.

The Coastal Cook of West Marin

Coconut Orange Chicken in a Crock

Super easy, really good.

3 pounds chicken pieces, skin
  removed
2 teaspoons grated fresh ginger,
  or ½ teaspoon ground
1 teaspoon salt
⅛ teaspoon pepper
1 (6-ounce) can frozen orange
  juice concentrate

1 (11-ounce) can Mandarin
  oranges
2 tablespoons cornstarch
1 tablespoon lite soy sauce
1 tablespoon brown sugar
½ cup shredded coconut
2 green onions, chopped
  (optional)

Spray inside of crockpot with nonstick cooking spray. Put chicken, ginger, salt, pepper, and frozen orange juice in crockpot and cook 6–8 hours on LOW.

Put meat on a beautiful serving platter and keep warm by covering with foil.

Drain oranges, reserving juice. Put juice from oranges and juice from chicken in a saucepan. Whisk in cornstarch, soy sauce, and brown sugar. Bring to a boil. Stir until thickened.

Pour some sauce over chicken in serving dish. Arrange oranges around chicken. Sprinkle with coconut and green onions, if desired. Pass remaining sauce at table. Yields 4–6 servings.

The 7 Day Cookbook

Sun-Dried Tomatoes & Artichoke Pasta

1 (12- to 16-ounce) package
  mostaccioli pasta
2 tablespoons olive oil
1 medium onion, chopped
2–4 cloves garlic, chopped
1 (14-ounce) can artichoke hearts
  in water, drained

1 (8-ounce) jar sun-dried
  tomatoes in oil
½ cup bread crumbs
½ cup chopped fresh parsley,
  or ¼ cup dried
1 cup pasta water
Parmesan cheese

Cook pasta. While pasta is cooking, heat oil in large skillet; add onion and garlic. Cook until onion is soft; add artichokes, sun-dried tomatoes, bread crumbs, and parsley; heat through. Add 2 ladles of water that pasta is cooking in, to artichoke mixture. Drain pasta and add to artichoke mixture. Transfer to serving dish; sprinkle with Parmesan cheese. Serves 10.

Tasty Temptations

Stardust Pesto Cheesecake

PESTO AND WINE SAUCE:

1 cup fresh basil leaves
⅓ cup grated Parmesan cheese
¼ cup fresh parsley leaves
¼ cup olive oil

2 tablespoons pine nuts
¼ cup dry white wine
½ cup chopped roasted red
  bell peppers (jarred)

Combine first 5 ingredients in a food processor; purée until smooth. In small saucepan, heat wine just until warm. Remove from heat. Stir in pesto and bell peppers; set aside.

PESTO CHEESECAKE:

½ cup pasta stars, cooked
1 tablespoon butter, softened
¼ cup bread crumbs, lightly
  toasted
½ cup plus 2 tablespoons
  freshly grated Parmesan
  cheese, divided
2 (8-ounce) packages light cream
  cheese, softened

1 cup ricotta cheese
¼ teaspoon salt
⅛ teaspoon cayenne pepper
3 large eggs (room
  temperature)
¼ cup pine nuts
Sprigs of fresh basil
2 fanned strawberries (garnish)

Cook pasta stars according to directions; drain; cool and set aside. Spread butter over bottom and side of 9-inch springform pan. In a small bowl, combine bread crumbs and 2 tablespoons Parmesan cheese. Coat the prepared pan; set aside.

In a large mixing bowl, beat cream cheese, ricotta cheese, ½ cup Parmesan cheese, salt, and cayenne pepper until light and fluffy. Add eggs, one at a time, beating well after each addition. Spoon ½ of the mixture into another bowl; stir in pasta stars. Add ½ cup pesto to remaining half and mix well. Spoon pesto mixture into prepared pan; smooth top. Spread cheese-star mixture evenly over the top; garnish with pine nuts.

Bake at 375° for 45 minutes. Cool on rack. Chill, tightly covered, for 8–10 minutes. Run knife around pan; remove side. Transfer to serving platter. Garnish with basil and fanned strawberries. Serve with wheat crackers. Makes 10–12 servings.

Fair's Fare

California produces some of the finest wines in the world. There are over 800 wineries and some 4,400 grape growers . . . and counting.

Steamed Artichokes
with Garlic Mayonnaise

4 large artichokes	1 bay leaf
½ lemon (juice only)	2 garlic cloves

Cut artichokes ½-inch from top cone and clip leaf tips. Squeeze juice from lemon over artichokes. Steam in 1 inch of boiling water, with bay leaf and garlic cloves, for 30 minutes. Remove and drain by holding artichoke upside down and squeezing. Place on serving dish and fan leaves out around the plate. Serve hot or cold with Pisto's Garlic Mayonnaise. Serves 4.

PISTO'S GARLIC MAYONNAISE:

2 eggs*	2 garlic cloves
Salt and pepper to taste	½ teaspoon tomato paste
1 teaspoon lemon juice	Pinch of saffron
1 teaspoon red wine vinegar	½ cup light olive oil
½ teaspoon dry mustard	

Place all ingredients except oil in a food processor. Process for 8 seconds. With machine running, slowly drizzle oil into mixture. Blend until thick. Chill for 1 hour. Spoon mayonnaise into center of each artichoke. Makes 1 cup.

*For those people concerned about raw eggs, pasteurized liquid eggs or pasteurized liquid egg whites can usually be successfully substituted.

Monterey's Cookin' Pisto Style

Chili Cheese Shrimp

16 ounces cream cheese, softened	½ cup sliced green onions
2 tablespoons Worcestershire	⅛ teaspoon Tabasco
¼ teaspoon grated lemon peel	12 ounces bottled chili sauce
1 tablespoon lemon juice	1 tablespoon horseradish
	12 ounces small shrimp, cooked

In a bowl, beat first 6 ingredients together until smooth. Spread into bottom of a shallow one-quart dish. Mix chili sauce and horseradish. Spread this over cream cheese mixture. Top with shrimp. Serve cold with crackers.

The Lafayette Collection

Colorado

CAPITAL: *Denver*

NICKNAME: *The Centennial State*

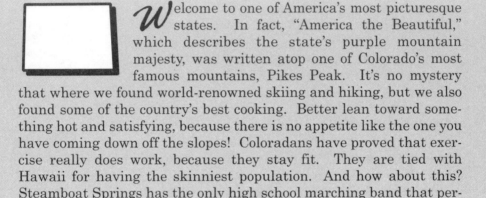

*W*elcome to one of America's most picturesque states. In fact, "America the Beautiful," which describes the state's purple mountain majesty, was written atop one of Colorado's most famous mountains, Pikes Peak. It's no mystery that where we found world-renowned skiing and hiking, but we also found some of the country's best cooking. Better lean toward something hot and satisfying, because there is no appetite like the one you have coming down off the slopes! Coloradans have proved that exercise really does work, because they stay fit. They are tied with Hawaii for having the skinniest population. And how about this? Steamboat Springs has the only high school marching band that performs on skis!

Ranch Biscuits

Biscuits that are light and high, but rich in flavor. Easily put together in the morning. Pat them out on floured wax paper to toss away the mess.

2 cups unbleached flour
4 teaspoons baking powder
2 teaspoons sugar
1 teaspoon salt
½ teaspoon cream of tartar

½ cup cold butter, cut into
  1-inch cubes
⅔ cup plus 2–3 tablespoons
  half-and half

Preheat oven to 450°. Combine flour, baking powder, sugar, salt, and cream of tartar in food processor bowl. Add butter and process until mixture resembles cornmeal. Transfer mixture to a bowl and stir in ⅔ cup half-and-half, adding more if dough seems dry. Mix gently and knead 5 or 6 times. Pat out to ½-inch thickness on lightly floured board, and cut into round or square biscuits. Bake on parchment-lined cookie sheet for 10 minutes.

Good Morning, Goldie!

Rocky Mountain Campfire Chili

2 pounds ground beef, elk, or
  deer (or mixed)
2 medium yellow onions,
  chopped
3 cloves garlic, minced
Oil
1 (16-ounce) can tomatoes,
  broken up
4 tablespoons tomato paste

4 ounces diced green chiles
2 pickled jalapeño peppers,
  chopped (optional)
3 tablespoons chili powder
1 teaspoon each: salt and cumin
1 tablespoon oregano
2 (14½-ounce) cans beef broth
5 cups water
1 (15-ounce) can pinto beans

Brown meat with onions and garlic in small amount of oil. Add tomatoes, tomato paste, chiles, jalapeños, seasonings, beef broth, and water. Bring mixture to a boil. Reduce heat to low and cook 4–5 hours, stirring occasionally. Adjust seasonings, if necessary. Add beans during last 30 minutes of cooking. Serve hot in bowls with an assortment of condiments such as grated cheeses, sliced olives, pico de gallo, chopped onions, etc. Yields 3 quarts.

Colorado Foods and More...

Boulder Black Bean Soup

The perfect supper after an awesome day of skiing!

2 teaspoons olive oil
1 medium onion, chopped
3 cloves garlic, minced
1 teaspoon dried whole oregano
½ teaspoon dried thyme
½ teaspoon cumin
¼ teaspoon cayenne pepper
3 cups canned black beans,
  rinsed and drained, divided

3 cups low-sodium chicken
  broth
2 tomatoes, chopped
½ cup chopped onion
  (optional)
½ cup shredded reduced-fat
  Monterey Jack cheese
  (optional)

Heat oil in a large saucepan over medium heat. Sauté onion and garlic until tender (about 5 minutes). Stir in oregano, thyme, cumin, and pepper; cook one minute longer. Place half of beans in a blender and purée until smooth, adding chicken broth as needed to make a smooth purée. Add purée and remaining whole beans and broth to saucepan. Bring to a boil over medium heat, then simmer uncovered for 20–30 minutes. Serve garnished with diced tomatoes, and if desired, onion and shredded cheese. Yields 8 servings.

Simply Colorado

Hot Apricot Buttered Rum

¼ cup packed brown sugar
2½ cups water
½ stick unsalted butter, cut
  in bits
½ tablespoon cinnamon
¼ tablespoon freshly grated
  nutmeg

3 whole cloves
½ cup dark rum
¼ cup apricot flavored brandy
Fresh lemon juice
4 sticks cinnamon

In a saucepan, stir together brown sugar, water, butter, cinnamon, nutmeg, and cloves. Simmer for 5 minutes, stirring occasionally. Stir in rum, brandy, and a squirt of lemon juice. Divide among 4 heated mugs and insert cinnamon stick. Makes 4 servings.

What's Cookin' in Melon Country

Pikes Peak Spiked Apple Crisp

5 cups peeled and sliced apples
  (Pippin, Jonathan, or Winesap)
½ teaspoon cinnamon sugar
1 teaspoon grated lemon rind
1 teaspoon grated orange rind
1 jigger Grand Marnier
1 jigger Amaretto di Saronno
¾ cup granulated sugar

¼ cup packed light brown
  sugar
¾ cup sifted flour
¼ teaspoon salt
½ cup butter or margarine
Cream, whipped cream, or ice
  cream for topping

Arrange apple slices in greased 2-quart round casserole. Sprinkle cinnamon sugar, lemon and orange rinds, and both liqueurs on top of apples. In a separate bowl, mix sugars, flour, salt, and butter with a pastry blender until crumbly. Spread mixture over top of apples. Bake uncovered at 350° until apples are tender and top is lightly browned, approximately one hour. Serve warm with cream, whipped cream, or vanilla or cinnamon ice cream. Makes 8 servings.

Colorado Cache Cookbook

"Pikes Peak or Bust" was a popular slogan during the gold-mining days. Though it is probably the most famous mountain in North America, Pikes Peak is only the state's 31st highest summit. It was atop this peak that Katherine Lee Bates was inspired to write "America the Beautiful."

Crested Butte Chili Cheese Supreme

2 tablespoons vegetable oil
1 medium green pepper, chopped
1 clove garlic, minced
1 (15.5-ounce) can kidney beans, drained
1 (16-ounce) can tomatoes, with juice, coarsely chopped
1 (15-ounce) can tomato sauce
1 tablespoon chili powder or to taste
1 (15-ounce) carton ricotta cheese

2 cups (8 ounces) shredded Monterey Jack cheese
1 (4-ounce) can chopped green chiles, drained
1 bunch green onions, finely chopped
3 eggs, beaten
1 (8-ounce) bag tortilla chips
2 cups (8 ounces) shredded mild or medium Cheddar cheese

Heat oil in skillet over medium-high heat. Sauté green pepper and garlic until tender. Add kidney beans. Set aside.

In saucepan, combine tomatoes, tomato sauce, and chili powder. Bring to a boil, then reduce heat and simmer uncovered for 15 minutes. Add to kidney bean mixture. Combine ricotta and Monterey Jack cheeses, chiles, onions, and eggs.

Spread ¼ of cheese mixture evenly in greased 9x13-inch glass baking dish. Arrange ¼ of chips over cheese. Spread ¼ of tomato mixture over chips. Repeat layer 3 more times. Cover with foil and bake at 325° for 30–40 minutes. Remove foil and top with Cheddar cheese. Bake 10–15 minutes more. Let stand 5 minutes before serving. Yields 10–12 servings.

West of the Rockies

Raggedy Ann Cookies

1 cup butter or margarine,
  softened
1 cup packed brown sugar
1 egg
1 teaspoon maple flavoring
2¼ cups flour

½ teaspoon baking powder
½ teaspoon salt
½ teaspoon cinnamon
1 cup shredded coconut
1 cup finely chopped nuts
  (optional)

Cream butter, brown sugar, egg, and flavoring until fluffy. Add flour, baking powder, salt, and cinnamon. Mix well. Stir in coconut and nuts, if desired. Drop by teaspoonful 2 inches apart on greased cookie sheet. Butter bottom of a glass, dip into granulated sugar, and press cookie flat. Bake at 350° for 10–12 minutes. Cool on rack. Yields 5 dozen.

The Colorado Cookbook

Durango Meatballs

1 pound each ground pork and
  ground round, mixed together
2 cups soft bread crumbs
2 eggs
½ cup finely chopped onion
2 tablespoons chopped parsley

2 teaspoons salt
2 tablespoons butter
1 (10-ounce) jar apricot
  preserves
½ cup barbecue sauce

Combine meat, bread crumbs, eggs, onion, and seasonings and mix lightly. Shape into medium-size meatballs and brown in butter. Place in a casserole and pour the apricot preserves and barbecue sauce over the meatballs. Bake at 350° for 30 minutes. Makes 4–5 dozen meatballs.

The Durango Cookbook

The town of Durango lies in the heart of the beautiful Four Corners region, the only place in the United States where four states—Colorado, New Mexico, Utah, and Arizona—meet.

Connecticut

CAPITAL: *Hartford*

NICKNAME: *The Constitution State*

With its wealth of village greens, white-steepled churches, and colorful seaports, Connecticut's scenery is some of New England's most beautiful. Since the 17th century, the Constitution State has been predominantly a manufacturing state and a world leader in industrial development. There are classic Ivy League schools, modern expressways, great corporate offices, and small farms. Here, the Connecticut Yankee has long been a symbol of ingenuity and inventiveness. Bordered by New York, Rhode Island, Massachusetts, and Long Island Sound, the food fare is indicative of the bounty of the rich land and abundant sea. We loved Mystic Seaport and all the good food we enjoyed there and while traveling around the countryside. Though its official nickname is the Constitution State, most people call Connecticut the Nutmeg State, and its residents, "Nutmeggers."

Shrimp Salad with Snow Peas and Water Chestnuts

½ pound snow peas, strings
  removed
¾ pound shrimp, cooked
1 cup sliced canned water
  chestnuts, drained

½ cup light vegetable oil
1 tablespoon rice vinegar
2 tablespoons honey
Juice of 1 lemon
2 tablespoons light soy sauce

Bring a large pot of water to a boil. Blanch the snow peas in rapidly boiling water for 30 seconds. Drain and refresh under cold water. Drain again.

Arrange peeled shrimp, snow peas, and water chestnuts in a serving dish. Combine all remaining ingredients for the dressing and pour it over the salad. Toss well and serve. Yields 4–6 servings for lunch.

Off the Hook

Bow House Brochettes

Flavor lives up to its wonderful aroma!

½ **pound sliced bacon**
1 **pound sea scallops, rinsed**
 and drained
2 **tablespoons unsalted butter,**
 melted

1½ **tablespoons firmly packed**
 brown sugar
1 **teaspoon ground cinnamon**

Cut bacon slices in half. Wrap bacon around scallop and secure with wooden toothpick. Combine butter, brown sugar, and cinnamon. Brush on bacon-wrapped scallops. Broil, turning as necessary, until bacon is crisp on all sides.

   Scallops and bacon may be assembled early in day and chilled. Recipe may be doubled. Yields 1½ dozen.

Connecticut Cooks II

Turtles

Keep copies of this recipe handy—everyone will ask for one.

CRUST:
2 **cups flour**
1 **cup brown sugar**

½ **cup (1 stick) butter, at room**
 temperature

Preheat oven to 350°. Mix Crust ingredients in mixer bowl at medium speed until well mixed and dough forms fine particles. With hands, pat dough into a 9x13x2-inch pan.

CARAMEL:
1 **cup (2 sticks) butter**
3 **tablespoons corn syrup**
1½ **cups brown sugar**

2 **cups chopped pecans**
12 **ounces chocolate chips**

In a saucepan over medium heat, mix butter, syrup, and brown sugar for Caramel. Bring to a boil; boil for one minute, stirring constantly. Sprinkle nuts over Crust; pour Caramel over all. Bake 18–22 minutes, until surface bubbles. Immediately after removing pan from oven, pour chocolate chips evenly over all. Let stand briefly to melt, then spread chocolate. Cool; cut into squares. Yields 48 squares.

Christmas Memories Cookbook

Broccoli and Crab Bisque

Good for weight-watchers and cholesterol-counters. Tastes creamy and elegant— but good for you!

1 head broccoli
4 potatoes
1½ cups diced carrots
1 pound crabmeat
1½ cups chopped onions
2 teaspoons margarine or oil
5 cups broth (fish, chicken, or vegetable)
¾ cup chopped celery
½ teaspoon black pepper
1 teaspoon lemon juice
¼ teaspoon thyme
1 bay leaf
¾ teaspoon (or less) salt
2 cups skim milk

Slice broccoli stems crosswise and reserve flowerets. Peel and dice potatoes and carrots. Slice crabmeat into ½-inch pieces.

Sauté onions in margarine until soft. Add broth (fish bouillon cubes are best), broccoli stems, half of potatoes and carrots, celery, pepper, lemon juice, thyme, bay leaf, and salt. Bring to a boil, reduce heat, and simmer for 15 minutes or until vegetables are tender.

Remove bay leaf. Purée vegetables and broth in blender. Return purée to pot. Add remaining half of diced potatoes and carrots; cook soup over low heat about 10 minutes or until vegetables are tender.

Add broccoli flowerets and cook for 5–10 minutes until broccoli is tender-crisp. Add milk and crabmeat; heat but do not boil. Serve with favorite croutons, if desired.

The Marlborough Meetinghouse Cookbook

Sausage Whirls

1 pound hot bulk sausage
½ cup chopped onion
1 tablespoon oil
2 cups flour

½ teaspoon salt
3 teaspoons baking powder
5 tablespoons butter
⅔ cup milk

In a large fry pan, sauté sausage and onion in 1 tablespoon oil until browned. Set aside. In a large bowl, combine flour, salt, and baking powder. Cut in butter with pastry blender until mixture resembles coarse crumbs. Stir in milk to make soft dough. Divide dough in half. Roll out each half on a floured surface making 2 (10x15-inch) rectangles ½ inch thick. Spread evenly with sausage and onion. Roll up as for jellyroll. Seal edges.

Wrap in plastic wrap and freeze until ready to use. Thaw bread and preheat oven to 400°. Bake "loaves" on greased baking sheet for 10 minutes until golden. Cool 10 minutes before slicing. Serve warm. Makes 40 pieces.

Movable Feasts Cookbook

Almond Cheesecake with Raspberries

1¼ cups graham cracker
  crumbs
⅓ cup butter, melted
¼ cup sugar
2 (8-ounce) packages cream
  cheese, softened
1 (16-ounce) can ready-to-spread
  vanilla frosting

1 tablespoon lemon juice
1 tablespoon grated lemon peel
3 cups Cool Whip
Raspberries
Sliced almonds

Stir together crumbs, butter, and sugar in a small bowl; press onto bottom and ½ inch up sides of a 9-inch springform pan or pie plate. Chill. Beat cream cheese, frosting, juice, and peel in a large mixing bowl at medium speed with electric mixer until well blended. Fold in whipped topping; pour over crust. Chill until firm. Arrange raspberries and almonds on top.

Sandy Hook Volunteer Fire Co. Ladies Aux. Cookbook

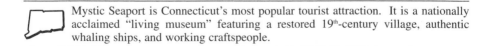

Mystic Seaport is Connecticut's most popular tourist attraction. It is a nationally acclaimed "living museum" featuring a restored 19th-century village, authentic whaling ships, and working craftspeople.

Reuben-in-the-Round

Great for late-night snack or as a party appetizer.

1 (8-ounce) package refrigerated
  crescent rolls
1 (12-ounce) can corned beef,
  shredded
¼ cup chopped green pepper
2 tablespoons ketchup

1 teaspoon horseradish
1 (8-ounce) can sauerkraut,
  well drained
½ teaspoon caraway seed
1 cup shredded Swiss cheese

Separate chilled dough into 8 triangles. Place 6 triangles in ungreased 8-inch pie pan, pressing edges together to form crust. Combine beef, pepper, ketchup, and horseradish; mix well. Spoon into crust. Spread sauerkraut over mixture. Sprinkle with caraway. Top with cheese. Cut remaining triangles into ½-inch strips. Stretch strips over filling to form lattice top. Bake at 350° for 20 minutes. Place aluminum foil strip around tin and bake for 15–20 minutes. Yields 8 servings.

Connecticut Cooks II

Scallop Puffs

One of the great pleasures of living at the eastern end of Long Island Sound is the scallops, both the bay scallops, from the waters at Niantic, and the large sea scallops. This recipe is a splendid way to use them.

½ pound sea scallops
2 tablespoons butter
1 teaspoon grated lemon rind
1½ garlic cloves, minced
½ teaspoon dried dill weed
1 cup shredded Swiss cheese

1 heaping cup mayonnaise
⅛ teaspoon black pepper
6 dozen 1½-inch bread rounds,
  lightly toasted
Paprika

Cut scallops in quarters. Melt butter. Add scallops, grated lemon rind, and garlic. Cook for 2–3 minutes. Add dill and cook 30 seconds more. Cool to room temperature. Add cheese, mayonnaise, and pepper and mix well. (Can be prepared up to a week in advance; cover and refrigerate.)

Place mixture on toast rounds, sprinkle with paprika, and run under broiler for 2–3 minutes. Serve hot. Puffs can be frozen after broiling. Makes 72 puffs.

The Lymes' Heritage Cookbook

Delaware

CAPITAL: *Dover*

NICKNAMES: *The First State*

*A*merica's first state, a "Small Wonder," Delaware is second in smallest size—96 miles long, and varies from 9 to 35 miles wide—only to Rhode Island. But it is big on history. Eleven years after the landing of the English pilgrims, the first white settlement was made on Delaware soil. Later, on December 7, 1787, it became the first state to ratify the U.S. Constitution. Betsy Ross's famous flag was said to have been first flown at the Battle at Cooch's Bridge on Route 4 in Newark. The Methodist Episcopal Church of America was organized in 1784 at Barratt's Chapel in Frederica. We love the museums there, particularly the Brandywine River Museum (Andrew Wyeth and family paintings), beautiful Longwood Gardens, and Winterthur (du Pont's winter home and gardens). When you go, plan to shop—there's no sales tax.

Crab Frittata

Good for brunch or a light supper.

1 clove garlic, mashed	3 eggs
⅔ cup chopped onion	½ cup nonfat milk
1 cup chopped zucchini	½ cup grated Parmesan
½ cup sliced mushrooms	cheese
2 tablespoons butter	1 (7½-ounce) can crabmeat,
1½ teaspoons salt	drained (or fresh)
¼ teaspoon pepper	Parsley

Sauté vegetables in butter; add salt and pepper. Cook, covered, for 5–7 minutes. Meanwhile, beat together eggs, milk, and cheese. Combine crab, vegetables, and egg mixture in buttered casserole. Sprinkle with parsley. Bake at 350° for 20 minutes, or until firm. Serves 2–4.

Winterthur's Culinary Collection

Steak Diane

6 filet mignon steaks, 1 inch thick	1 teaspoon butter
	1 teaspoon vegetable oil

Pound steaks to ½ inch thick. Melt butter and oil in sauté pan on medium-high heat, but do not burn butter. Add steaks and brown on one side until blood comes on top; then turn and cook for one minute longer (will be rare). You may cook for one more minute if you want medium rare, but do not overcook because they can dry out.

SAUCE:

2 teaspoons butter	4 teaspoons fresh parsley
6 shallots, minced	1 teaspoon Worcestershire
6 fresh mushrooms, sliced	Salt and pepper to taste
4 teaspoons minced fresh chives	2 ounces brandy

Melt butter in saucepan and add shallots, mushrooms, chives, and parsley. When shallots soften, add Worcestershire, salt and pepper. Now add Sauce to meat and simmer 2 minutes. Add brandy and touch with lighted match. Serves 6.

A Taste of Tradition

Charlotte au Chocolat

1 (12-ounce) package semisweet chocolate pieces	4 dozen ladyfingers, split
6 eggs, separated	Whipped cream and chocolate candy wafers for topping (optional)
2 tablespoons sugar	
2 cups heavy cream, whipped	

Melt chocolate pieces in top of double boiler. Cool. Beat in egg yolks, one at a time; beat well after each addition. Beat egg whites until frothy. Gradually beat in sugar until stiff peaks form. Beat ¼ of egg white mixture into chocolate. Fold in remaining mixture. Fold in whipped cream. Line bottom and sides of 9-inch springform pan with ladyfingers. Spoon ⅓ chocolate mixture into pan and top with layer of ladyfingers. Repeat layers, ending with chocolate mixture. Garnish with whipped cream and candy wafers, if desired. Chill 4 hours. Cut in thin wedges to serve. Serves 16.

Flavors of Cape Henlopen

Crab Salad

1 pound fresh backfin crabmeat
½ small red onion, diced fine
1 stalk celery, diced fine
Juice of 1 lemon
1 rounded tablespoon Grey
  Poupon Mustard

1 tablespoon sour cream
2 tablespoons mayonnaise
Ground black pepper to taste
Old Bay Seasoning to taste

Inspect crabmeat, removing any shell. Mix remaining ingredients. Pour over crab and mix gently. Serve as salad on bed of lettuce or to stuff a tomato or as an appetizer on crackers. Serves 4.

South Coastal Cuisine

Kennett Square Mushrooms

20–25 fresh medium-size
  mushrooms (approximately
  ½ pound)
2 tablespoons butter
1 small onion, minced
1 tablespoon Worcestershire

⅓ cup soft, fine bread crumbs
½ cup shredded sharp
  Cheddar cheese
Salt and pepper to taste
Parsley
2 tablespoons water

Select mushrooms with closed caps. Pull stems from mushrooms and chop finely. Melt butter in skillet and add stems and onion. Sauté until tender and translucent. Stir in remaining ingredients except water. If preferred, parsley may be sprinkled on top instead of mixed in with other ingredients. Fill mushroom caps with mixture, mounding over top. Arrange mushrooms in oven-proof serving dish. At this point mushrooms can be refrigerated up to 24 hours. Before serving, add 2 tablespoons of water to dish. Bake at 350° for 20 minutes. Serve hot. Yields 20–25 mushrooms.

Winterthur's Culinary Collection

 Lewes, Delaware, is situated where the Delaware Bay and Atlantic Ocean meet at Cape Henlopen. Founded as a whaling station by Dutch settlers in 1631, Lewes also holds the distinction of being "the first town in the first state."

Lasagna and Spinach Roll Ups

1 (16-ounce) box lasagna noodles
1 (1-pound) container cottage
  cheese
1 (1-pound) container ricotta
  cheese
¼ cup grated Parmesan cheese
2 eggs, beaten
1 (15-ounce) can spinach,
  drained well
1 teaspoon pesto, bought or
  homemade

¼ teaspoon ground nutmeg
1 teaspoon dried oregano
1 teaspoon garlic powder
1 teaspoon dried basil
1 teaspoon salt
¼ teaspoon black pepper
2 (26-ounce) cans spaghetti
  sauce, or homemade
1 cup shredded mozzarella
  cheese

Cook lasagna noodles according to directions on package; drain, rinse, and cool. In a large bowl, mix cottage cheese, ricotta cheese, Parmesan cheese, and beaten eggs. Now add spinach, pesto, nutmeg, oregano, garlic powder, basil, salt, and pepper, and mix well. Take one whole noodle and put ¼ cup cheese mixture at one end and roll up like a log; continue to do this with all noodles. Place them in a baking dish, in one layer. Pour spaghetti sauce over them and bake for 40 minutes, covered, so it does not dry out. Then remove cover, sprinkle mozzarella cheese over the top, and bake for 5 more minutes.

A Taste of Tradition

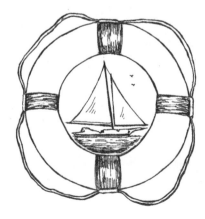

Delaware Succotash

2 thin slices salt pork
1 pint shelled lima beans, or
  1 package frozen, thawed
Water
8 ears fresh corn or frozen,
  thawed

1 large ripe tomato, cubed
1 teaspoon salt
¼ teaspoon pepper
Dash of nutmeg

Lay salt pork in bottom of a saucepan and cover with lima beans. Add enough water to cover, and cook over low heat until beans are tender. Cut kernels from fresh corn and combine with beans, cubed tomato, and seasonings. Cover and continue cooking over low heat for 10–15 minutes. Stir frequently. Yields 6 servings.

South Coastal Cuisine

Energy Bars

1 cup quick-cooking rolled oats
½ cup all-purpose flour
½ cup Grape-Nuts Cereal
½ teaspoon ground ginger
1 egg, beaten
⅓ cup applesauce
¼ cup honey

¼ cup packed brown sugar
2 tablespoons cooking oil
1 (16-ounce) package mixed
  dried fruit bits
¼ cup sunflower seeds
¼ cup chopped walnuts

Preheat oven to 325°. Line an 8x8x2-inch baking pan with aluminum foil. Spray foil with nonstick coating. In large mixing bowl, combine oats, flour, Grape-Nuts, and ginger. Add egg, applesauce, honey, brown sugar, and oil. Mix well; stir in fruit, sunflower seeds, and walnuts. Spread mixture in prepared pan. Bake at 325° for 30–35 minutes. Cool; cut. Makes 24 bars.

Each bar contains 100 calories and 3 grams fat.

Flavors of Cape Henlopen

Florida

CAPITAL: *Tallahassee*

NICKNAME: *The Sunshine State*

*J*ust thinking of Florida brings on a smile . . . and thoughts of vacation . . . and staying warm in the winter. Sunny Florida . . . swaying palms, warm tropical breezes, lapping ocean waves, and bountiful orchards. Florida has ideal growing conditions for citrus fruits, grows vegetables in the winter, and has a fantastic variety of seafood everywhere you turn. There are 882 islands or "keys" in the Florida Keys large enough to show up on maps, and 4,510 more that are 10 acres or larger. Orlando attracts more visitors than any other amusement park destination in the United States. Gatorade was first developed in Gainesville for the Florida Gators football players to help them combat dehydration. In 1944 Miami Beach pharmacist Benjamin Green cooked cocoa butter in a granite coffee pot on his wife's stove, and invented the first suntan cream. In the Sunshine State, having this is a very good thing.

Mango Colada

A piña colada with mango . . . what could be more refreshing?

6 ounces coconut cream
6 ounces pineapple juice
4 ounces mango purée

4 ounces spiced white rum
8 ice cubes

Place all ingredients, except ice, in a blender and add ice cubes one at a time. Blend until smooth. Makes 4 servings.

The Mongo Mango Cookbook

Almond Orange Garden Salad

Try this delicious dressing on all of your salad favorites.

SUNLIGHT SALAD DRESSING:

1 cup vegetable oil
¼ cup white wine vinegar
¼ cup sugar
1 teaspoon salt

1 teaspoon black pepper
3 teaspoons freshly chopped
    parsley, or 1 teaspoon dried

Combine dressing ingredients in a jar, and shake until well mixed.

SALAD:

¼ cup sugar
1 cup sliced almonds
½ head iceberg lettuce
½ head romaine lettuce
6 green onions, chopped

1½ cups fresh oranges, peeled
    and sectioned, or 2 (11-ounce)
    cans Mandarin oranges,
    drained

Add sugar to frying pan with almonds, and cook over medium heat, stirring and watching closely. When almonds are browned, pour them onto foil and let cool. Tear clean lettuce into bite-size pieces and place in a salad bowl. Add onions and oranges. Pour Sunlight Salad Dressing over Salad to taste, and toss lightly. Top with almonds and serve. Yields 8 servings.

A Slice of Paradise

Imperial Crab Casserole

1 pound backfin crabmeat
1 tablespoon chopped pimento
1 tablespoon chopped green
  pepper
6 saltine crackers, crushed

2 tablespoons mayonnaise
1 tablespoon prepared mustard
1 egg, beaten
Old Bay Seasoning

Grease 9x13-inch casserole. Mix together all ingredients, except Old Bay Seasoning. Pile ingredients loosely in casserole. Sprinkle seasoning on top.

TOPPING:

2 egg yolks
2 cups mayonnaise

Paprika

Beat egg yolks with mayonnaise. Spread mixture over crabmeat mixture. Sprinkle paprika on top. Bake at 425° for 20–25 minutes.

Sing for Your Supper

Orange Rum Cream Cake

1¾ cups sifted cake flour
1 tablespoon baking powder
¼ teaspoon salt
½ cup shortening

1 cup sugar
8 egg yolks, beaten
1 teaspoon grated orange rind
½ cup milk

Have all ingredients at room temperature. Sift together twice the flour, baking powder, and salt. Cream shortening till fluffy; gradually add sugar. Blend till mixture is creamy. Stir in egg yolks and orange rind until well mixed. Alternately add dry ingredients and milk, beating after each addition. Turn into 2 greased 8-inch cake pans, and bake in 350° oven for 30 minutes. Cool 10 minutes; turn onto cake rack. Fill with Orange Rum Filling and frost with whipped cream.

ORANGE RUM FILLING:
3 tablespoons butter, softened
¾ teaspoon grated orange rind
1½ cups sifted confectioners'
  sugar, divided

Dash salt
2 tablespoons orange juice
1 tablespoon rum
Whipped cream

Cream butter with grated orange rind. Gradually add ½ cup sifted confectioners' sugar, blending well. Add dash of salt; mix well. Add remaining 1 cup confectioners' sugar alternately with 2 tablespoons orange juice, beating till smooth after each addition. Blend in rum. Spread on cake layer. Frost with whipped cream.

Famous Florida Recipes

Gwen and husband Barney pause for a smoothie at Disney World. At Epcot, they sampled foods from many other countries, so much of which has influenced American cooking.

Black Beans and Rice

1 pound dried black beans, washed and drained
6 cups water
½ cup olive oil
1 large onion, coarsely chopped
1 green bell pepper, stem and seeds removed, coarsely chopped
1 clove garlic, minced
2 bay leaves
2 teaspoons salt
¼ teaspoon freshly ground black pepper
1 smoked ham bone (optional)
1 slice bacon, minced
¼ cup wine vinegar
Cooked yellow rice
Raw rings of onion or scallions, cut into ¼-inch rounds

Cover beans with water. Bring to a boil and boil for 2 minutes. Remove from heat; cover pan and let stand for 1 hour.

Heat olive oil in skillet. Add onion, pepper, and garlic. Sauté for about 5 minutes. Add to beans. Add bay leaves, salt, pepper, ham bone, and bacon. Bring to a boil and simmer, covered, for 2 hours or until tender, adding more water if necessary. Remove bay leaves and add wine vinegar. Serve with yellow rice, and garnish with onion rings. Serves 6–8.

Variation: This dish can be improved through the use of any flavorful stock (chicken, ham, vegetable, dry white wine, etc.), rather than water. Also for added flavor, as dish simmers, consider adding ½ cup sliced, pimiento-stuffed olives, 1 teaspoon ground oregano, and/or ¼ teaspoon ground cumin.

Note: To cook yellow rice, just cook rice as you normally do, but add a drop or 2 of yellow food color. In Key West, most cooks use an inexpensive condiment called BIJOL, which gives rice a rich yellow color.

Cookin' in the Keys

Shrimp Log

1 (8-ounce) package cream
  cheese, softened
1 cup minced cooked shrimp
2 tablespoons chili sauce
2 tablespoons chopped stuffed
  olives

2 tablespoons chopped green
  onion
1 teaspoon lemon juice
Sliced stuffed olives

In bowl, stir cream cheese until smooth. Blend in cooked shrimp, chili sauce, chopped olives, onion, and lemon juice. Shape into a log, and garnish with sliced stuffed olives; chill thoroughly. To serve, spread on wheat crackers. Makes about 1½ cups.

Garden of Eatin'

Margaritaville Key Lime Pie

This tropical dessert recipe comes from singer Jimmy Buffett's Margaritaville Café.

CRUST AND FILLING:
1 (9-inch) graham cracker
  pie crust
2 egg yolks
1 (14-ounce) can sweetened
  condensed milk

1 egg white
½ cup Key lime juice

Bake pie crust at 350° for 5 minutes. Beat egg yolks with an electric mixer 2 minutes. Blend yolks into milk. In separate bowl, beat egg white with electric mixer until fluffy. Gently fold white into mixture. Fold in lime juice. Pour filling into pie crust. Refrigerate 2–3 hours before adding Topping.

TOPPING:
5 egg whites
2 teaspoons cream of tartar

½ cup sugar

Whip egg whites and cream of tartar with electric mixer until foamy. Continue to whip while slowly adding sugar. Beat until peaks form. Score filling with a fork. Spread Topping over Filling. Bake at 425° for 5 minutes or until topping starts to brown. Yields 8 servings.

Calypso Café

Fish Seminole

4 fish fillets
¼ cup seasoned flour
2 eggs, beaten
Oil for sautéing
½ pound scallops
¼ cup diced shallot
½ pound fresh mushrooms,
  sliced

½ teaspoon salt
1 teaspoon chopped garlic
¼ teaspoon white pepper
Butter for sautéing
½ pound cooked crabmeat

Dredge fish in flour and dip in egg. Sauté in a skillet in a small amount of oil until browned on both sides. Transfer to an oven and bake at 450° until fish flakes easily with a fork, about 7–10 minutes.

To make topping, sauté scallops and next 5 ingredients together in a small amount of butter. Add crabmeat and cook until hot. Spoon topping over cooked fish. Yields 4 servings.

Calypso Café

Banana Cake

2 cups sugar
2 sticks butter, softened
2 eggs
½ cup milk

1½ teaspoons baking soda
2 cups flour
2 small bananas, mashed
1 teaspoon lemon juice

Cream together sugar, butter, and eggs. Add milk and baking soda, alternating with flour. Last, add bananas that have had lemon juice added to them. Bake in 2 large cake pans, greased and lined with wax paper rounds which you have cut to fit, at 350° for about 30 minutes. Cool.

FROSTING:
1 (8-ounce) package cream
  cheese, softened
1 (1-pound) box powdered sugar

1 teaspoon vanilla
Chopped nuts

Combine cream cheese, powdered sugar, and vanilla. Spread on cooled cake layers, and sprinkle top layer with chopped nuts.

Village Royale: Our Favorite Recipes

Georgia

CAPITAL: *Atlanta*

NICKNAME: *The Peach State*

*A*h, sweet Georgia . . . you can just feel the warm summer breezes wisping through the screen porch while you're sipping sweet tea in your rocking chair. And if you're lucky, somebody is about to call you to dinner. Georgia cooks have been enjoying the bounty of the land for centuries. Margaret Mitchell, the author of *Gone With the Wind,* was born in Atlanta, and the charm—and cooking of the Old South are still steeped in its culture. Dougherty County has about 250,000 pecan trees, more than any other U.S. county . . . no wonder pecans are Georgia's second leading crop! Coca-Cola was invented in Georgia in 1886. Gainesville claims to be the poultry capital and has a city ordinance (just for fun) against eating their delicious local fried chicken with a knife and fork! Good idea! When it comes to food, Georgians get serious!

Frozen Peach Daiquiri

1 pint frozen fresh peaches
9 ounces cold water
6 ounces golden rum*
3 packets daiquiri mix

Cut frozen peaches into chunks and put into blender or food processor, then add the water, rum, and daiquiri mix. Blend at high speed until smooth. Makes 4 "normal" drinks. Frozen peaches preferred, as then no ice or ice cubes are needed in the drink. Serve with jalapeño dip and corn chips.

*Golden rum is preferred over clear or "white" rum.

Head Table Cooks

Chocolate Bread Pudding

My children request this! Men love it!

2 squares unsweetened baking
  chocolate
4 cups milk
2 eggs

⅔ cup sugar
1 teaspoon vanilla
¼ teaspoon salt
2 cups bread crumbs

In saucepan, melt chocolate in milk; do not boil. In bowl, beat eggs and add sugar. Combine with chocolate and milk, then add vanilla and salt. Pour bread crumbs over, and stir until all are soaked. Pour into greased 1½-quart casserole dish. Set in pan of hot water and bake at 350° for 1 hour.

SAUCE:
⅓ cup soft butter
1 cup light brown sugar

3 tablespoons milk

Cream butter with sugar. Gradually add milk, drop-by-drop, beating all the time.

Variation: Put whipped cream on top.

Frederica Fare

Tarragon Chicken
with Angel Hair Pasta

6 boneless chicken breast halves
3 tablespoons butter
2 cloves garlic, minced
1 teaspoon dried whole tarragon,
  crumbled
1 cup heavy cream

¾ cup grated Parmesan cheese
¼ teaspoon salt
½ cup dry white wine
¼ teaspoon cayenne pepper
1 pound angel hair pasta,
  cooked

Lightly pound chicken between pieces of wax paper. Sauté in butter over medium-high heat, about 1 minute on each side. Add garlic, tarragon, cream, Parmesan cheese, salt, wine, and cayenne pepper. Stir until blended; cook over medium heat until chicken is done and sauce is slightly reduced, about 15 minutes. Serve over angel hair pasta. Serves 6.

Peachtree Bouquet

Sassy Stuffed Chicken

1 medium onion, finely chopped
3 tablespoons butter, divided
1 (10-ounce) package frozen
  chopped spinach, thawed
  and squeezed dry
1 pound ricotta cheese
1 egg, lightly beaten
1 tablespoon mixed fresh
  oregano and basil

¼ cup chopped parsley
Pepper to taste
Powdered nutmeg to taste
4 whole chicken breasts,
  skinned, boned, and halved
Paprika
1 lemon, thinly sliced
Fresh spinach leaves

Sauté onion in 1 tablespoon butter over medium heat until soft, about 10 minutes. Combine with spinach, cheese, egg, oregano, basil, parsley, pepper, and nutmeg. Mix well. Pound each chicken breast lightly to flatten. Trim away excess fat. Place approximately 2 tablespoons spinach-cheese filling on each chicken breast and roll up. Fasten with string or toothpicks. Place in one layer in a glass baking pan. Dust with paprika and dot with remaining butter. Bake at 350° until golden brown. Garnish with lemon slices and serve on spinach leaves. Yields 4 servings.

Potlucks & Petticoats

Margaret Mitchell, author of *Gone With the Wind,* was born in Atlanta. Her book, published in June 1936, is still one of the best-selling books of all time. Mitchell was awarded the Pulitzer Prize for her sweeping novel in May 1937. The novel has been translated into 36 languages, and was made into an equally famous motion picture starring Vivien Leigh and Clark Gable. The movie had its world premiere at the Loew's Grand Theater in Atlanta on December 15, 1939. On August 11, 1949, while crossing the intersection of Peachtree and 13th, Margaret Mitchell was struck by a speeding car. She died five days later and is buried in Atlanta's Oakland Cemetery with other members of her family. She was 48 years old.

Almond Florentines

A Savannah favorite.

2½ cups sliced almonds
1 cup sugar
½ cup unsalted butter, melted
5 tablespoons unbleached
  all-purpose flour

2 egg whites, slightly beaten
Pinch salt
½ teaspoon vanilla extract

Preheat oven to 350°. Line cookie sheets with parchment paper—no substitute! Toss almonds and sugar together. Stir in melted butter. Stir in flour, egg whites, salt, and vanilla until well blended. Drop by spoonfuls onto sheets, or pick up a blob of batter in your hand and squeeze out one cookie's worth at a time, scraping off onto sheet with your other thumb. Space about 2 inches apart. Bake one sheet at a time for 10 minutes, or until golden brown on bottom and edges. Makes 6 dozen 2-inch cookies.

Gottlieb's Bakery 100 Years of Recipes

Savannah Red Rice

¼ pound bacon
½ cup chopped onion (Vidalia)
½ cup chopped celery
¼ cup seeded and chopped
  green pepper
2 cups rice, uncooked

2 (16-ounce) cans tomatoes,
  puréed
3 teaspoons salt
¼ teaspoon pepper
1 teaspoon sugar
⅛ teaspoon Tabasco

In a large frying pan, fry bacon until crisp; remove from pan. Crumble and reserve. Sauté onion, celery, and green pepper in bacon grease until tender. Add rice, tomatoes, crumbled bacon, and seasonings. Cook on top of the stove for 10 minutes. Pour into large, greased casserole dish, cover tightly, and bake at 350° for 1 hour. Serves 8.

Savannah Style

Stone Mountain, 16 miles east of Atlanta, is the largest exposed granite mountain in the world, and is second only to Ayers Rock in Australia as the world's largest monolith. At its summit, the elevation is 1683 feet, about double that of the surrounding area. The Confederate Memorial Carving of Stonewall Jackson, Robert E. Lee and Jefferson Davis on Stone Mountain is the largest bas-relief sculpture in the world.

Crab Maire

4 green onions, chopped
½ cup chopped parsley
½ cup butter
2 tablespoons flour
1 pint half-and-half

½ pound Swiss cheese, grated
1 tablespoon sherry
Salt and pepper to taste
1 pound crabmeat

Sauté green onions and parsley in butter. Stir in flour; add half-and-half to make sauce. Add all other ingredients except crabmeat. Cook over low heat until cheese is melted. Add crabmeat and heat. Place in chafing dish and serve with Melba toast rounds or toast points. Yields 50 appetizer servings.

Quail Country

Peach Cream Pie

Delicious made with Georgia peaches, fresh or from the freezer.

2 cups vanilla wafer crumbs
1 stick margarine, melted
1 (14-ounce) can sweetened
   condensed milk
½ cup lemon juice

1 (1-pint) carton frozen peaches
1 (8-ounce) carton frozen
   whipped dessert topping,
   thawed

Make crust of vanilla wafer crumbs and melted margarine. Press into 9-inch pie plate and chill. Blend condensed milk and lemon juice until thick. Partially thaw frozen peaches; put them into blender and blend for a few seconds until smooth. Pour peaches into milk mixture and blend well. Fold in dessert topping with spoon and pile into crumb crust. Yields 1 (9-inch) pie.

A Taste of Georgia

Hawai'i

CAPITAL: *Honolulu*

NICKNAME: *The Aloha State*

*A*loha! This said-with-a-smile Hawaiian greeting is also the official state nickname. It means more than hello and goodbye—it's the way people treat each other . . . a way of life . . . a state of mind. One of the most beautiful places on earth, Hawaii is a string of 137 islands in the Pacific Ocean, about 2,400 miles from the continental United States. With beautiful flowers and trees, canyons, lava fields, waterfalls, and beaches everywhere, Hawai'i is truly paradise. The average daytime temperature ranges from 78 to 85 degrees, and the gentle breeze absolutely caresses you. The pineapple and coconut and other native fruits are so fresh and delicious. It's the only state that grows cacao beans and coffee—their outstanding Kona Coffee is world famous. We also found that Spam, introduced in World War II, is a popular dish. Hawai'i's alphabet only has 12 letters, so though easy to learn to pronounce, some of their words get strung out. Hawai'i's state fish is the humuhumu nukunuku a pua'a—now that's a mouthful! Hawaiians always say, "Mahalo," which means thank you . . . and like "Aloha," it also comes with a smile.

Mai Tai

The Mai Tai has become one of the most popular drinks in the islands.

2 ounces light rum
1 ounce dark rum
1 ounce Triple Sec orange
  liqueur

½ ounce amaretto
½ ounce lime juice
Crushed ice

Mix the rums, Triple Sec, amaretto, and lime juice in a 7-ounce glass. Add crushed ice and garnish.

Hawaii's Best Tropical Food & Drinks

Oven Kalua Pig

Kalua pig is a popular dish in Hawai'i, often served at luaus. "Kalua" means "the pit" in Hawaiian, and refers to the method the pig is cooked—in an underground earthen oven called an imu.

2 tablespoons Hawaiian salt
¼ cup soy sauce
1 teaspoon Worcestershire
2 cloves garlic, crushed
1 (½-inch) slice of ginger,
  crushed

1 tablespoon liquid smoke
1 (4- to 5-pound) pork butt
Ti or banana leaves

Mix together salt, soy sauce, Worcestershire sauce, garlic, ginger, and liquid smoke. Place pork on several ti or banana leaves. Rub with seasonings and let stand one hour. Fold leaves over to wrap the pork. Wrap the leaf-enclosed pork in foil. Place in a baking pan and bake in a 325° oven for 4–5 hours. Unwrap pork, cool, and shred meat. Serves 8–10.

Ethnic Foods of Hawaii

Editor's Extra: Kosher or sea salt can be substituted for Hawaiian salt.

Quick Chicken Luau

1 (10-ounce) package frozen
  leaf spinach
1 (10¾-ounce) can cream of
  chicken soup

8 chicken thighs (or breasts)
1 (12-ounce) can coconut milk

Thaw spinach by leaving it at room temperature for several hours, or defrost in the microwave (3–4 minutes). Squeeze water out of it, using your hands. Spread spinach out in a greased 9x13-inch baking pan. Spread soup over it. Place chicken over the soup. Pour coconut milk over chicken. Bake in a 350° oven for one hour. Serves 4.

Note: Traditional chicken luau is made out of taro tops called luau leaves. Spinach is a quick substitute.

Aunty Pua's Keiki Cookbook

Party Shrimp Curry

Honolulu parties often have curry as a main dish. Pale pink shrimp in a coconut-accented sauce, surrounded with pretty bowls of condiments, is impressive. The host or hostess can prepare the dinner ahead of time and with only a few last-minute touches, it will be ready for guests.

6 tablespoons butter (⅓ cup)
1 medium-size onion, finely
 chopped
⅓ cup flour
2 tablespoons freshly grated
 ginger, or 1 tablespoon dry
2–3 tablespoons curry powder
2 cups milk (regular or
 coconut)

1 cup canned or fresh coconut
 milk
1 pound medium, raw shrimp,
 peeled and deveined
Salt to taste
Dash of cayenne pepper
 (optional)

Melt butter in large saucepan. Cook onion just until limp (do not brown). Add flour, ginger, and curry. Stir over a low flame to blend. Gradually add regular and coconut milk, stirring until the mixture is smooth. Add shrimp, with salt to taste, and the cayenne, if desired. Cook over a low flame just until shrimp turn pink. This will take about 5 minutes. At this point, the curry may be refrigerated until party time.

The condiments for the curry might include chopped peanuts or macadamia nuts, minced green onions, finely diced cucumbers, chutneys, and grated coconut. Curry is served with plenty of hot steamed rice. A dish of sliced fresh tropical fruits is often added to the festive table. Individual portions of curry may be served in papaya shells. This will serve 4, and can be increased for large parties.

Honolulu Hawaii Cooking

Hawai'i encompasses a land area of 6,422.6 square miles in the Pacific Ocean, about 2,400 miles from the west coast of the continental United States. Stretching from northwest to southeast, the major islands are: Ni'ihau (Nee-ee-how), Kaua'i (ka-Wah-ee), O'aho (Oh-Wa-who), Moloka'i (mo-lo-Kah-ee), Lana'i (la-Nah-ee), Koho'olawe (kaw-ho-oh-la-vay), Maui (Mow-ee, rhymes with Now-ee), and Hawai'i (ha-Wa-ee or ha-Ve-ee).

Huli Huli Chicken

This aromatic chicken turned (huli huli) on the spit is a staple at beach picnics, roadside stands, and at fundraisers.

SAUCE:

¼ cup ketchup
¼ cup shoyu (soy sauce)
½ cup chicken broth
⅓ cup sherry
½ cup fresh lime juice
¼ cup frozen pineapple juice
  concentrate

½ cup brown sugar
1 tablespoon crushed fresh
  ginger
1 clove garlic, crushed
1 teaspoon Worcestershire

Mix Sauce ingredients in bowl.

**3 chicken fryers, halved or
  quartered**

**Hawaiian salt and pepper
  to taste**

Thread chicken onto rotisserie spit. Use clean 1½-inch paintbrush to coat Sauce over cleaned chicken pieces, then sprinkle with salt and pepper. Grill on rotisserie, turning and basting frequently with Sauce until done, 45–60 minutes.

For grilling, place on rack over coals, turning and basting for about 45 minutes. Or roast in 325° preheated oven, basting frequently, for 90 minutes. Serves 6.

Kona on My Plate

The ukulele is the sound, and the lei is the symbol of Hawaii. Made of flowers, leaves, shells, seeds, or feathers, leis welcome millions of worldwide visitors to Hawaii each year.

Piña Colada Cake

1 (18¼-ounce) package yellow
  cake mix
1 (3¾-ounce) package vanilla
  pudding
1 (15-ounce) can Coco Lopez
  Cream of Coconut, divided
½ cup plus 2 tablespoons rum,
  divided

⅓ cup vegetable oil
4 eggs
1 (8-ounce) can crushed
  pineapple, drained
Whipped cream, pineapple
  chunks, maraschino cherries,
  and toasted coconut for
  garnish

Preheat oven to 350°; well grease and flour a 10-inch Bundt or tube pan. In a large mixing bowl, combine cake mix, pudding mix, ½ cup cream of coconut, ½ cup rum, oil, and eggs. Beat well. Stir in pineapple. Pour into prepared pan; bake for 50–55 minutes. Cool 10 minutes.

    With a table knife or skewer, poke holes about 1 inch apart in cake almost to the bottom. Combine remaining cream of coconut and remaining 2 tablespoons rum; slowly spoon over cake. Chill thoroughly. Store in refrigerator. Garnish as desired. Serves 12.

Dd's Table Talk

Spam Fried Rice

Good with fried eggs.

1½ cups diced Spam
Leftover rice, about 4 cups
  (cooked)

1 egg
1 tablespoon shoyu (soy sauce)
3 stalks green onions, chopped

Fry Spam in a bit of oil in a skillet. Turn heat to low and add rice. Mix egg with shoyu and add to the rice and Spam. Add chopped green onions just before serving.

Hawaii's Spam Cookbook

Hawaiians consume some 4.3 million cans of Spam a year. Spam was introduced to the islands during World War II when military personnel brought it with them from the mainland.

Liliko'i Cheesecake

As soft and sweet as a Hawaiian breeze.

CRUST:

1⅔ cups graham crumbs (or 22 squares finely rolled)
3 tablespoons honey

¼ cup butter or margarine, softened

Mix together crumbs, honey, and margarine, and press firmly into a 9-inch springform pan.

CHEESECAKE:

1 envelope or 1 tablespoon unflavored gelatin
½ cup liliko'i (passion fruit) juice, divided

½–¾ cup sugar
½ cup boiling water
2 (8-ounce) packages cream cheese, softened

In a large bowl, soften gelatin in a little of the fruit juice; mix in sugar. Add boiling water and stir until gelatin is completely dissolved. Stir in remaining liliko'i juice. With electric mixer, beat in cream cheese until smooth. Pour into Crust; chill until firm (about 2 hours). Makes about 8 servings.

Note: For a sweeter cake, use ¾ cup sugar.

Cook 'em Up Kaua'i

Editor's Extra: Use your wire whip on your mixer and beat it a couple of minutes to make this really creamy. Fun to add a few chocolate swirls on the plate, or some kiwi slices, and/or a dab of whipped cream to each serving.

Gwen is dwarfed by one of Hawai'i's gargantuan banyon trees.

Idaho

CAPITAL: *Boise*

NICKNAME: *The Gem State*

*I*daho is largely unspoiled, providing a virtual playground where adventure abounds. You can play in over 19,000 miles of hiking trails, 14,000 miles of biking trails, 3,000 miles of white water rivers, and 17 ski areas. And the widest variety of game in the United States—trophy elk, mule deer, bighorn sheep, antelope, bear, moose, cougar, mountain goat, white-tailed deer, waterfowl, upland game birds—abound freely in these areas. Idaho was settled by Basque immigrants who came from Spain to work mainly as sheepherders. Idahoans have excelled at how to please the palate around the campfire as well as at a suburban table. Dutch oven cooking is fun, practical, and delicious—bring on the sourdough bread. Potatoes aren't the only thing they grow, though they do that well. Nearly 85% of all the commercial trout sold in the United States is produced near Twin Falls. The Gem State produces gems—the beautiful Star Garnet, jasper, opal, jade, topaz, zircon, and tourmaline. The whole state is a gem.

Onion Roasted Potatoes

1 envelope onion soup mix
2 pounds all-purpose potatoes,
  cut into large chunks
⅓ cup olive or vegetable oil
Chopped parsley for garnish
  (optional)

Preheat oven to 450°. In large plastic bag, add soup mix, potatoes, and oil. Close bag and shake until potatoes are evenly coated. Empty potatoes into greased shallow baking or roasting pan. Discard bag. Bake, stirring occasionally, 30–40 minutes, or until potatoes are tender and golden brown. Garnish, if desired, with chopped parsley. Makes 8 servings.

Spragg Family Cookbook

Idaho Centennial Apple Pie

CHEESECAKE FILLING:

1 (8-ounce) package cream
  cheese, softened
⅓ cup sugar
1 egg

½ teaspoon vanilla
Pastry for 2 (9- or 10-inch)
  pies

Combine cream cheese, sugar, egg, and vanilla in a small bowl with an electric mixer until light. Pour into one unbaked pie crust. (At this point, you can put it in a gallon freezer bag to make later.)

APPLE FILLING:

1 cup sugar
3 tablespoons cornstarch
½ teaspoon cinnamon
¼ teaspoon salt

6 cups peeled and sliced apples
  (Jonathan when in season)
¼ cup apple juice
2 tablespoons butter

Combine sugar, cornstarch, cinnamon, and salt in a large saucepan. Add apples, apple juice, and butter. Place on medium heat. Bring to a boil. Reduce heat. Cover and simmer for 2 minutes. Spoon over Cheesecake Filling.

Roll dough for top crust. Lift onto filled pie. Trim ½ inch beyond edge of pie plate. Fold under the bottom crust and flute. Decorate with pastry scraps and cut vents in crust. Bake at 400° for 40 minutes or until nicely browned.

Another Cookbook

The Appaloosa is the Idaho state horse. The name is a variation of the Indian name for "palouse horse," named after the Palouse River in Idaho. The Nez Perce Indians, in their desire for the strongest, fastest and most sure-footed mounts, selectively bred them. But over time, these distinctive horses became lost or severely diluted due to indiscriminate breeding. In 1938, the Appaloosa Horse Club was formed in Moscow, Idaho, dedicated to preserving and improving the Apppaloosa breed.

Venison North Idaho

2 venison steaks, thick loin
½ clove garlic
1 tablespoon olive oil
2 tablespoons butter
Salt and pepper to taste
½ cup chopped mushrooms

½ bay leaf
1 teaspoon Worcestershire
2 tablespoons currant or apple
  jelly
¼ cup dry sherry
½ cup heavy cream

Rub the surface of steaks gently with the garlic. Heat olive oil and butter until sizzling in frying pan, and sauté steaks quickly in this until both sides are brown. Season with salt and pepper to taste. Combine rest of ingredients and pour over steaks. Bake in 350° oven for 70 minutes.

Recipes Logged from the Woods of North Idaho

Potato Cake

This recipe is about 140 years old. It's so moist, you don't need to frost it.

⅔ cup butter or shortening
2 cups flour
½ cup milk
2 teaspoons baking powder
¼–1 teaspoon ground cloves
½–1 teaspoon cinnamon
½ teaspoon salt
½ cup cocoa, or 2 squares
  chocolate, melted

2 cups sugar
1 cup hot mashed potatoes
4 eggs (beat yolks and whites
  separately, add whites last)
¼–1 teaspoon nutmeg
1 teaspoon vanilla
1 cup chopped nuts

Combine all ingredients; mix well and bake in greased 9x13-inch cake pan at 375° for 40 minutes.

Idaho's Wild 100!

What makes Idaho potatoes different? Idaho's clean air, climate, rich volcanic soil, and fresh water from melting snow in nearby mountains create ideal conditions for potato growing. The mountains collect snow all winter, which melts and flows crystal clear into large surface and underground reservoirs. That water is then used to irrigate the potatoes. Look for the "Grown in Idaho" seal as assurance that you are getting Genuine Idaho Potatoes.

Roasted Pepper Salad

2 large green bell peppers	Dash salt
2 large yellow bell peppers	Freshly ground pepper
2 large red bell peppers	6 tablespoons Spanish olive oil
2 tablespoons red wine vinegar	

Char peppers over gas flame or in broiler, turning occasionally, until skin blackens. Place in plastic bag; let stand for 19 minutes to steam. Peel and seed peppers, then cut into ½-inch-wide strips and place in bowl. Mix together vinegar, salt and pepper. Whisk in oil in a slow steady stream. Stir into peppers. Allow to stand at least 2 hours, and up to 24 hours, stirring occasionally. Serve at room temperature. Serves 4.

Basque Cooking and Lore

One Pot Bachelor Cookout

Many a lonely cowpoke in a remote line camp thirty miles from town will appreciate this simple rugged feast. Next time the cow boss comes around, have him bring all the necessary fixin's.

10–12 Idaho spuds, peeled	1 small clove garlic, minced
1 pound thick-sliced bacon	1 bay leaf
3 onions (Walla Walla Sweets), chopped	1 green pepper, chopped
	1 red pepper, chopped
Salt, pepper, and Tabasco to taste	1 small yellow squash, sliced
	4 carrots, sliced
2 tablespoons all-purpose seasoning	1 zucchini, sliced
	10 slices cheese

Cut potatoes into 1-inch chunks. In Dutch oven, fry bacon crisp, then crumble; add onion, and cook until onions are transparent. Add potatoes and seasonings. Place vegetables on top. Cook 30–40 minutes until done. Remove from heat; add cheese slices on top. Cover and let cheese melt over the mess.

Old-Fashioned Dutch Oven Cookbook

Idaho Tacos

1 pound ground beef
1 envelope taco seasoning
4 hot baked potatoes
1 cup (4 ounces) shredded
  sharp Cheddar cheese

1 cup chopped green onions
Salsa (optional)

In a skillet, brown beef; drain. Add taco seasoning; prepare according to package directions. With a sharp knife, cut an X in the top of each potato; fluff pulp with a fork. Top with taco meat, cheese, and onions. Serve with salsa, if desired. Yields 4 servings.

Ashton Area Cookbook

Papa's Favorite Trout

Jack Hemingway says, "This was Papa's favorite trout recipe. Mmmmm!"

1 dozen (6- to 8-inch) little
  brookies, filleted, but leave the
  blood line along backbone

Salt and pepper
1 stick butter
Juice of 2 lemons

Salt and pepper trout inside and out. Melt butter in a large skillet until it froths. Add trout and brown on both sides. Add lemon juice prior to turning trout over with spatula. Baste continuously until butter and trout are browned. Eat right away! Serves 6–8.

Ketchum Cooks

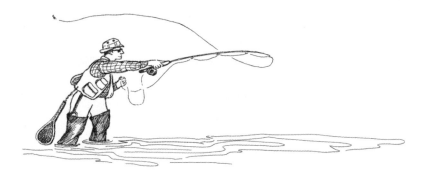

Illinois

CAPITAL: *Springfield*

NICKNAME: *Land of Lincoln*

*I*llinois is a land of diversity and prosperity. The state has been a part of several wars, including the French and Indian War, the Revolutionary War, and the Civil War. In 1871 the city of Chicago was almost completely destroyed by fire, supposedly started when a cow owned by Mrs. O'Leary kicked over a lantern. Illinois was home to President Abraham Lincoln and his wife Mary Todd Lincoln, and President Ronald Reagan was born here, too. Entertainment is world-class, with live theater, talk shows, and museums all over the state. The Bulls and Bears light up the sports arenas. Southern Illinois is considered one of the best hunting areas in the Midwest. Would you believe they dye the Chicago River green on St. Patrick's Day?

Fresh Gooseberry Pie

3 cups fresh gooseberries,
  divided
1½ cups sugar
3 tablespoons quick cooking
  tapioca
⅛ teaspoon salt
Almond Pastry for 2-crust pie
2 tablespoons butter or
  margarine

Crush ¾ cup gooseberries and add to sugar, tapioca, and salt. Stir in remainder of berries. Cook and stir until mixture thickens. Turn into pastry-lined 9-inch pie pan. Dot with butter. Adjust top crust and flute edges; cut vents. Brush with milk. Bake in hot oven (400°) for 35–45 minutes, or until crust is golden. Serve slightly warm.

ALMOND PASTRY:

Before adding water to blended flour and shortening in making pastry for 2-crust pie, add 1 teaspoon almond extract. Also excellent for peach and cherry pies.

What's Cooking "Down Home"

Harry's Chicken Vesuvio

This recipe is a specialty of Chef Abraham Aguirre, chef at Harry Caray's restaurant, "Holy Cow!!!"

½ chicken, cut into 4 pieces
½ teaspoon salt
½ teaspoon pepper
2 teaspoons oregano
2 teaspoons granulated garlic
2 ounces frozen peas
1 teaspoon sugar

1 baking potato, peeled, cut
  into quarters
7 tablespoons olive oil, divided
2 large garlic cloves
½ cup dry white wine
2 teaspoons chopped parsley

Rinse chicken and pat dry. Season with salt, pepper, oregano, and garlic. Combine peas, sugar, and enough boiling water to cover in bowl; mix well. Let stand for 1 minute; drain. Sauté potato in 1 tablespoon olive oil in skillet until golden brown; drain. Heat 6 tablespoons olive oil to 300° in 10-inch skillet. Add garlic cloves. Cook for 2 minutes, stirring occasionally. Add chicken. Sauté until brown on both sides. Add potato; mix well.

Deglaze skillet with white wine. Spoon into baking pan. Bake in 400° oven for 20–30 minutes or until chicken is tender. Transfer chicken to serving platter. Arrange potato and peas around chicken. Pour sauce over top. Sprinkle with parsley. Yields 4 servings.

The Cubs 'R Cookin'

Red Pepper Soup

This soup is absolutely gorgeous! It is not a spicy soup since it uses sweet peppers.

4 red bell peppers, chopped
1 large onion, chopped
2 tablespoons margarine
¼ teaspoon ground cumin

¼ teaspoon cayenne pepper
3 cups chicken broth
½ teaspoon lemon juice

Sauté peppers and onion in margarine until soft. Add cumin and cayenne with chicken broth and simmer until vegetables are very soft.

Purée solids, then run them through a strainer to eliminate pepper skins. Return it all to soup pot and add lemon juice. Yields 6 cups.

Angiporto, Inc.

Marvelous Mocha Pie

20 chocolate Oreo cookies,
  crushed

¼ cup butter, melted
1 quart coffee ice cream

Melt butter. Mix well with crushed cookies and press into pie plate. Spread 1 full quart ice cream over crust and freeze.

CHOCOLATE SAUCE:

3 (3-ounce) squares
  unsweetened chocolate,
  melted
¼ cup butter

⅔ cup sugar
⅔ cup evaporated milk
1 teaspoon vanilla

Bring chocolate, butter, and sugar to a boil. Gradually add evaporated milk. Cook until thickened. Let cool; add vanilla. Spread over ice cream and return to freezer until sauce sets.

TOPPING:

1 cup whipping cream,
  whipped
Toasted almonds, sliced or
  slivered

Kahlúa (optional)

Before serving, top with whipped cream; garnish with nuts. A small amount of Kahlúa may be spooned over whipped cream before serving.

Soupçon II

Born in Kentucky, Abraham Lincoln moved to Illinois in 1830. Lincoln loved Springfield. When he left, he said, "For more than a quarter of a century, I have lived among you and . . . have received nothing but kindness at your hands." Lincoln Log Cabin in Lerna is the last home of Thomas and Sarah Bush Lincoln, parents of Illinois' favorite son, Abraham Lincoln.

Chicago Deep Dish Pizza

2½–3 cups flour, divided
¼ cup cornmeal
1½ teaspoons salt
1 teaspoon sugar
1 package dry yeast
1 cup very hot water

2 tablespoons salad oil
1 tablespoon olive oil
Prego Pizza Sauce
Assorted pizza toppings
Mozzarella cheese

In mixer bowl, combine ½ cup flour, cornmeal, salt, sugar, and yeast. Mix well. With mixer at low speed, gradually add hot water and salad oil. Increase speed to medium and beat one minute. Stir in enough flour to make soft dough.

On lightly floured board, knead 5 minutes. Place in oiled bowl, turning dough to oil top. Cover and let rise until doubled, about 45 minutes. Punch down, and let rest 10 minutes.

Preheat oven to 400°. Roll out dough and fit into deep dish pizza pan, or any oven-proof pan. Prick with fork. Bake dough about 4 minutes and brush lightly with one tablespoon olive oil. Cover with sauce, toppings, and cheese, and bake about 20 minutes more.

Our Best Home Cooking

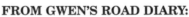

FROM GWEN'S ROAD DIARY:
In October of 1995, we had a filming segment with CLTV in the *Chicago Tribune* test kitchen, where these lovely cooks had made two beautiful Topsy Turvy Upside Down Apple Pies from our *Best of the Best from Illinois Cookbook*. When the filming was done, we asked if we could bring the pies to our next-morning TV spot on WGN. "Yes!" the film director replied. "Let us film the two of you running to your van with the pies like you are on your way." Talk about exciting! With cameras following us, we ran down the corridor, into the elevator, onto the street, and into our van, each carrying a prized pie! Very early the next morning, I made my first national TV appearance on WGN and I was so nervous, I didn't think I would be able to speak! Somehow, on air, the pie actually turned out of the pan beautifully . . . and it spoke for itself.

Illini Pork Medallions

2 large pork tenderloins
  (1¼ pounds each)
2 tablespoons oil
1 medium onion, sliced
½ cup thinly sliced celery
¼ pound fresh mushrooms,
  sliced
¼ cup butter, melted
1 tablespoon flour

½ cup beef stock, or 1 beef
  bouillon cube, dissolved in
  ½ cup hot water
½ cup white wine
1 teaspoon salt
¼ teaspoon freshly ground
  black pepper
Cooked rice

GARNISH:
Spiced crab apples   Orange slices

In hot skillet, brown meat on all sides in oil and set aside. Sauté
onion, celery, and mushrooms in butter until tender. Combine flour
and stock, and stir into vegetables. Stir in wine. Arrange tenderloins in a 9x13-inch pan and sprinkle with salt and pepper. Pour vegetable mixture over all. Cover and bake for 1½ hours at 325°. Cook
to internal temperature of 180° for fresh pork. Remove pork from
pan and cut into ½-inch-thick slices. Arrange on platter; garnish
with spiced crab apples and orange slices. Serve with rice. Makes 6
servings.

Honest to Goodness

Holiday Mashed Potatoes

12 medium potatoes, cooked
1 (8-ounce) package cream
  cheese, cut in chunks
¼ cup margarine
½ cup sour cream

½ cup milk
2 eggs, slightly beaten
1 teaspoon salt
¼ cup finely chopped onion

Mash potatoes while hot. Add cream cheese and margarine.
Combine sour cream and milk. Add to potato mixture. Add beaten
eggs, salt, and onion. Put in greased casserole. (May be prepared the
day before serving and refrigerated in greased casserole.) Bake
uncovered at 350° for 45 minutes.

A Cause for Applause

Italian Beef

1 (6-pound) rump roast
3 large onions, quartered
1 teaspoon salt

¼ teaspoon coarsely ground
   black pepper

Place beef in roaster, half filled with water. Add onions, salt, and pepper. Bake in moderate (350º) oven, covered. Roast until tender. Take from oven. Remove from roaster, transferring to a container in which meat and seasoning can stand overnight.

Next day, remove fat. Slice beef very, very thin (almost shave it). Strain liquid and add:

½ teaspoon garlic salt
½ teaspoon oregano
¼ teaspoon basil

½ teaspoon seasoned salt
1 teaspoon Ac'cent
½ teaspoon Italian seasoning

Bring all ingredients to a boil. Remove from stove. Place thinly sliced beef in layers in pan; sprinkle each with seasoning (salt and pepper). Pour remaining liquid over to cover beef. Place in 350º oven for 1 hour. Serve warm on buns or hard bread and serve with small hot peppers.

Cookbook 25 Years

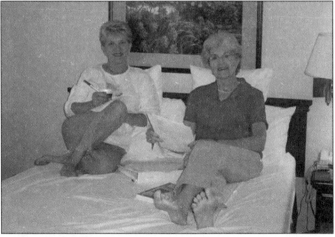

Barbara and Gwen usually have to do "homework" to consolidate notes, plan new research, rehearse for a show, edit recipes, etc. The end of the day on the road is rarely the end of the work.

Indiana

CAPITAL: *Indianapolis*

NICKNAME: *The Hoosier State*

*I*ndiana . . . a land of farms and fields and colorful trees, of sandy dunes and rocky caves, of Indy car races and sports hall-of-famers . . . a state that is a continuous network of charming towns and old-fashioned Hoosier hospitality. The Indiana Extension Homemakers Association is one of the largest in the nation, with some 17,000 members . . . they just love to get together around good old home cooking. In Mentone, you can see the world's largest egg (3,000 pounds), constructed to symbolize the area being the largest egg producer in the Midwest. And as for the origin of the word Hoosier, there are many suggestions . . . "Who's your mom? Who's your dad?" Who knows?

Hoosier Biscuit

1 teaspoon salt
1 pint milk
3–4 cups flour
2 tablespoons yeast

1 teaspoon cream of tartar
2 tablespoons hot water
2–3 eggs

Add a teaspoon of salt to a pint of new milk, warm from the cow. Stir in flour until it becomes a stiff batter, add great spoonfuls of lively brewer's yeast, put it in a warm place, and let it rise as much as it will. When well raised, stir in a teaspoon of saleratus (cream of tartar) dissolved in the hot water. Beat up 3 eggs (2 will answer), stir with the batter, and add flour until it becomes a tolerable stiff dough. Knead it thoroughly, set it by the fire until it begins to rise, and then roll out, cut to biscuit form, put it in pans, cover it over with a thick cloth, set by the fire until it rises again, then bake in a quick oven (400°) for about 30 minutes, or until golden brown.

The Conner Prairie Cookbook

Burgoo

Every fall burgoo festivals in Southern Indiana serve as fund raisers for area churches and schools whose volunteers make up hundreds of gallons at a time and cook it overnight in huge pots over slow fires. Legend has it that burgoo developed as a result of pioneer women wanting to clean out their pantries each year in order to have canning jars for the new crops coming in; the thick, chowdery potage was what resulted from dumping last year's harvest into a community pot with whatever meat (including wild game) was available. A party always ensued. Nowadays, burgoo is available year round at several area taverns.

3 pounds cheap beef roast
2 pounds pork roast
4 cups dry great Northern beans
1 bunch celery
6 medium turnips, peeled
8 medium potatoes, peeled
8 medium onions
½ pound fresh green beans
3 pounds carrots, scraped
1 small head green cabbage
3 (16-ounce) cans corn
3 (16-ounce) cans hominy
3 quarts tomatoes, canned or peeled fresh
1 (48-ounce) can chicken broth
½ lemon, chopped (rind and all)
3 tablespoons mixed pickling spice, tied up in a cheesecloth bag
6–8 ounces ketchup
Salt and pepper to taste

Precook meats and dry beans. Grind meats and vegetables in a food chopper or food processor (do not purée).

Combine all ingredients in a pot. If using more than one pot, blend burgoo back and forth between pots as it cooks. Cook 5 hours over low heat, stirring often and on a regular basis to prevent sticking on bottom. Season with salt and pepper to taste. Yields 10 gallons.

Note: Recipe may be halved. Burgoo freezes well.

Festival Foods and Family Favorites

Oven Fried Chicken

1 frying-size chicken, cut up
⅓ cup plain flour
1 teaspoon salt
Dash of pepper
1 egg

2 tablespoons water
¾ cup cornflake crumbs
¼ cup grated Parmesan cheese
¼ cup margarine, melted

Coat chicken with combined flour and seasonings. Dip chicken in combined egg and water; coat with combined crumbs and cheese. Place in 9x13-inch baking pan; drizzle margarine over chicken. Bake at 375° for 1 hour or until tender.

Our Favorite Recipes II

Skillet Lasagna

1 pound ground beef
1 envelope spaghetti sauce mix,
  divided
1 pound cream-style cottage
  cheese
3 cups noodles (uncooked)

1 (29-ounce) can tomatoes,
  undrained
1 cup water
1 (8 ounce) package shredded
  mozzarella cheese

Lightly brown hamburger; sprinkle ½ of spaghetti mix over meat. Spread cottage cheese over meat. Next, add noodles in layers. Sprinkle remaining spaghetti mix. Add tomatoes and water and continue cooking slowly for 30–35 minutes. Sprinkle cheese over top. Return cover and let stand 10–15 minutes before serving.

Amish Country Cookbook II

The Indianapolis Motor Speedway is a National Historic Landmark. The Speedway was built as a combination race track and testing facility in 1909. The 500-Mile Race was first held in 1911. Today it is the world's largest one-day sporting event. The Brickyard 400, a NASCAR event, was first held in August, 1994.

Indiana Raspberry Tart

A unique recipe combining cooked and uncooked berries with exceptional results.

PASTRY:

1 cup all-purpose flour
2 tablespoons sugar
⅛ teaspoon salt

½ cup (1 stick) butter or
  margarine, cold
2–3 tablespoons cold water

Preheat oven to 400°. In medium bowl, combine flour, sugar, and salt. Cut in butter until crumbly. Sprinkle with water, 1 tablespoon at a time, until pastry mixture is just moist and holds together. Press pastry into bottom and 1-inch up side of a 9-inch springform pan. Set aside.

FILLING:

¼ teaspoon ground cinnamon
⅔ cup sugar
¼ cup all-purpose flour

6 cups fresh raspberries,
  divided
Whipping cream

Combine cinnamon, sugar, and flour in small bowl. Sprinkle half the flour mixture over the bottom of Pastry. Top with 4 cups raspberries. Sprinkle remaining flour mixture over raspberries.

Bake tart on lowest oven rack, 50–60 minutes, or until golden and bubbly. Remove from oven; cool on wire rack. Remove side of springform pan carefully after tart has completely cooled. Top with remaining 2 cups raspberries. Cut into wedges.

To serve, pour 2 tablespoons cream on individual plate; arrange a tart wedge on cream. Serves 10.

Back Home Again

Rockville is the Covered Bridge Capital of the World. There are 32 covered bridges in Parke County alone. A ten-day festival is held there each October, bringing over one million people to the county.

Fresh Tomato Pie

2 tablespoons butter
2 large onions, thinly sliced
12 slices bacon, divided
2 cups fresh soft bread crumbs, divided
3–4 fresh ripe tomatoes, thinly sliced

2 cups grated Cheddar cheese
3 eggs
½ teaspoon salt
⅛ teaspoon pepper

Butter a 9-inch pie plate. Melt butter in a medium-size skillet over medium heat. Sauté onions for 3–5 minutes. Set aside.

Cook 9 slices bacon; drain and crumble. Reserve 3 slices. Place 1 cup bread crumbs in prepared pie plate. Place ingredients in layers as follows: tomatoes, onions, cheese, and bacon. Repeat layers until all ingredients are used. The pie will be mounded but cooks down.

Beat eggs well; add salt and pepper. Pour over pie. Sprinkle with remaining 1 cup bread crumbs. Cook 3 slices of bacon halfway in the microwave to remove of some of the grease before draping them on top of the pie. Bake at 350° for 35–40 minutes. Garnish with parsley and serve.

Hopewell's Hoosier Harvest II

Overnight Chicken Casserole

5 chicken breasts, or 1 chicken, stewed, boned, and diced
2 cups chicken broth
1 (7-ounce) package elbow macaroni, uncooked
1 (10¾-ounce) can cream of mushroom soup
1 (10¾-ounce) can cream of celery soup

¼ pound diced Velveeta or shredded sharp cheese
3 hard-boiled eggs, diced
1 (4-ounce) package slivered almonds
Onion salt or flakes to taste

Mix together and pour into a 9x13-inch casserole. Store covered in the refrigerator overnight. Bake uncovered for 1 hour at 350°. Serves 12.

Mincemeat and Memories

Peaches 'N Cream Pie

¾ cup flour
½ teaspoon salt
½ cup milk
1 (3¼-ounce) package dry
  vanilla pudding mix
  (not instant)
1 teaspoon baking powder
1 egg
3 tablespoons soft margarine
  or butter

1 (15- to 20-ounce) can sliced
  peaches, well drained,
  reserve juice
1 (8-ounce) package cream
  cheese, softened
3 tablespoons reserved juice
½ cup plus 1 tablespoon sugar,
  divided
½ teaspoon cinnamon

Grease and flour a deep 9-inch pie pan. Combine and beat first 7 ingredients for 2 minutes at medium speed. Pour into prepared pie pan. Place peaches over batter.

In a small bowl, combine cream cheese, juice, and ½ cup sugar, and beat for 2 minutes at medium speed. Spoon over peaches to within 1 inch of edge. Combine remaining 1 tablespoon sugar and cinnamon and sprinkle over cream cheese filling. Bake at 350° for 30–35 minutes. Cool. Refrigerate.

Love Cookin'

FROM GWEN'S ROAD DIARY:
People are always asking us about unusual foods and things that we discover that are beyond the norm. A reporter friend in Evansville told us that one of the taverns there had pork brain sandwiches on the menu and had for a long time. So, of course, we had to go see for ourselves! I must report that it wasn't bad at all. Indeed our travels have led us to taste the likes of rattlesnake, ostrich, alligator, buffalo, moose, reindeer, ants—you name it—in disguised forms of grilled, pickled, chocolate covered, battered and fried. Our endeavor to discover America's BEST required that we open our minds and our taste buds, something we would recommend for everybody.

Iowa

CAPITAL: *Des Moines*

NICKNAME: *The Hawkeye State*

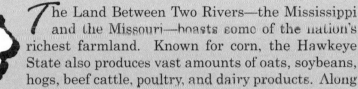

The Land Between Two Rivers—the Mississippi and the Missouri—boasts some of the nation's richest farmland. Known for corn, the Hawkeye State also produces vast amounts of oats, soybeans, hogs, beef cattle, poultry, and dairy products. Along the Grant Wood Scenic Byway, you'll recognize the things that inspired this Iowa painter: rolling hills, church spires, corn stalks, rounded haystacks. The *American Gothic* house of his famous painting is in Eldon. Iowans use new and innovative ideas to create recipes using available resources while always searching for different ways to bring good food to the family table. Eskimo Pies, the popular ice cream treats, were invented in the town of Onawa in 1920.

Iowa Chops

½ cup whole-kernel corn
½ cup bread crumbs
Pinch of salt and pepper
¾ tablespoon parsley
Pinch of sage

½ tablespoon chopped onion
½ cup finely chopped, peeled apple
1 tablespoon milk
2 Iowa pork chops, thick cut

In a bowl, combine ingredients, except chops, until well mixed. Cut a slit in the side of chop and stuff with mixture.

BASTING SAUCE:
¼ cup honey
¼ cup mustard
¼ teaspoon rosemary leaves

½ teaspoon salt
Pinch of pepper

Combine Basting Sauce ingredients and blend until smooth.

In frying pan, brown stuffed chops, then bake in 350° oven for about one hour, basting chops often with sauce.

Spanning the Bridge of Time

Almond Cookies
(Bitterkoekjes)

½ pound almond paste   ¾ cup sugar
2 egg whites, unbeaten

Mix ingredients together with a fork. Drop by teaspoon onto greased cookie sheet. Bake at 300° for 20 minutes. Remove from cookie sheet promptly to prevent sticking.

Dutch Touches

Nutty Cereal Snack

1 (12-ounce) package square
  bite-size rice cereal (12 cups)
1 (12-ounce) package M&M's
  (1½ cups)
2 (2-ounce) packages slivered
  almonds
1 (3.75-ounce) package shelled
  sunflower seeds

1 cup plus 2 tablespoons
  margarine or butter
1½ cups sugar
1½ cups light corn syrup
1½ teaspoons vanilla

In a very large container, combine cereal, M&M's, almonds, and sunflower seeds; set aside. In a large saucepan, melt margarine. Add sugar and syrup to saucepan and stir to combine. Bring mixture to a boil over medium heat. Boil gently for 3 minutes, stirring frequently. Remove pan from heat and stir in vanilla. Pour syrup over cereal mixture, while stirring, until pieces are coated. Turn out onto wax paper and let stand, covered with wax paper, for several hours.

Iowa Granges Celebrating 125 Years of Cooking

The *Field of Dreams* movie site is a baseball diamond carved from a corn field where the Academy Award-nominated movie was filmed in the summer of 1988. The "field" is located on two farms three miles northeast of Dyersville.

Skillet Sweet Corn

Cream corn right off the cob.

6 ears corn
6 tablespoons butter
½ cup light cream

½ teaspoon salt
½ teaspoon granulated sugar
Ground pepper to taste

Husk corn and remove silks. Slice off kernels with a long sharp knife or electric knife. Using the back of a dinner knife, scrape the milky substance from the cob into the corn. Heat butter in a skillet, add corn and milky substance, and cook and stir 3–4 minutes or until desired tenderness. Add cream and seasonings. Stir over low heat for 2–3 minutes. Makes 4 servings.

A Cook's Tour of Iowa

Pride of Iowa Cookies

1 cup brown sugar
1 cup white sugar
1 cup shortening
2 eggs
1¾ cups flour
1 teaspoon baking soda
1 teaspoon baking powder

½ teaspoon salt
1¾ cups oatmeal
½ cup nuts (optional)
1 cup chocolate chips
½ cup flaked coconut
   (optional)

Cream sugars, shortening, and eggs. Sift flour, baking soda, baking powder, and salt. Add oatmeal, then stir into creamed mixture. Add nuts, chips, and coconut, if desired. Drop onto lightly greased cookie sheet. Bake at 350° for 10–12 minutes.

Country Cupboard Cookbook

Caramel Ice Cream Dessert

1 stick butter, melted
2 cups graham cracker crumbs
1½ cups brown sugar

1 cup chopped pecans
1 cup caramel topping
½ gallon ice cream, softened

Mix melted butter, graham cracker crumbs, and brown sugar. Reserve ¼ of the mixture. Press remaining crumb mixture in the bottom of a 9x13-inch pan. Bake at 350° for 15 minutes. Let cool. Layer nuts on top of baked crumbs, then caramel topping, then softened ice cream. Top with reserved crumb mixture. Freeze before serving.

SEP Junior Women's Club 25th Anniversary Cookbook

Berry Delicious Bread

1 (10-ounce) package frozen
  strawberries, thawed
¾ cup sugar
⅔ cup oil
2 eggs

1½ cups flour
1 teaspoon baking soda
½ teaspoon salt
½ teaspoon cinnamon
¾ cup chopped nuts (optional)

Grease and flour a 9x5-inch loaf pan (or can be baked in smaller loaf pans). Combine strawberries, sugar, oil, and eggs. Beat on medium speed for 2 minutes. Add remaining dry ingredients. Stir until moistened. Pour into pan. Bake in preheated oven at 350° for 50–60 minutes. Cool in pan for 15 minutes, then remove.

Applause Applause

 Swing to the Big Band sounds of Glenn Miller in Clarinda. The house where the popular orchestra leader and hit-maker of the swing era was born has been restored with period furnishings and is open for visitors.

Pasghetti Pizza

1 (16-ounce) package spaghetti
2 eggs
½ cup milk
4 cups shredded mozzarella, divided
¾ teaspoon garlic powder
Salt to taste
1 pound ground beef, browned and drained
1½ teaspoons oregano
1 (32-ounce) jar spaghetti sauce
1 package sliced pepperoni

Break spaghetti into 2-inch pieces. Cook and drain. In large bowl, beat eggs. Add milk, one cup cheese, garlic powder, and salt. Add spaghetti and stir. Spread this mixture into greased 10x15-inch jellyroll pan. Bake 15 minutes at 400°. Spread ground beef over spaghetti and sprinkle with oregano.

Spread spaghetti sauce over this, then put on the sliced pepperoni. Top with remaining cheese. Lower temperature to 350° and bake 20 minutes until cheese is bubbly and browned. Let stand 5 minutes before cutting.

Spitfire Anniversary Cookbook

FROM GWEN'S ROAD DIARY:
On research trips, it was always maddening that most of the stores were only open from 10 a.m. to 5 p.m., especially in small communities, and this is where we did a lot of research. So after-hours, we went to malls and restaurants, garnering local food information from people, menus, books, wherever, never wasting a moment of our precious time. We set up our promotion trips ourselves, weaving each city's TV, radio, and newspaper interviews into the mapped-out days. We often had to push to drive to the next town, getting to our hotel well into the night. I always unwound at the end of the day by keeping a diary to record daily happenings . . . people, places, thoughts, plans, and how today's experiences might help us to improve on whatever lie ahead tomorrow.

Kansas

CAPITAL: *Topeka*

NICKNAME: *The Sunflower State*

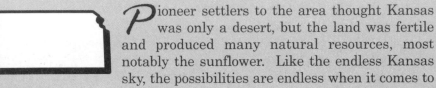

Pioneer settlers to the area thought Kansas was only a desert, but the land was fertile and produced many natural resources, most notably the sunflower. Like the endless Kansas sky, the possibilities are endless when it comes to good food in the Sunflower State. Sumner County is known as the Wheat Capital of the World. All the wheat grown in Kansas in a single year would fit in a train stretching from western Kansas to the Atlantic Ocean. Ask almost anyone, though, and you'll find it's the barbecue they take most seriously. Restaurants, organizations, associations, and individuals all boast about their excellent barbecue recipes . . . and we can tell you firsthand, they have every right to brag.

Barbecued Steak

1 cup ketchup
½ cup water
¼ cup vinegar
¼ cup chopped green pepper
¼ cup chopped onion
1½ tablespoons Worcestershire

1 tablespoon prepared mustard
2 tablespoons brown sugar
½ teaspoon salt
⅛ teaspoon pepper
4 pounds round steak, cut
  ½ inch thick

In saucepan, combine all ingredients except steak. Bring to a boil, then simmer for about 5 minutes over low heat. Keep barbecue sauce hot. Cut steak into serving-size portions. Place pieces in a large roasting pan. Pour hot barbecue sauce over meat. Cover and bake at 325° for 1½–2 hours. Makes 8–10 servings.

Recipes & Remembrances/Courtland Covenant Church

Speedy Overnight Casserole

3 cups chopped cooked chicken
  or turkey
2 cups uncooked large elbow
  macaroni
1 (10¾-ounce) can cream of
  mushroom soup
1 (10¾-ounce) can cream of
  chicken soup
1 soup can milk

1 soup can chicken broth
1 small onion, chopped
1 (8-ounce) can sliced water
  chestnuts
½ teaspoon salt
½ pound grated cheese (save
  some for topping)
1 cup crushed potato chips

Mix all ingredients except chips. Put in 9x13-inch pan. Sprinkle reserved cheese and potato chips on top. Cover with foil. Refrigerate overnight.

    Bake, covered, for 1½ hours at 350°. This freezes well.

Home at the Range III

Cinnamon Trail Mix

2 cups toasted oat cereal
2 cups hexagon-shaped corn
  cereal
2 cups pretzel bits
¾ cup raisins

½ cup sunflower seeds
2 tablespoons reduced-fat
  margarine
2 tablespoons brown sugar
1 tablespoon cinnamon

In a large bowl, combine cereals, pretzel bits, raisins, and sunflower seeds. Toss gently. Melt margarine in microwave or saucepan, and stir in brown sugar and cinnamon. Pour over cereal mixture. Toss to coat. Bake 8–10 minutes in a 350° oven.

Sisters Two II

A few Kansas facts: Kansas' name is from the Kansa or Kaw Indians. The cottonwood tree is often called the "pioneer of Kansas" because of its abundance on the plains. The official state song of Kansas is "Home on the Range."

Kansas Mud

1 (8-ounce) package cream
  cheese, softened
1 cup powdered sugar
½ cup margarine, softened
2 (3-ounce) packages vanilla
  instant pudding

3 cups milk
1 teaspoon vanilla
1 large carton Cool Whip
1 large package Oreo cookies,
  crushed

Cream together cream cheese, powdered sugar, and margarine. Mix pudding, milk, and vanilla together, then add to above mixture. Fold in Cool Whip. Fold in crushed Oreo cookies, reserving some cookie crumbs to add to top. Line flowerpot with foil, add dessert, top with reserved cookie crumbs (dirt), and add artificial sunflower.

125 Years of Cookin' with the Lord

Sunflowers are native to American soil and have been growing wild in Kansas for centuries.

German Chocolate Caramel Brownies

1 (14-ounce) package caramels,
  unwrapped
1 (5-ounce) can evaporated
  milk, divided
1 (18¼-ounce) package
  German chocolate cake mix

¾ cup margarine, melted
1 cup (6 ounces) chocolate
  chips

Melt caramels and ⅓ cup evaporated milk together. Mix together cake mix, margarine, remaining ⅓ cup evaporated milk, and chocolate chips. Grease a 9x13-inch pan. Press ½ dough in pan; spread with caramel mixture. Top loosely with rest of dough. Bake 30 minutes at 350°.

Home at the Range II

Chicken Pot Pie

How wonderful! Chicken pot pie you can make without deboning a chicken and peeling vegetables.

2 (9-inch) deep-dish frozen pie
  shells
1 (10-ounce) can chunk chicken,
  drained
1 (15-ounce) can mixed
  vegetables, drained

1 (2.8-ounce) can French fried
  onion rings
2 (10¾-ounce) cans condensed
  cream of chicken soup
¼ teaspoon salt

Prick bottom of pie shell all over with fork. Bake uncovered at 375° for 10 minutes. Combine chicken, vegetables, onion rings, soup, and salt. Fill bottom pie shell with mixture. Place second pie shell on top. Prick with fork in 6 places. Set on a foil-covered oven rack to catch spills. Bake uncovered at 375° for 40 minutes. Yields 6 servings.

The Give Mom a Rest (She's on Vacation) Cookbook

Kansas ranks first in the United States in quail and prairie chicken harvest.

Peanut Clusters

The chocolate bark/butterscotch chips combination is my family's favorite, but they are all delicious. This is a recipe that children can easily make on their own. It is foolproof. If the mixture is too thin to drop into nice mounds, let it cool a little to thicken.

1 (24-ounce) package almond bark, vanilla or chocolate
2 cups (12 ounces) baking chips (chocolate, vanilla, or butterscotch)

4²⁄₃ cups (24 ounces) salted peanuts

Melt almond bark and chips together in the microwave or place in a low oven. Keep away from all water. Stir until smooth. Stir in peanuts. Drop teaspoonfuls onto wax paper. Let cool to harden. Yields 5 dozen.

The Give Mom a Rest (She's on Vacation) Cookbook

Border Burgers

2 pounds lean ground beef
1 (4-ounce) can diced green chiles
1½ cups finely shredded Cheddar cheese, divided
½ teaspoon salt

½ teaspoon pepper
½ teaspoon cumin
4 hamburger buns, separated
2 (15-ounce) cans chili with beans, heated
1 cup chopped red onion

Combine ground beef, green chiles, ¾ cup Cheddar cheese, salt, pepper, and cumin in bowl; mix well. Shape into 8 (¾-inch-thick) patties. Grill 4–6 inches above hot coals for 8 minutes for rare, 12 minutes for medium, and 15 minutes for well done, turning once or twice. Move patties to edge of grill. Place buns cut-side-down on grill. Grill for one minute or until light brown. Remove from grill. Arrange patties on buns on serving platter. Top with chili; sprinkle with cheese and onion. Yields 8 servings.

The Kansas City Barbeque Society Cookbook

Kentucky

CAPITAL: *Frankfort*

NICKNAME: *The Bluegrass State*

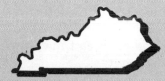

Kentucky . . . the mere mention of its name brings a vision of gentle bluegrass countryside with thoroughbred horses grazing behind miles of painted wooden fences. The cooking heritage of the Bluegrass State goes back to simple mountain-folk food, beginning when Daniel Boone crossed the Cumberland Gap in 1775 . . . and Kentuckians have been blazing new trails in cooking ever since. While the Colonel introduced his fried chicken to the world, the Brown Hotel was making its Hot Brown Sandwich famous, too. Many favorite recipes are directly attributable to the Kentucky Derby, such as Derby Pie and Mint Juleps. Kentucky is the state where both Abraham Lincoln, President of the Union, and Jefferson Davis, President of the Confederacy, were born . . . less than one hundred miles and one year apart. One of the world's largest gold depositories is at Fort Knox military reservation. In 1893, two Louisville sisters wrote the most popular, most sung, most recognizable song in the world . . . "Happy Birthday to You."

Kentucky Colonels

½ pound butter, softened
2 pounds confectioners' sugar, divided
Dash salt
½ cup crème de menthe or bourbon
½ rectangle paraffin
12 ounces semisweet chocolate

Gradually blend butter with sugar (reserve some for rolling balls), salt, and liqueur. Roll into balls the size of marbles. Roll balls in powdered sugar. Refrigerate until firm. Melt paraffin in double boiler. Slowly add chocolate, and, if desired, 1 tablespoon liqueur. Do not let water under pan boil. Dip balls in chocolate. Place on wax paper and refrigerate. If necessary, thin chocolate with a few drops of salad oil. Makes 120.

The Cooking Book

Broccoli Bisque

1 cup sliced leeks
1 cup sliced mushrooms
3 tablespoons butter or
  margarine
3 tablespoons flour

3 cups chicken broth
1 cup broccoli florets
1 cup light cream or milk
1 cup grated Jarlsburg cheese

In a large saucepan, sauté leeks and mushrooms in butter until tender (do not brown). Add flour and cook, stirring, until bubbling. Remove from heat and gradually blend in chicken broth. Return to heat; cook and stir until smooth and thick. Add broccoli; reduce heat and simmer 20 minutes or until broccoli is tender. Blend in cream and cheese, and cook until cheese melts. Season to taste.

Bluegrass Winners

Berea Kentucky Corn Sticks

1/2 cup flour
2 cups white cornmeal
1/2 teaspoon salt
1 teaspoon baking powder
1/2 teaspoon baking soda

2 cups buttermilk
2 eggs, well beaten
4 tablespoons lard or
  shortening, melted

Sift flour, cornmeal, salt, and baking powder together. Mix baking soda with buttermilk. Add to dry ingredients. Mix. Add eggs and beat. Add lard. Mix well. Pour into well-greased, hot corn stick pans. Place on lower shelf of oven at 450°–500° for 8 minutes. Move to upper shelf and bake 5–10 minutes longer. Yields 12–14 large corn sticks.

A Taste from Back Home

Kentucky's blue grass is not really blue—it's green. But in the spring, it produces bluish-purple buds that give a rich blue cast to a large field.

The word "bluegrass" also describes a kind of country string band music developed by Bill Monroe in the late 1940s. Monroe, "the Father of Bluegrass," comes from Kentucky and chose the state nickname for his band, the Blue Grass Boys, featuring a young Earl Scruggs on five-string banjo, Lester Flatt on guitar, and Chubby Wise on fiddle. This was the group that was to be the model for all bluegrass groups to come, carving a permanent name for bluegrass in the annals of American popular culture.

Mr. Closson's Mint Julep

This recipe comes from Burton Closson. The technique of steeping mint leaves in bourbon caught the attention of cookbook committee members.

SIMPLE SYRUP:

Boil equal amounts of sugar and water. Cool and refrigerate.

MINT-FLAVORED BOURBON:

Fresh mint leaves (enough to stuff the bottle)

1 quart bourbon (Old Rip Van Winkle)

Wash and dry mint leaves. Add to bourbon and let steep in the bottle for 3 days. Remove leaves and discard them. To serve, fill julep glass with crushed ice. Pour 1–1½ tablespoons Simple Syrup over ice. Fill glass with Mint-Flavored Bourbon. Stir. Garnish with sprig of mint.

The Kentucky Derby Museum Cookbook

Louisville Hot Brown

This is an adaptation of Cissy Gregg's two-sauce recipe—a simpler and quicker recipe. Its authorship is unclear, and it has been printed a number of times over the years.

1 small onion, chopped
4 tablespoons butter
3 tablespoons flour
2 cups milk
½ teaspoon salt
¼ teaspoon white pepper
¼ cup shredded Cheddar

¼ cup grated Parmesan
8 slices toast, trimmed
Cooked chicken or turkey breast slices
Crisp-fried bacon, crumbled
Mushroom slices, sautéed

Sauté onion in butter until transparent; add flour and combine. Add milk, salt, and pepper and whisk until smooth. Cook on medium heat until sauce thickens, stirring occasionally. Add cheeses and continue heating until they blend. Remove from heat.

Put one slice of toast in each of 4 oven-proof individual serving dishes. Top each piece of toast with slices of chicken or turkey. Cut remaining toast slices diagonally and place on sides of sandwiches. Ladle cheese sauce over sandwiches. Place sandwiches under broiler until sauce begins to bubble. Garnish with crumbled bacon and sautéed mushroom slices and serve immediately.

The Courier–Journal Kentucky Cookbook

Chocolate-Nut Pie

½ cup margarine, melted
1 cup sugar
½ cup flour
2 eggs, slightly beaten

1 teaspoon vanilla
¾ cup English walnuts
¾ cup chocolate chips
1 (9-inch) unbaked pie shell

Mix in order given. Pour into unbaked pie shell. Bake at 350° for 30 minutes.

My Old Kentucky Homes Cookbook

Editor's Extra: If you like a crispier crust, prebake it 5 minutes in 450° oven.

The Downs

3 cups cooked and diced
  chicken breasts
2 hard-boiled eggs, chopped
¼ cup chopped black olives
¼ cup chopped celery
½ cup mayonnaise
1 tablespoon lemon juice

Salt to taste
12 slices white bread, crusts
  removed
1 (10¾-ounce) can cream of
  chicken soup, undiluted
1 cup sour cream
1 cup grated Cheddar cheese

Combine chicken, eggs, olives, and celery. Blend in mayonnaise and lemon juice. Salt to taste. Spread chicken mixture on bread to make a sandwich. Place 6 sandwiches in a 9x13-inch casserole. Combine soup and sour cream. Pour over sandwiches. Cover and refrigerate overnight.

Bake at 325° for 20 minutes. Add grated cheese and bake until cheese melts. Serves 6.

Fillies Flavours

Raspberry Carousel

1 (3-ounce) box raspberry
  gelatin
2 cups boiling water, divided
¾ cup cranberry juice
1 cup diced apples
¼ cup sliced celery

½ cup chopped walnuts
1 (3-ounce) box lemon gelatin
1 (8-ounce) carton whipped
  topping
¼ cup mayonnaise (optional)

Dissolve raspberry gelatin in 1 cup boiling water. Add cranberry juice and chill until thickened, about 1 hour. Fold in apples, celery, and nuts. Spoon in 6-cup mold and chill until set, about 15 minutes. Dissolve lemon gelatin in remaining boiling water. Chill until slightly thickened, about 45 minutes. Combine whipped topping and mayonnaise. Fold into gelatin. Spoon into mold. Chill until firm, at least 4 hours. Unmold on crisp salad greens.

Lake Reflections

Black Bottom Pie with Bourbon

Delicious! Different! Dazzle your guests!

1 envelope unflavored gelatin
¼ cup cold water
1 cup sugar, divided
3 tablespoons cornstarch
2 cups milk
4 large eggs, separated
3 tablespoons Kentucky
  bourbon

1½ ounces unsweetened
  chocolate, melted
1 teaspoon vanilla
¼ teaspoon cream of tartar
1 (9-inch) pie shell, baked

Sprinkle gelatin into cold water. In saucepan, stir together ½ cup sugar and cornstarch. Gradually stir in milk. Add egg yolks. Cook over medium heat, stirring constantly until mixture becomes as thick as mayonnaise. Remove from heat. Reserve one cup of mixture. Into remaining hot mixture, stir gelatin and bourbon. Refrigerate until cooled thoroughly (about 30 minutes).

Stir chocolate and vanilla into reserved one cup of mixture. Spread over bottom of pie shell. Refrigerate. When refrigerated mixture is cooled, beat egg whites with cream of tartar; gradually add remaining ½ cup sugar, beating until soft peaks form. Fold into chilled gelatin mixture. Spoon over chocolate layer in pie shell. Refrigerate at least 3 hours before serving. Yields 1 (9-inch) pie.

To Market, To Market

Louisiana

CAPITAL: *Baton Rouge*

NICKNAME: *The Pelican State*

*L*ouisiana is a party: it's Mardi Gras; it's jazz; it's football; it's finding any excuse at all to cook up some good food and have a party! Abbeville has a festival around a 5,000-egg omelet—now there's a party. Food may be a necessity of life, but in Louisiana, it is a celebration of life. And everybody who cooks and eats these full-of-taste Cajun and Creole dishes seems to know that they're a part of this special magic. Scared to try it? First you make a roux, then you add the Holy Trinity (chopped onions, bell pepper, and celery), and anything added after that is guaranteed to be good! Of course you'll have to use some of that good ole Louisiana Tabasco sauce to spice it up. And here's a crawfish tale: It is said some of the lobsters in Nova Scotia wanted to relocate with the Acadians to Louisiana, but the trip was so hard and long that they lost a lot of weight! In season, crawfish are everywhere; we had crawfish dogs at a service station in Breaux Bridge—talk about good!

Creamy Smooth Pecan Pralines

2 cups sugar
½ cup white Karo syrup
½ cup water

2 cups pecan halves
½ stick margarine
1 tablespoon vanilla

Combine sugar, syrup, water, and pecans in heavy 3-quart saucepan. Stir over medium heat until sugar is dissolved and mixture comes to a boil. Cook, stirring occasionally, until mixture reaches soft-ball stage (small amount forms soft ball when dropped into cold water). Remove saucepan from heat; add margarine and vanilla.

Allow candy to cool. Whip until mixture gradually changes to lighter color and becomes creamy. Drop by tablespoonfuls onto buttered cookie sheet. Push mixture from tablespoon with a teaspoon to hasten dropping before praline becomes too firm to shape.

Tony Chachere's Cajun Country Cookbook

Crawfish Pistolettes

1 onion, chopped	Tony Chachere's Creole
1 bell pepper, chopped	Seasoning to taste
2 ribs celery, chopped	1 (10¾-ounce) can cream of
1 clove garlic, chopped	mushroom soup
1 stick butter	3 tablespoons chopped parsley
2 pounds crawfish tails	30 pistolettes (like French
1 (4-ounce) can mushroom	mini-rolls)
pieces, drained	

Sauté vegetables in butter. Add crawfish, mushrooms, and seasoning. Cook for 15 minutes. Add mushroom soup and parsley. Simmer 5 minutes on low heat. Let cool. Cut off tip of pistolette. Remove some of the bread from inside and replace with crawfish mixture. Replace bread tip. Spread melted butter and garlic powder on top of pistolette. Bake at 450° for 8 minutes.

Variation: Add ½ pound melted Velveeta cheese.

St. Philomena School 125th Anniversary

Crawfish Étouffée II

2 tablespoons butter	1 teaspoon chili powder
2 medium onions, chopped fine	1 tablespoon Worcestershire
2 bell peppers, chopped fine	1 tablespoon Louisiana Hot
4 ribs celery, chopped fine	Sauce
1 clove garlic, minced	Salt and pepper to taste
1 (8-ounce) can tomato sauce	1 pound crawfish tails
1 package dry spaghetti mix	

Heat butter in large skillet. Add onions, bell peppers, celery, and garlic. Sauté ingredients. Add tomato sauce, spaghetti mix, chili powder, Worcestershire, hot sauce, salt and pepper to taste. Let simmer for 30 minutes. Add crawfish; cover tightly and cook on low heat for about one hour. Serve over rice. Serves 4.

The Louisiana Crawfish Cookbook

Pralines & Cream Dream

1 cup light brown sugar
¼ cup light corn syrup
½ cup half-and-half
2 tablespoons butter

1 cup coarsely chopped pecans
½ teaspoon vanilla
Vanilla ice cream

In a small saucepan, combine brown sugar, corn syrup, and half-and-half. Place over medium heat and cook for 7–8 minutes. Stir in butter, pecans, and vanilla. Remove and cool completely. To serve, spoon alternate layers of ice cream and praline sauce in a wine glass or parfait glass. Serves 6.

Kay Ewing's Cooking School Cookbook

Stuffed Eggplant

4 medium eggplants
1 cup finely chopped onions
½ cup finely chopped celery
¼ pound margarine
12 stale saltine crackers
2 eggs
2 pounds boiled shrimp,
  peeled and deveined

1 pound white crabmeat
Parsley and green onions
  to taste
Cajun seasoning to taste
Italian bread crumbs

Cut each eggplant into 2 equal parts; remove middle (leave thick shell) and chop. In saucepan, sauté chopped eggplant, onions, celery, and margarine until done. Crush crackers and put in bowl with eggs. Mix well with chopped boiled shrimp, eggplant mixture, crabmeat, parsley, and green onions. Season to taste. Boil shells of eggplant for 10 minutes or until tender, then stuff with mixture. Top each eggplant with Italian bread crumbs. Bake 20–25 minutes at 350°.

Secrets of the Original Don's Seafood & Steakhouse

Cajuns love to go two-steppin' to the rhythms of "chank-a-chank." Cajun music is a blend of German, Spanish, Scottish, Irish, Anglo-American, African-Caribbean, and American Indian influences with a base of western French and French Acadian folk tradition. Broken down more graphically, some call it bluegrass with a French accent, or European folk music. The instruments are the fiddle, accordion, and triangle. A fais do-do is a Cajun party with music, dancing, and plenty of food. Lagniappe is a little something extra.

Shrimp Creole

¼ cup flour
¼ cup bacon grease
2 cups chopped onions
½ cup chopped green onions
2 cloves garlic, minced
1 cup chopped green pepper
1 cup chopped celery, with
  leaves
1 teaspoon thyme
2 bay leaves
3 teaspoons salt
½ teaspoon pepper
1 (6-ounce) can tomato paste

1 (16-ounce) can tomatoes and
  liquid, coarsely chopped
1 (8-ounce) can tomato sauce
1 cup stock (made from boiling
  shrimp heads and shells), or
  1 cup water
4 pounds peeled and deveined
  raw shrimp
1 teaspoon Tabasco
½ cup chopped parsley
1 tablespoon lemon juice
2 cups cooked rice

In a 4-quart Dutch oven, make a dark brown roux of flour and bacon grease. Add onions, green onions, garlic, green pepper, celery, thyme, bay leaves, salt, and pepper, and sauté uncovered over medium fire until onions are transparent and soft, about 30 minutes. Add tomato paste, and sauté 3 minutes. Add tomatoes, tomato sauce, and stock (or water). Simmer very slowly, partially covered, for one hour, stirring occasionally. Add shrimp and cook until shrimp are just done, about 5 minutes. Add Tabasco, parsley, and lemon juice. Stir, cover, and remove from heat. Serve over rice.

    This dish is best when allowed to stand several hours or overnight. Let cool and refrigerate. It also freezes well. Remove from refrigerator one hour before serving. Heat quickly, without boiling, and serve immediately.

The Plantation Cookbook

Seafood Gumbo

½ cup oil
½ cup all-purpose flour
2 cups finely chopped onions
2 teaspoons chopped green
  onions
1 cup finely chopped celery
1½ gallons water (boil shrimp
  peelings for stock water)
4 cloves garlic, minced
  (optional)

Salt, black pepper, and cayenne
  pepper to taste
2 pounds shrimp, peeled and
  deveined
½ teaspoon finely chopped
  parsley
½ pint shelled oysters
1 pound claw crabmeat
Gumbo filé (optional)

Make a roux with oil and flour. Pour off excess oil from roux; add onions and celery. Cook until onions are wilted, then add water and garlic. Cook in heavy uncovered pot over medium heat for one hour, and season to taste with salt, black pepper, and cayenne. Add shrimp and parsley to mixture; cook another 10–15 minutes. Add oysters and crabmeat to gumbo; allow to come to a boil. Serve in soup plates with cooked rice. Serves 6. Use a dash of filé in each plate, if desired.

Secrets of the Original Don's Seafood & Steakhouse

FROM GWEN'S ROAD DIARY:
Scheduled for a very early morning TV appearance in the Quarter in New Orleans and being familiar with the city, I saw no need for us to do a "dry run" as we usually did to find the location the night before . . . better to allow plenty of time in the morning when it was quiet. What we didn't count on was the fog! "We couldn't see the street signs from our van! When we finally found the designated lift door on a side street, we parked hurriedly and knocked on the door. No answer. We knocked louder with our watches telling us there was no more time, and in the process, woke a person who looked like he had partied all night, who wasn't very happy about our disturbance. The door finally opened before we had to confront him. Once inside the studio, we were treated like we had stepped out of a limousine."

Crawfish Remoulade

2 teaspoons horseradish
  mustard
½ cup tarragon vinegar
2 tablespoons ketchup
½ teaspoon paprika
1 clove garlic, minced

1 teaspoon cayenne pepper
1 cup salad oil
½ cup chopped green onions
½ cup chopped celery
2 teaspoons salt
3 pounds cooked crawfish

Combine all ingredients except crawfish in blender. Pour over crawfish and marinate overnight. Serve chilled.

Roger's Cajun Cookbook

Editor's Extra: Equally good with shrimp.

Blackened Rib Eye

Because the cooking process is very fast in this recipe, thickness is the only way to achieve the desired stage of cooking. Use the suggested chart to choose the correct thickness of your steak. Be sure to have great ventilation before cooking. I suggest you do this outside if possible, since butter will smoke and pop during the cooking process.

¼ inch = Well done
⅜ inch = Medium-well done
½ inch = Medium done

⅝ inch = Medium-rare done
¾ inch = Rare done
1 inch = Very rare done

2 rib eye steaks, cut to desired
  thickness
1 tablespoon cayenne pepper
1 tablespoon whole oregano
1½ teaspoons crushed
  rosemary

1½ teaspoons paprika
1½ teaspoons salt
1½ teaspoons black pepper
¼ cup butter, divided

Clean steaks and pat dry. Mix cayenne pepper, oregano, rosemary, paprika, salt, and black pepper in bowl until completely blended. Next, sprinkle mixture over both sides of steak until completely coated. Heat skillet to hot and add 2 tablespoons butter to pan. Butter will smoke and pop and turn slightly brown. Lift the skillet off the fire and move the butter around until almost melted. Next, place back on fire and as soon as the butter begins to smoke again, place both steaks in butter for 60 seconds each side. Remove steaks from pan and add remaining butter, scraping the bottom as you stir in the butter. As soon as the butter is melted, pour over each steak and serve.

'Dat Little New Orleans Creole Cookbook

Maine

CAPITAL: *Augusta*

NICKNAME: *The Pine Tree State*

*W*ith 3,500 miles of coastline, 6,000 lakes and ponds, and 2,295 square miles of inland waters, it's no wonder Maine is able to harvest some 57 million pounds of lobster, 128 million pounds of finfish, and 7 million pounds of shellfish each year! They also boast the largest blueberry crop in the nation. Conifer and hardwood forests cover 90% of the state. Maine is so beautiful, beckoning visitors to its parks—Acadia National Park is the second most visited national park in the nation—and to picturesque lighthouses and harbors. Did you realize that Maine is the only state whose name has one syllable? And it is the only state to share its border with only one other state.

Lobster Stew

The lobster feed is enjoyed by inlanders as well as those on the coast. One of the delicious aftermaths of a lobster feed is a lobster stew. The coral (eggs in some lobsters) and tomalley (lobster liver) add good flavor, plus the meat from claws and body of the crustacean, picked by patient lobster "pickers." We find that it takes about 5 (1¼-pound) lobsters to make 1 pound or 3 cups of clear meat.

¼–½ cup butter or margarine	Salt and pepper to season
2–3 cups lobster meat	Coral and tomalley
2 quarts milk	

In a kettle, melt butter over low heat and sauté lobster meat, stirring until meat is pink in color. Add milk and continue cooking, stirring frequently. Reduce heat; do not boil. A double boiler at this stage is recommended. The stew will have blossomed to a rosy color. Add coral and tomalley. Heat to serve hot. Many cooks prepare the stew early in the day, then refrigerate and reheat it when needed.

Memories from Brownie's Kitchen

Ski Day Chicken Casserole

Actually, good for any day.

8 tablespoons butter or
  margarine, divided
¼ cup flour
1½ cups chicken broth
1 cup sour cream
⅛ teaspoon nutmeg
⅛ teaspoon pepper
Salt to taste
¼ cup dry sherry

½ pound flat egg noodles,
  cooked and drained
4½ cups cut-up cooked
  chicken
½ pound mushrooms,
  sliced and sautéed
1 cup soft bread crumbs
½ cup freshly grated
  Parmesan cheese

Melt 4 tablespoons butter; stir in flour, and add chicken broth and sour cream, stirring until thick. Add nutmeg, pepper, and salt. Remove from heat and stir in sherry. Arrange noodles in a greased 9x13-inch baking dish. Cover with chicken, mushrooms, and sauce. Melt remaining 4 tablespoons butter and mix with crumbs. Top casserole with crumbs and cheese. Bake in preheated 350° oven for 30 minutes or until hot and bubbly. May be made a day in advance, refrigerated, and baked when needed. Serves 8.

Merrymeeting Merry Eating

Blueberry Buckle

½ cup shortening
½ cup sugar
1 egg, beaten
2 cups flour

½ teaspoon salt
½ cup milk
2½ cups blueberries

Cream shortening with sugar; add egg and beat. Sift flour with salt and add to creamed mixture alternately with milk. Spread into a greased 8x8-inch pan and spread blueberries over top. Cover with Topping. Bake at 375° for 45 minutes.

TOPPING:
½ cup sugar
½ cup flour

¾ teaspoon cinnamon
½ cup margarine

Mix dry ingredients together. Cut in margarine.

Maine's Jubilee Cookbook

Yankee Bean Soup

This is a soup that could be made from scratch, but I doubt that you would bother. Rather, it is a a perfect way to stretch leftover baked beans to make a full meal instead of a snack.

Purée leftover baked beans with beef stock to thin the purée slightly. Heat soup and add sliced, cooked hot dogs. Molasses, ketchup, and mustard may be added if you want to accentuate the Yankee bean flavor.

The Loaf and Ladle Cook Book

Stonington Baked Fish Fillets

We love this with fresh peas and red potatoes.

**2 pounds fish fillets (a thick
   fish, haddock or cod, is best)**

¼ teaspoon paprika
3 tablespoons lemon juice

Cut fish fillets into serving pieces. Place in a buttered shallow baking dish. Sprinkle with paprika and lemon juice.

WHITE SAUCE:
2 tablespoons butter
3 tablespoons flour
1 tablespoon dry mustard
1¼ cups milk

Salt and pepper to taste
½ cup buttered bread crumbs
1 tablespoon minced parsley

In a small saucepan, melt butter over medium heat. Whisk in flour quickly, and add dry mustard and milk. Salt and pepper to taste. Cook, stirring constantly for 3–4 minutes until thickened. Pour sauce over fish; sprinkle with crumbs and parsley. Bake at 350° until browned. Serves 6.

Seafood Secrets Cookbook

Eastport, Maine, is the most easterly city in the United States. The residents of Washington County are usually the very first Americans to greet the sun each morning when it rises. On approximately 200,000 acres of open land in this county, 80% of the nation's wild blueberry crop is raised.

Filling Station
Sour Cream Coffee Cake

Sara Dix's original bakery was located in the building at the base of Winthrop Hill. One day a tractor-trailer lost its brakes coming down the hill and crashed into the bakery, fell through the floor, and landed in the basement. Needless to say, this was a real crimp on "business as usual." However, Sara adapted, sold baked goods and sandwiches/soups out of her house, and then relocated to her current location—a converted gas station with an art deco look.

1½ cups sugar
¾ cup butter
1½ teaspoons vanilla
3 eggs
3 cups all-purpose flour

1½ teaspoons baking powder
1½ teaspoons baking soda
¾ teaspoon salt
1½ cups dairy sour cream
1 cup blueberries

Heat oven to 325°. Grease a tube pan. Beat sugar, butter, vanilla, and eggs in a bowl at medium speed. Add flour, baking powder, baking soda, salt, and sour cream. Fold in blueberries. Bake 45–50 minutes. Test with a toothpick; if it comes out clean, the coffee cake is done. Cool 20 minutes and remove from the pan.

A Taste of Hallowell

Lobster à la Newburg

½ pint cream
1 tablespoon butter, softened
1 tablespoon flour
Yolks of 2 eggs
Salt and cayenne pepper
 (few grains)

1 large lobster, cooked, cut
 in pieces
Juice of half a lemon
Wine glass of sherry

Make a cream of the cream, butter, flour, and egg yolks; season with salt and very little cayenne. Put lobster meat in a double boiler and when hot, add creamed mixture, allowing it to just come to a boil, then add lemon juice and sherry.

All-Maine Cooking

Yankee Pot Roast

Really good. This recipe is for the famous Clay Hill Farm pot roast.

1 (4- to 6-pound) round roast
  or rump roast
2 cups red wine
2 cups tomato juice
1 large onion, minced
2 carrots, finely minced

1 clove garlic, minced
½ cup brown sugar
2 bay leaves
¼ teaspoon nutmeg
Salt and pepper to taste

Do not brown the pot roast. Place meat in a heavy roasting pan that has a tight-fitting lid. Mix all other ingredients together and pour over meat. Cover and cook at 300° for about 45 minutes per pound. Turn roast over about halfway through cooking time. Let roast rest; thicken gravy and serve.

Visions of Home Cook Book

FROM GWEN'S ROAD DIARY:
You simply must see lighthouses when you go to Maine, and it's not hard to do . . . but in our desire to make it happen right away, we somehow "missed the boat"! Checking in late, we got up early in the morning so that we could work our excursion into our schedule before the stores opened, and headed out to see our first Maine lighthouse. The closer we got, the foggier it got, and by the time we got there, it was pea soup! "Where is the lighthouse?" we asked. "It's right there," a local jogger pointed. And as he did, a low, bellowing fog horn so befitting the scene pierced the morning quiet. "The fog will lift soon," he assured us. But though we sat on the huge boulders and enjoyed the splashing of the water against them—wondering if someone was cooking breakfast inside that lighthouse—it never did lift before our appetites for breakfast motivated us to move on. But, we got to see others. Lighthouses are intriguing. Wonder why that is?

Maryland

CAPITAL: *Annapolis*

NICKNAME: *The Old Line State*

*M*aryland is known for its bountiful crab. Indeed the Chesapeake Bay is an integral part of Maryland and its heritage and cuisine. Besides producing a wealth of fish and shellfish, the Bay has enriched the land surrounding it, and so provides ideal growing conditions for corn and berries, apples and peaches, fresh beans and other vegetables. There's so much history in Maryland. Francis Scott Key, a Maryland lawyer, wrote "The Star-Spangled Banner" on September 14, 1814, while watching the bombardment of Fort McHenry in Baltimore Harbor. Annapolis is known as the Sailing Capital of the World. The United States Naval Academy was founded there in 1845. Intrigued by the beauty of this place—including all the handsome young cadets—we wondered if it was called a campus or a base. Neither—it's the Yard.

Maryland's Finest Crab Imperial

1 (1-pound) container fresh
  backfin lump crabmeat
¼ teaspoon salt
Dash of pepper
1 tablespoon chopped pimento
1 tablespoon chopped green
  pepper
1 whole egg, beaten
1 cup heavy mayonnaise
  (or Miracle Whip)
½ teaspoon Worcestershire
Dash of paprika

Remove all shell from lump crabmeat so as not to break up the lumps. Place crabmeat in bowl and add salt and pepper. Sprinkle with pimento and chopped green pepper. In another bowl, beat egg and fold in mayonnaise and Worcestershire. Place enough of this dressing mixture in the crabmeat to allow it to stick together. Pack the crabmeat mixture lightly in a crab shell for baking or in a shallow pan. Bake at 350° for 30 minutes. Remove from oven and sprinkle top with paprika.

A Family Tradition

4th of July Bean Casserole

Made with bacon and ground beef, this is a tasty side dish for a barbecue, but could be served as a main dish any time of year.

½ pound bacon, diced
½ pound ground beef
1 cup chopped onion
1 (28-ounce) can pork and
  beans
1 (17-ounce) can lima beans,
  rinsed and drained
1 (16-ounce) can kidney
  beans, rinsed and drained

½ cup barbecue sauce
½ cup ketchup
½ cup sugar
½ cup packed brown sugar
2 tablespoons prepared
  mustard
2 tablespoons molasses
1 teaspoon salt
½ teaspoon chili powder

Preheat oven to 350°. In a skillet over medium-high heat, cook bacon, beef, and onion until meat is brown and onion is tender. Remove from heat and drain. Place in a greased casserole dish. Add beans and mix well. In a separate bowl, combine barbecue sauce, ketchup, sugars, mustard, molasses, salt, and chili powder and stir into beef mixture. Cover and bake for 45 minutes. Uncover and bake for 15 minutes longer, or until browned and bubbly. Serves 12 as a side dish. If serving this savory baked casserole as a main course, offer hot corn bread and a green salad to make a full meal.

In the Kitchen with Kendi

Baked Chicken Reuben

4 boned, skinless chicken
  breasts
¼ teaspoon salt
⅛ teaspoon pepper
1 (16-ounce) can sauerkraut,
  drained

Low-fat Russian or Thousand
  Island dressing
4 slices fat-free Swiss cheese
1 tablespoon chopped parsley
Chopped chives

Preheat oven to 325°. Coat a small glass or ceramic baking dish with vegetable oil cooking spray. Arrange chicken pieces in the dish and sprinkle with salt and pepper. Cover chicken with sauerkraut. Pour desired amount of dressing evenly over all and top with cheese and parsley. Cover with foil and bake one hour, or until fork-tender. Sprinkle with chopped chives to serve. Serves 4.

Bountiful Blessings

Soft Shell Crabs

Clean soft shell crabs; remove eyes and sandbag, the "dead man's fingers" under the points, and the "apron" on the lower back shell. Dry well; salt and pepper them, and sprinkle lightly with flour. Fry in deep hot fat. They will brown quickly. Dry out on brown or absorbent paper. Serve with lemon wedges or tartar sauce.

Maryland's Way

Maryland Risotto

¾ cup olive oil, divided
4 cloves garlic, chopped
1 cup diced onion
3 cups Arborio rice
1 cup dry white wine
3 cups diced canned or fresh
  tomatoes

Pinch saffron threads
1 pound small shrimp, peeled
1 pound lump crabmeat, shells
  removed
Salt and pepper to taste
Grated Parmesan cheese

Bring 12 cups of water to a boil, then cover and simmer. Heat 6 tablespoons olive oil in a large sauté pan. Add garlic and onion. Add rice and stir until coated, 2–3 minutes. Add wine and tomatoes; cook until liquid is absorbed. Gradually add one cup of the hot water and then add saffron. As water is absorbed, continue to add hot water, one cup at a time, stirring constantly.

In a separate skillet, heat remaining 6 tablespoons oil. Add shrimp; cook until opaque, 5–6 minutes. Add crabmeat; toss to combine. Add to rice and mix well. Add additional hot water if risotto is too tacky. Serve in bowls and season with salt, pepper, and Parmesan cheese. Serves 8 as entrée.

Recipe from Executive Chef Michael Cajigao, Phillips by the Sea, Ocean City

Coastal Cuisine

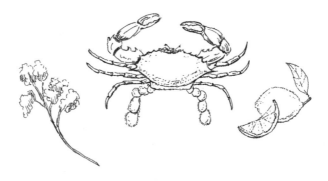

Eastern Shore Crab Cakes

An old receipt from the Eastern Shore of Maryland.

1 pound crabmeat
Salt and pepper to taste
1 egg
¼ pound butter
1 tablespoon lemon juice

1 hard-boiled egg
1 tablespoon Worcestershire
Bread crumbs (from 2–3 slices
   bread)

Put crabmeat in a bowl and season to taste with salt and pepper. Add slightly beaten egg, melted butter, lemon juice, cut-up hard-boiled egg, and Worcestershire. Then add just enough soft bread crumbs to make it into cakes. Fry the cakes a golden brown.

Maryland's Way

Marinated Pork Tenderloin with Creamy Mustard Sauce

Savory tenderloin is grand for spring entertaining and excellent served with spinach salad. A dash of ginger added to the marinade can create a delightful oriental touch.

¼ cup soy sauce
¼ cup bourbon

2½ tablespoons brown sugar
1 (2-pound) pork tenderloin

In a 7x11-inch baking dish, combine first 3 ingredients, then add tenderloin. Cover and refrigerate for 2 hours or more, turning the meat at least twice. Remove meat from marinade and place on a rack in a roasting pan. Reserve marinade for basting, and bake for 45 minutes at 325°, basting occasionally.

MUSTARD SAUCE:
⅔ cup nonfat sour cream
⅔ cup light mayonnaise

2 tablespoons dry mustard
3 green onions, finely chopped

Combine all ingredients in a small mixing bowl; cover and chill. Serve pork either warm or cold with Mustard Sauce on side. Serves 6 as an entrée.

Of Tide & Thyme

Butter "Fork" Cookies

1 stick margarine, softened	1 egg
1 stick butter, softened	2½ cups flour
1¼ cups sugar	1 teaspoon vanilla

Cream butters and sugar in mixer until light and fluffy (about 15 minutes). Add egg. Mix well. Mix in flour and vanilla until well combined. Drop dough from teaspoon onto cookie sheet. Press down until thin with fork dipped in ice cubes and water. Bake at 350° about 8–10 minutes. Remove from pan after one minute. Cool on rack. Makes about 100 cookies. Store in covered tin can.

More Favorites from the Melting Pot

Chafing Dish Crab Dip

Easy, and can be made ahead. Perfect for a party!

1 pound fresh backfin crabmeat, picked	Salt and white pepper to taste
1 (8-ounce) package cream cheese, softened	4 tablespoons mayonnaise
	3 tablespoons sherry/wine
2 tablespoons milk	Pinch seafood seasoning
1 medium onion, chopped	Dash paprika
2 tablespoons horseradish	Toasted almonds
Dash hot pepper sauce	Crackers

Combine all ingredients except almonds and crackers. Bake at 375° for 10–15 minutes. Sprinkle with toasted almonds, and serve in chafing dish with crackers. Serves 10–12.

Of Tide & Thyme

More than half of the Atlantic coast's breeding population of great blue herons nests in Chesapeake Bay. The bay, the nation's largest estuary, and surrounding areas provide both the ideal food and habitat necessary for great blue heron survival. As a result, the great blue heron is rivaled only by the blue crab as the symbol of Chesapeake Bay wildlife.

Massachusetts

CAPITAL: *Boston*

NICKNAME: *The Bay State*

 **M**assachusetts is alive with colonial history the whole state seems to take pride in preserving. So much of our country's heritage has roots there. Four of our nation's presidents, John Adams, John Quincy Adams, John Fitzgerald Kennedy, and George Herbert Walker Bush, were born in Norfolk County. Glaciers formed the islands of Nantucket and Martha's Vineyard during the ice age—such intriguing places to visit. We loved the Berkshires, too. Boston is not only the Bay State's capital, but the largest city in New England. Many famous dishes come from "Beantown," including Boston Baked Beans, Boston Brown Bread, Baked Boston Scrod, and the official state dessert of Massachusetts, Boston Cream Pie. The Boston Tea Party reenactment takes place in Boston Harbor every December, and the Boston Marathon is run during Patriot's Day.

Boston Baked Beans

2 pounds beans: pea beans, navy beans, or small white beans
1 teaspoon baking soda
1 pound salt pork
1 medium onion
⅔ cup dark molasses
8 tablespoons dark brown sugar
2 teaspoons dry mustard
⅔ teaspoon salt
½ teaspoon pepper
Hot water (about 2 cups)

Soak beans overnight in a 2-quart bean pot. In morning, parboil them for 10 minutes with a teaspoon of baking soda. Run cold water through beans in a colander or strainer.

Dice salt pork and onion in small pieces. Put half of each on bottom of pot. Put half of beans. Add rest of pork and onion, then rest of beans. Mix other ingredients with hot water (add water a little at a time, as necessary, to keep beans moist—don't flood the beans). Pour over beans to cover. Bake in 300° oven for 6 hours. Serves 10.

A Culinary Tour of the Gingerbread Cottages

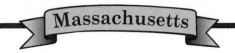

Hot Mulled Cider

You can use a crockpot, but it will take longer to heat. This is the recipe we use at the annual Harvest Craft Fair.

1 quart hot tea	3 sticks cinnamon
1 gallon apple cider	1 teaspoon allspice
Juice of 5 lemons	1 teaspoon whole cloves
Juice of 5 oranges	½ teaspoon salt (optional)
1¼ cups brown sugar	Pinch of mace

Simmer ingredients, uncovered, 15 minutes in a large 10- to 12-quart pan, stirring from time to time. Serve hot with thin slices of oranges in each cup. Makes 20–30 servings.

Note: This cannot be frozen, but it can be refrigerated and reheated.

Tasty Temptations from the Village by the Sea

Lobster Tarts

1 pie crust dough	2 tablespoons lemon juice
2 tablespoons butter	1 tablespoon flour
1 (6-ounce) container frozen lobster, or 8 ounces fresh lobster	½ cup warm light cream
	1 egg yolk
2 tablespoons finely chopped onion	2 tablespoons brandy
	Cheddar cheese
1 tablespoon finely chopped parsley	

Using pie crust dough, make 36 mini tarts using either tart pan or small muffin pan. Lightly bake. Melt butter; add lobster, onion, and parsley. Sprinkle with lemon juice and flour. Add cream, which has been blended into yolk and brandy. Fill tarts with mixture and sprinkle with cheese. Bake at 375° for about 20 minutes.

A Taste of New England

Provincetown, Massachusetts, the birthplace of the commercial fishing industry of the United States, was the wealthiest town per capita in New England in the 1840s and '50s. It is still considered the gourmet seafood capital of the Atlantic seaboard, supplying fresh fish for the tables of gourmets everywhere.

Steamed Clams

Clams for steaming should be bought in the shell and always alive. The old-fashioned rule for steaming is to let the clams boil up and lift the cover three times. Then they are done. Save clam liquor, as it is delicious to drink. Liquor should be drained and clear. Serve clams with individual dishes of melted butter. Some prefer a few drops of vinegar or lemon juice added to the butter. Also, serve clam liquor with the clams.

4 quarts clams　　　　　　　**Melted butter**
½ cup hot water

Wash clams thoroughly. Scrub with a brush and change water several times.

　　Put into a large kettle. Allow ½ cup hot water for 4 quarts of clams; cover closely, and steam until shells partially open, care being taken that they are not overdone. Serves 4–6.

Come Savor Swansea

FROM GWEN'S ROAD DIARY:
On Cape Cod we stopped in a lovely grocery store where we were fascinated with the array of things we had never seen . . . like clams of all sizes and colors and shapes, and mushrooms of a dozen varieties. I could never be able to describe these to my diary, so I went back to the car for the movie camera. We got so engrossed in our task—Barbara pointing out fun new things she was discovering, and me filming these beautifully displayed items—that we were not aware of being watched until I felt a tap on the shoulder. It was the manager, who told us in no uncertain terms that they did not allow filming, and that we would have to leave. Only time we've ever been thrown out of a grocery store! But we wouldn't take anything for the experience . . . or the film!

Best Crab Dip Ever

1 (8-ounce) package cream
  cheese, softened
1 tablespoon milk
1 (7½-ounce) can crabmeat,
  drained
2 tablespoons chopped onion
½–1 teaspoon horseradish
¼ teaspoon salt
2 tablespoons sherry
Slivered almonds (optional)

Mix the cream cheese and milk. Add other ingredients and mix well.
Put in a small baking dish with a cover. Bake at 350° for 20–30 minutes. Garnish with almonds, if desired. Serve in a chafing dish (or
one that can be kept warm) with crackers.

A Taste of New England

Seafood Chowder

May be prepared ahead and frozen.

WHAT YOU NEED:
½ cup finely minced onion
¼ cup butter, melted
2 cups chicken or fish stock
1 cup chopped celery
1 cup thinly sliced carrots
1 teaspoon salt
⅛ teaspoon freshly ground
  pepper
½ bay leaf
½ teaspoon thyme
½ pound haddock fillets,
  bite-size pieces
3 cups milk, divided
¼ cup flour
½ cup heavy cream, mixed
  with ½ cup milk
1 cup crabmeat, flaked
  (fresh, frozen, or canned)
1 cup minced clams (fresh or
  canned, drained)
3 tablespoons finely chopped
  parsley

WHAT YOU DO:
In a large pot, sauté onion in melted butter until tender. Add stock,
celery, carrots, salt, pepper, bay leaf, and thyme. Bring to a boil and
simmer gently 10–15 minutes. Add haddock and simmer another 10
minutes, or until fish flakes away easily. Make a smooth paste by
mixing 1 cup milk with flour. Add to hot mixture; cook and stir until
mixture thickens. Add remaining 2 cups milk, then stir in
cream/milk mixture, crabmeat (if frozen, drain), and clams; reheat
but do not allow to boil. Before serving, sprinkle with parsley.

Cape Collection–Simply Soup

New England Boiled Dinner

6 pounds brisket or rump of
  corned beef
½ clove garlic
6 peppercorns
6 carrots
3 large yellow turnips, cut in
  quarters

4 small parsnips
8 small onions, peeled
6 medium-size potatoes, pared
  and cut in quarters
1 head cabbage, quartered

Place corned beef in cold water with garlic and peppercorns and cook slowly until tender, skimming now and then. If you use very salty corned beef, drain when it comes to a boil and use fresh water for the rest of the cooking time. Allow from 4–5 hours for simmering, testing tenderness with a fork. When done, remove meat, and cook vegetables in stock. When vegetables are done, return meat to pot and reheat.

Serve with grated fresh horseradish beaten with sour cream, or use prepared horseradish with sour cream, adding a little lemon juice. Serves 4–8, depending on size of the beef.

Note: We like the beef sliced thin, not in chunks. We arrange the slices overlapping on an ironstone platter, arrange the vegetables around them with a slotted spoon, and serve the stock—never thicken it—in an ironstone tureen.

My Own Cookbook

Berkshire Apple Pancake

This popular Red Lion Inn recipe uses two products from the bounty of the Berkshires—apples and maple syrup.

3 apples	¾ teaspoon vanilla
3 eggs, beaten	¾ teaspoon ground cinnamon
3 cups flour	5 tablespoons butter, melted
1½ tablespoons baking powder	¼ cup firmly packed light
¾ teaspoon salt	brown sugar
5 tablespoons sugar	Warm maple syrup, for serving
2 cups milk	

Preheat oven to 450°. Peel and core apples. Coarsely chop 2½ apples. Slice remaining ½ apple into thin spirals for garnish on top. Brush spirals with lemon juice to prevent them from darkening, and set them aside.

Mix the eggs, flour, baking powder, salt, sugar, milk, vanilla, cinnamon, and chopped apples together in a bowl. Beat until they are combined, although batter will remain lumpy. Melt butter in a 10-inch cast-iron frying pan. Pour batter into pan, and arrange reserved apple spirals on top.

Bake pancake in oven at 450° for 15 minutes. Then turn oven down to 350° and continue to bake pancake an additional 40 minutes, or until toothpick inserted in center comes out clean. Remove pan from oven and allow it to rest for 5 minutes. Sprinkle brown sugar over top of pancake, cut into wedges, and serve with warm maple syrup.

The Red Lion Inn Cookbook

Every year since 1776, on July 4th, the Declaration of Independence is read from the same balcony it was first read from, the Old State House. Built in 1713, it is the oldest public building in Boston. The oldest wooden building in Boston is Paul Revere's House. It was nearly 100 years old when the patriot took his famous midnight ride to warn "every Middlesex village and farm" that the British were coming.

Michigan

CAPITAL: *Lansing*

NICKNAMES: *The Great Lakes State*

*F*rom maple-syrup springs to wild-berry summers, pumpkin-squash falls to steamy-soup winters, the bounty and beauty of the Michigan seasons are enjoyed from both sides of the kitchen window. Thousands of islands surround the Great Lakes State providing a tremendous seafood bounty. Hold your right hand out with your fingers closed and you have the shape of Michigan's Lower Peninsula, and this is how many people point out a particular place in the state on their palm and fingers. Lots of dry beans (more than any other state) and sugar beets are produced in the tip of the thumb. Michigan is known for their cherries and also has an abundance of plums, fifteen varieties of apples, and a whole lot of peppers. (Did you know peppers, like tomatoes, are fruits?) Michigan boasts the second largest variety of agricultural products of any state in the nation, and naturally cooks up an abundance of good recipes. And of course, Battle Creek is the Cereal Capital of the World.

Dried Cherry Chicken Salad

1 cup dried tart red cherries
4 chicken breast halves, cooked,
   torn into large pieces
3 stalks celery, coarsely chopped
2 Granny Smith apples, coarsely
   chopped
1 cup coarsely chopped pecans
1¼ cups mayonnaise
½ cup chopped parsley
1 tablespoon raspberry vinegar
Salt and pepper to taste

Mix cherries, chicken, celery, apples, and pecans in a large bowl. Combine the mayonnaise, parsley, and raspberry vinegar in a bowl; mix well. Add to chicken mixture and toss lightly to coat well. Season with salt and pepper. Chill 2 hours or longer. Serve on a bed of red leaf lettuce. Garnish with additional cherries. Serves 6.

The Dexter Cider Mill Apple Cookbook

Swedish Rice Pudding

6 eggs, beaten
½ cup white sugar
1 cup brown sugar (not packed)
Pinch salt
½ teaspoon cinnamon
¼ teaspoon nutmeg
4½ cups mixture of whole milk
and half-and-half, scalded

2 tablespoons butter, melted in
hot milk
2 tablespoons vanilla (less,
if desired)
2 cups rice, cooked the day
before
Raisins (optional)

Beat eggs; add sugars, salt, cinnamon, and nutmeg. Mix well. Slowly add heated milk and melted butter. Mix. Add vanilla and rice; mix. Add raisins, if desired. Put into a buttered large casserole. Sprinkle a little brown sugar and cinnamon over top. Place casserole into a pie pan with hot water. Bake 1–1½ hours at 325° or until knife inserted comes out clean. Let cool.

Halvorson-Johnson Family Reunion Cookbook

Acorn Squash à la Cherries

5 acorn squash
5 tablespoons butter
5 teaspoons brown sugar

1¼ cups tart cherries (out of
a 21-ounce can), drained

Cut squash in half and remove seeds. Add to each, one tablespoon butter, one teaspoon brown sugar, and ¼ cup cherries. Bake at 350°, covered with foil, for 60 minutes, or until tender. Serves 10.

Bringing Grand Tastes to Grand Traverse

Tart Cherry Almond Bread

3 cups all-purpose flour
2 teaspoons baking powder
1 teaspoon baking soda
½ teaspoon salt
¼ cup butter or margarine,
  softened
1 cup plus 1 teaspoon sugar,
  divided

2 eggs
1 cup buttermilk
2 teaspoons almond extract
1 cup pitted tart cherries,
  drained
3 tablespoons sliced almonds

Preheat oven to 350°. Combine flour, baking powder, baking soda, and salt. Set aside. In a large bowl, beat together butter and one cup sugar. Add eggs and mix well. Stir in buttermilk and almond extract. Stir in flour mixture. Chop drained cherries; stir into batter. Spread batter in greased 9x5-inch loaf pan. Sprinkle one teaspoon sugar and sliced almonds over batter. Bake at 350° for 70 minutes, or until toothpick inserted in center comes out clean. Cool 10 minutes, then turn out of pan onto cooling rack. Yields 1 loaf.

Good Food from Michigan

Open Fire Walleye Fish Fry

Here's one for walleye that's a bit different. It works best over an open fire.

½ cup Jiffy, Bisquick, or
  pancake mix
1 teaspoon Italian seasoning
1 teaspoon poultry seasoning
1 egg

1½ cups club soda or beer
  (maybe more)
2 walleye fish fillets
Some flour

Combine all ingredients, except walleye and flour, for the batter. This batter must be thin. You may add milk or more club soda (or beer) until it is the consistency of a thin pancake batter. Roll fillets in flour. Dip in batter, and fry in deep fat or oil until brown at the edges. Flip and cook until done. Serves 4.

Mrs. Boone's Wild Game Cookbook

Michigan Meat Balls

2 pounds hamburger
1 cup sour cream
1 package Lipton Dry Onion
  Soup Mix
1 egg
1½ cups bread crumbs

½ cup flour
1 teaspoon paprika
¼ cup butter
1 (10¾-ounce) can cream of
  chicken soup
¼ cup water

Mix hamburger, sour cream, soup mix, egg, and crumbs. Mix well. Form into walnut-size balls. Roll in flour and paprika and brown in butter. Blend soup with water; pour over meat balls and simmer. Crockpot works good.

Country Cookbook

Company Pork Chops

6 Ida Red apples, peeled,
  thickly sliced
6 pork chops
2 teaspoons butter or
  margarine

6 tablespoons brown sugar
6 tablespoons ketchup

Preheat oven to 375°. Line a large baking dish with enough foil to overlap casserole and seal. Arrange apple slices in a single layer in prepared dish. Brown pork chops in butter in a skillet. Arrange over apples. Sprinkle with brown sugar and spread with ketchup. Fold foil over pork chops, sealing with a double fold. Bake at 375° for one hour or until pork chops and apples are tender. Serve immediately. Serves 6.

The Dexter Cider Mill Apple Cookbook

Visitors from all over the country come to marvel at the millions of tulips that line the city streets in Holland at their annual Tulip Time Festival in May. Dutch dancers dressed in traditional Dutch costumes and the gorgeous tulips highlight the 10-day festival, among the top five festivals in the United States.

Plum Sauced Barbecued Ribs

8 pounds pork spareribs

Cut ribs into 2–3 rib portions. In large Dutch oven, bring salted water to boiling; reduce heat. Simmer ribs, covered, for 45 minutes or until tender; drain.

SAUCE:

½ **cup chopped onion**	¼ **cup chili sauce**
2 **tablespoons butter or**	¼ **cup soy sauce**
margarine	2 **teaspoons prepared mustard**
1 **(17-ounce) can purple plums**	1 **teaspoon ground ginger**
1 **(6-ounce) can frozen**	1 **teaspoon Worcestershire**
lemonade, thawed	

In large saucepan, cook onion in butter until tender. Drain plums, reserving syrup; remove pits and discard. Place plums and syrup in blender or food processor; cover and process until smooth. Add plum purée and remaining ingredients to onions. Simmer, uncovered, for 10 minutes, stirring occasionally. Grill ribs over low coals about 25 minutes, turning 3–4 times and brushing often with Sauce until well coated. Pass remaining Sauce. Makes 8 servings.

What's Cookin'

FROM GWEN'S ROAD DIARY:
Barbara and I have been fortunate to have caught many state fairs and county festivals. Tasting the homemade wares of blue ribbon recipes from all across the state is quite a treat. Not only do we get to taste regional, ethnic, and specialty foods, but we got to meet their makers and bakers and find out how they do it. Often "the secret" is in the method as well as the ingredients.

Minnesota

CAPITAL: *Saint Paul*

NICKNAME: *The North Star State*

Also called the Land of 10,000 Lakes, Minnesota is truly a beautiful state rich in forest and, yes, 10,000 mirror-like lakes. Wow, talk about great fishing and hunting and wildlife adventures! Corn, soybeans, hay, wheat, sugar beets, wild rice, oats, and barley are plentiful. We heard Minnesota won the contest for the best flour in the world at the Paris 1900 World's Exposition. Because of its flour mills and dairy products, Minnesota is known as the Bread and Butter State. To know Minnesota cooking is to know its people. Many Swedish immigrants settled there and traditions like smorgasbord are still popular . . . Yah! Bloomington's Mall of America is the Midwest's number one tourist destination. Candy maker Frank C. Mars of Minnesota introduced the Milky Way candy bar in 1923 and the five-cent Three Musketeers in 1937 (it originally contained three bars in one wrapper). And here's one for the kiddies: Tonka Trucks were developed and continue to be manufactured in Minnetonka.

Finnish Oven Pancake

4 eggs
¾ teaspoon salt
¼ cup honey
2½ cups milk

1 cup unsifted flour
4 tablespoons butter or margarine, softened

Preheat oven to 400°. Put a 9x10-inch glass baking dish in the oven for 10 minutes. Beat eggs, salt, honey, and milk; add flour and mix. Add butter to glass baking dish. When butter is melted, pour batter in slowly. Bake for 30–35 minutes or until set. Makes 4–6 servings.

Finn Creek Museum Cookbook

Rhubarb-Strawberry Coffee Cake

FILLING:

3 cups chopped rhubarb
1 (16-ounce) package frozen
   strawberries

1 cup sugar
⅛ cup cornstarch
2 tablespoons lemon juice

Combine and cook fruit for 5 minutes. Mix sugar and cornstarch and stir in lemon juice. Cook and stir until thick; cool.

BATTER:

3 cups flour
1 cup sugar
1 teaspoon baking soda
1 teaspoon salt
1 teaspoon baking powder

1 cup butter
1 cup buttermilk
2 eggs, beaten
1 teaspoon vanilla

Sift dry ingredients in bowl and cut in butter. Quickly stir in buttermilk, eggs, and vanilla until moist. Spread half of Batter in a 9x13-inch pan; add Filling. Dot with remaining Batter.

TOPPING:

½ cup flour
¾ cup sugar

¼ cup butter
½ teaspoon cinnamon

Mix ingredients; sprinkle on top of Batter. Bake at 350° for 40 minutes.

Potluck Volume II

We did it!

The story of how two ladies,
Gwen McKee and Barbara Moseley,
went out to find America's best recipes and in the process,
created the BEST OF THE BEST STATE COOKBOOK SERIES.

THE COMPLETE
BEST OF THE BEST STATE COOKBOOK SERIES

Preserving America's Food Heritage

Big Sky—*Montana and Wyoming.* **Great Plains**—*Kansas, Nebraska, North Dakota and South Dakota.* **Mid-Atlantic**—*Delaware, Maryland, New Jersey, and Washington, D.C.* **New England**—*Connecticut, Maine, Massachusetts, New Hampshire, Rhode Island, and Vermont*

We did it!

The story of how two ladies, Gwen McKee and Barbara Moseley, went out to find America's best recipes and in the process, created the BEST OF THE BEST STATE COOKBOOK SERIES.

The process began in the early 1980s. After being involved in the development and publication of numerous cookbooks, Gwen McKee and Barbara Moseley were frequently asked what were their favorite cookbooks and recipes. From their own cookbook collections, they had highlighted recipes they thought were special. From this, the idea was born, "Why not collect all those highlighted recipes from different cookbooks into one cookbook?" They quickly realized that this ambitious undertaking could best be accomplished on a state-by-state basis. The BEST OF THE BEST STATE COOKBOOK SERIES had begun!

From the very beginning, Gwen and Barbara established goals. They would search for cookbooks that showcased recipes that captured local flavor. They would insist on kitchen-friendly recipes that anybody anywhere could cook and enjoy. They would make the books user friendly, and edit for utmost clarity. The criteria for including a recipe was that it have three distinguished features: great taste, great taste, and great taste!

Early in the BEST development, the purchase of a used van turned out to be just the right vehicle for their travels. With stacks of boxes, luggage, grocery bags, cooking paraphernalia, etc., it proved to be the ideal way to pack up and head out for discovery! This was one of four vans that took Gwen and Barbara across the country.

PHOTO BY COOKIE SNYDER

*I*n 1982, *Best of the Best from Mississippi: Selected Recipes from Mississippi's Favorite Cookbooks* was published. Its success prompted going next door to Louisiana, Gwen's native state. The Louisiana edition, published in 1984, has been reprinted seventeen times and is the best-seller of all the states.

The two editors then took on Texas—four trips were required just to cover the territory! But cover it they did, selecting eighty cookbooks from all over Texas to contribute their most popular recipes to *Best of the Best from Texas Cookbook.* At 352 pages and almost 500 recipes, Texas is one of the largest cookbooks in the SERIES.

With three states under their belt, Gwen and Barbara now had a mission and a motto: **Preserving America's Food Heritage.**

Gwen and Barbara did a lot of work on the recipes before they ever got in the kitchen to test them.

...We're under way! 1982-1985

Tasting the local fare is one of the best bonuses of a trip through any region in search of great recipes. In Hurricane Mills, Tennessee, Gwen and Barbara visited Loretta Lynn's Kitchen and found tasty local vittles and recipes for how to fix them.

*T*he editors committed themselves to tracking down those classic family recipes that have been refined and perfected over generations. It had become an interesting, sometimes fascinating, often exhilarating process . . . and they knew they were hooked on wanting to explore each state and taste their cuisine.

Talking to townfolk was always fun and informative. Gwen and Barbara would usually be directed to someone else if that person couldn't help them— "Go see Norma at the drugstore; she has lots of cookbooks."

Over the next four years, Gwen and Barbara concentrated on those neighboring states that were convenient to get to. In the early days before the Internet, their normal method of finding local cookbooks was to travel throughout the state. Gwen usually did the driving, and Barbara—with map in lap—the navigating. They stopped at bookstores,

In North Carolina, they drove a long way to taste Pete Jones' famous barbecue at his Skylight Inn in Ayden—a restaurant that has a replica of our nation's capitol on the roof! Here Pete treated them to the delicious flavor of true wood-smoked North Carolina barbecue. No wonder it has won so many awards—well worth the drive.

gift and kitchen shops, restaurants, bed and breakfasts, chamber of commerce offices, tourist bureaus, and any other place that might offer the possibility of discovering a popular local cookbook. Without fail, in every state, the BEST thing was the people they met and the information they so proudly shared.

The road was not always so easy and enjoyable as it may sound. They occasionally had car problems, but invariably were helped by friendly people, including truckers, motorcyclists, even the police! They missed turns, became hopelessly lost, and sometimes made wonderful cookbook discoveries while finding their way back.

Throughout the '90s, Gwen and Barbara continued to search with renewed dedication to finding and preserving those little recipe gems that might be tucked away in a modest church cookbook published in a small community. Junior League

While traveling across the country, Gwen and Barbara were invited by Paula Cunningham, owner of McClanahan Publishing in Kuttawa, Kentucky, on a sea plane ride over the Land Between the Lakes. They all dined that night on wonderful Kentucky Baked Pork Chops.

... We're covering the South! 1986-1990

Bringing food to book signings helped us show people how delicious the recipes were. Teammate Tupper England (between Barbara and Gwen) has illustrated every one of the cookbooks in the SERIES.

cookbooks, because they are developed by local members and contain recipes from their city and community, have been particularly valuable contributors to the SERIES.

They also continued to meet and make wonderful new friends. In Indiana, they spent a few days with Chris and Mike Sikorski. Chris has the distinction of being the first member of the Best of the Month Club (individuals who have signed up to receive a copy of each new edition in the Series). Chris tried recipes, gave us her comments, and became a dear friend. This is true of many of our Best Club members.

Gwen and Barbara stayed an extra day in Cincinnati just to try the different varieties of chili that the city is

famous for. They had seafood chowder in Boston, Hot Browns in Louisville, lobster in Maine, buffalo stew in Wyoming, Huli Huli Chicken in Hawaii, gumbo in Louisiana . . . and after each culinary experience, they sought out the BEST recipes that would enable the rest of America to enjoy all of these regional classics.

There were always adventures on the road. Near Farmington, Maine, Gwen and Barbara found themselves among hundreds of motorcyclists. When they stopped for gas in the midst of them, they discovered that these burly, leathered, tatooed guys (and gals) were genuinely intrigued by their pursuit of

Hot Cheese in a Jar

2 pounds Velveeta cheese, melted
1 medium onion, grated
1 (5.33-ounce) can evaporated milk
1 pint Miracle Whip salad dressing
1 (8-ounce) can seeded, deveined
  jalapeño peppers, chopped fine
  (cut off stems)

Melt cheese in top of double boiler. Add onion, milk, Miracle Whip, and peppers to melted cheese, and mix well. Pour into 6 (8-ounce) jelly jars. Cool, screw on caps, and refrigerate.

This recipe was often made before road trips and a supply taken along. Many times the editors relied on this treat to make it through some long days of travel. The recipe was con-tributed by Cowtown Cuisine *and is included in* Best of the Best from Texas Cookbook *(page 28). It is truly a classic.*

America's BEST recipes, and offered some favorite dishes of their own. It seemed that talking about food was a common denominator that just about everybody delighted in doing. Almost always, it translated to finding a local cookbook that had just the recipe they were after.

*I*n addition to the over 300 wonderful recipes that each BEST cookbook contains, Gwen and Barbara have added other features that make the cookbooks more useful and enjoyable. Glossaries were included in those books with words or phrases that might not be understood in other parts of the country (Louisiana's French and Cajun words, Texas' and New Mexico's Spanish terms, Hawaii's pronunciations, etc.).

Sometimes the forked road beckoned in both directions, and the girls didn't know which way to turn. Their trips were sketched out, but left lots of room for wherever the spirit led them. This was a photo op for a chapter opening picture at Indiana Dunes, but they were never quite sure where they would wind up in search of America's favorite recipes.

... We're halfway there! 1991-1996

In their quest for the BEST, Gwen and Barbara learned that every region has a particular food or signature dish. As soon as they arrived in Maine, they embraced the state's culinary spirit by diving into some drawn-buttered boiled lobster at the first roadside restaurant with a lobster on its sign!

Cookbooks" section of each BEST cookbook. This section provides a brief description of each contributing cookbook, a reproduction of the book's cover, plus price and ordering information.

*I*n the late '90s, the editors finished the Midwest and set their sites on the "big" states of the West. These states with their vast areas provided major challenges to locating those local cookbooks that might contain that special recipe.

In the Southwest, the Arizona and New Mexico editions became instant favorites. The popularity of the Mexican influence on the cuisine of this region, abundantly represented in these cookbooks, surely contributed to their appeal.

The California edition, like Texas and New England, required more pages to accommodate the large number of contributing cookbooks. The great variety of recipes selected makes these cookbooks particularly interesting and enjoyable to use.

"Editor's Extras" have occasionally been added to the original recipes to ensure complete understanding, suggest an alternate ingredient if the original was not available, or offer an embellishment or variation the editors particularly liked and wanted to share.

Sprinkled throughout each BEST cookbook is a series of short "quips" that provide interesting facts about each state. These are fun and informative, and help to convey the unique features of the state.

Each cookbook contains photographs and illustrations that capture some of the visual highlights of each state.

One of the most popular features, particularly for anyone who collects cookbooks, is the "Catalog of Contributing

Often shrouded in a thick fog, the Golden Gate Bridge sways 27 feet to withstand winds of up to 100 miles per hour. Its two great cables contain enough strands of steel wire (about 80,000 miles) to encircle the equator three times, and the concrete poured into its piers and anchorages would pave a five-foot sidewalk from New York to San Francisco.

An example of the illustrations and "quips" that are scattered throughout the BEST OF THE BEST cookbooks.

With the California edition, the editors made one of their few bad decisions. In order to speed up production, they bound the book as a paperback rather than the normal ring-bound format. The Best of the Month Club members immediately voiced their displeasure. The editors listened and responded, and *Best of the Best from California Cookbook* is now ringbound like all the others. This binding format allows for convenient lay-flat usage, and like the recipes themselves, creates an overall comfortable, user-friendly feel for the cookbooks.

Gwen and Barbara knew from the beginning that they did not want the BEST OF THE BEST cookbooks to be hardbound, oversized, full-color, expensive books that would stay on the coffee table and not be allowed to go in the kitchen. It was

Barbara and Gwen are always at home in the kitchen, no matter where they are. Though space was limited in this tiny Manhattan apartment, fresh produce at the corner market was not. It was a fun experience cooking New York recipes with friends in this cozy kitchen.

...We're going strong! 1997-2000

their hope that each BEST OF THE BEST cookbook would become a family favorite used again and again for their consistently superb recipes.

There were two major developments that helped the Series gain national recognition. In the mid '80s, Cracker Barrel Old Country Stores began carrying the BEST OF THE BEST STATE COOKBOOKS when they had only about 65 stores in their chain. Over the years, this wonderful relationship has grown as the BEST SERIES developed. Now most of the more than 500 Cracker Barrel stores now carry the BEST cookbook of the state where the store is located. Many customers play the game of getting a new BEST book only at a Cracker Barrel store each time they go to a new state.

In 1997, the electronic shopping giant, QVC, came to Mississippi as part of their nationwide search for new products. BEST OF THE BEST FROM MISSISSIPPI was one of the twenty or so products that were selected to air on the Mississippi show. It sold out in two minutes, faster than any other product, and earned the honor of being included with other state winners on a special show from the main QVC Studios in West Chester, Pennsylvania. Since then, Gwen has appeared numerous times on QVC showcasing many of the BEST OF THE BEST STATE COOKBOOKS. This relationship has been a successful collaboration, allowing a tremendous number of people to become aware of the Series.

In addition to bookstores, many small gift stores and kitchen shops have given valuable support to the BEST cookbooks over the years.

Talented food stylist Bobbi Cappelli, shown at left with Gwen and Barbara, makes the BEST OF THE BEST recipes for QVC on-air presentations. She makes the dishes look as good as they taste. The hosts and crew are treated to delicious samplings when the shows are over.

Barbara and Gwen were usually expected to cook when they booked a TV appearance, a difficult thing to do on the road. Sometimes they had to prep the food in their hotel room. For this Miami show, they cooked the fish for Black Bart's Seafood Ambrosia in a hot pot!

*I*n 2000, after nearly two decades, Gwen and Barbara were still going strong. They had completed thirty-six states, had met and become friends with many delightful people, had seen a great portion of their beautiful country, and were even more committed to their goal of *Preserving America's Food Heritage.*

From 2001 to 2003, Gwen and Barbara completed eight BEST cookbooks and covered eleven states (*Best of the Best from the Mid-Atlantic Cookbook* includes Maryland, Delaware, and New Jersey. *Best of the Best from Big Sky Cookbook* covers Montana and Wyoming). From Cape May, New Jersey, to Glacier Bay, Alaska, this was a demanding stretch. However, the Series had now gained widespread recognition, and a devoted following, so the process of searching for those special local recipes was a great deal easier.

In Anchorage, Alaska, Gwen dined on Chef Matt Little Dog's incredible bread pudding at Simon and Seaforts, and after begging for his recipe, he agreed to share his secret in the *Best of the Best from Alaska Cookbook.* Incidentally, it became the best-selling cookbook in Alaska shortly after it became available there.

Gwen and Barbara were now a long way from home in the Pacific Northwest and Alaska, but still discovering wonderful cookbooks and selecting from them the popular recipes of the region.

Oregon's fruit-growing district, "The Fruit Loop" offered delicious fresh fruit picked right off the tree that inspired recipes like Boysenberry Swirl Cheesecake. "We enjoyed fresh fruit and fruit-coated hazelnuts for days . . . didn't buy nearly enough."

Seattle's Pike Place Market was an exciting experience. The great variety of vegetables, fruits, and fish on display challenged the editors to find recipes that could fully exploit such an abundance of fresh ingredients. They feel they have met the challenge with *Best of the Best from Washington Cookbook.*

The state fair in Palmer, Alaska, was another unique occasion to taste some local fare. The exhibit at the fair contained remarkable blue-ribbon winning fruits and vegetables.

"It helps our research to find out all we can about the food of the state, and Pike Place Market is the place to do that in Seattle," says Barbara. "Just look at this gorgeous seafood."

Gwen and husband, Barney, attended the Alaska State Fair in Palmer, and were aghast at how big the long summer days grow these vegetables. It was a wonderful place to get a first-hand look and taste of some of Alaska's food products.

In beautiful Hawaii, the editors encountered many helpful people, including Jeff and Bennett at Booklines Hawaii, who were virtual gold mines of information, as they either publish or distribute almost every current cookbook related to Hawaiian cooking. And sweet Faith in Kauai proudly offered her own extensive cookbook collection for us to review, many of which were of a vintage nature.

Utah and Nevada, the final two states, offered an opportunity for the editors to experience not only the tasteful cuisine but also the unique beauty of the desert, quite different from their lush, green, southern landscapes.

*T*here are forty-one volumes in the complete BEST OF THE BEST STATE COOKBOOK SERIES. This is due to the fact that some states were combined into one cookbook. *Best of the Best from New England Cookbook,* for instance, consists of Rhode Island, Connecticut, Massachusetts, Vermont, New Hampshire, and Maine.

Best of the Best from the Mid-Atlantic

On the drive up the North Shore on Oʻahu (in Punaluʻu), you can't miss the bright yellow Shrimp Shack truck. Irene serves up delicious pan-fried shrimp herself, delivering it personally to you on her umbrella-topped picnic tables. Her recipe has been written up in magazines, and she has been featured on the Food and Travel channels. When Gwen asked her if she would share her recipe, she sweetly agreed.

... We're getting close! 2001-2003

Cookbook includes recipes collected from cookbooks published in Maryland, Delaware, and New Jersey.

The recipes from North Dakota, South Dakota, Nebraska, and Kansas were combined into *Best of the Best from the Great Plains Cookbook.* *Best of the Best from Big Sky Cookbook* contains the most popular recipes from the leading cookbooks of Montana and Wyoming.

The Series also includes second editions from Louisiana and Texas. These states published early in the process are the two bestsellers in the Series. *Best of the Best from Louisiana II Cookbook* (1998) and *Best of the Best from Texas II Cookbook* (1996) are part of the forty-one book BEST OF THE BEST STATE COOKBOOK SERIES.

Completely new editions have been created for Mississippi and Florida, and

Passing along her love for cooking, Gwen enjoys letting her grandchildren have fun with her in the kitchen. What better way to Preserve America's Food Heritage!

BEST OF THE BEST
Statistics

- Total cookbooks evaluated: over 10,000

- Total cookbooks selected to contribute recipes: 2,689

- Recipes evaluated: hundreds of thousands

- Total number of recipes selected: 17,214

- Road miles traveled: approximately 70,000

- Phone calls made: over 125,000

- Days on the road: approximately 900

- Percent of people who were asked to taste BEST recipes and agreed: 100%

BEST SELLING
STATES
(based on lifetime monthly average)

1. LOUISIANA
2. TEXAS
3. ARIZONA
4. VIRGINIA
5. NORTH CAROLINA
6. OHIO
7. MINNESOTA
8. TEXAS II
9. LOUISIANA II
10. TENNESSEE

Total number of BEST cookbooks sold: 1,800,000 (through 2004)

others are in production. These cookbooks consist of new contributors and new recipes and are now part of the forty-one book collection. The original editions are still available while the current supply lasts.

The BEST OF THE BEST cookbooks range in size from 288 to 380 pages and contain between 350 and 500 recipes. They are ringbound for convenience of use, and are enclosed in heavy, laminated covers that resist stains and spills.

Each cookbook contains a mix of contributing cookbooks ranging from a modest little community cookbook to a grandiose bestseller.

The editors are particularly pleased that, although some of the smaller contributing cookbooks may go out of print, their most popular and tasteful recipes are not lost, but are preserved in their state's BEST OF THE BEST cookbook.

*N*ow that the Series has been completed, what next? Gwen and Barbara, both grandmothers many times over, are not ready to retire. "There are still cookbooks to be discovered and tasteful recipes to be preserved," says Barbara. "We plan to keep cookin'."

"Regardless of what we do in the future," Gwen adds, "we set out to collect, capture, and celebrate the food of America on a state-by-state basis, and that mission has been accomplished.

We did it!"

... We did it! 2004

Swedish Meat Balls

1½ pounds ground beef
½ cup minced onion
1 cup oatmeal
1 tablespoon minced parsley
1½ teaspoons salt

⅛ teaspoon pepper
1 teaspoon Worcestershire
1 egg
½ cup milk

Mix together and shape into walnut-size balls. Brown in ½ cup hot oil. Remove meat.

GRAVY:
¼ cup flour
1 teaspoon paprika
½ teaspoon salt

⅛ teaspoon pepper
2 cups boiling water
¾ cup milk

Stir into oil the flour, paprika, salt, and pepper. Stir in the water and milk. Heat. Return meat to Gravy and simmer 15–20 minutes.

Wannaska Centennial

No-Flop Flounder

2 (10-ounce) packages frozen
  spinach, thawed and drained
1 cup dairy sour cream
1 tablespoon flour
½ teaspoon salt
¼ teaspoon nutmeg
Dash of pepper

1 pound flounder or orange
  roughy
2 tablespoons butter
¼ teaspoon salt
1½ teaspoons paprika
½ cup shredded Swiss cheese

Combine spinach with sour cream, flour, salt, nutmeg, and pepper; mix well. Spoon into shallow greased casserole or baking dish. Rinse fish; dry with paper towels. Place fish on top of spinach mixture in a single layer. Melt butter; brush on fish. Sprinkle fish with salt, paprika, and cheese. Bake at 375° for 30 minutes. Makes 3–4 servings.

From Minnesota: More Than a Cookbook

With so many thousands of lakes, there are lots and lots of fishermen in Minnesota. And it goes on all the time; in winter, they just saw a hole in the ice and pull 'em out. Some of the best fishing is on a frozen Minnesota lake. Fishing huts are quite cozy and offer a contrast to the open lakes of summer. These winter fishing-folks are likely sitting in their shirt sleeves, playing cards, and catching fish in a style unseen during warm-weather ventures.

Norwegian Macaroons

1¼ cups flour
1¼ teaspoons baking soda
1 cup sugar
1 cup butter, melted
1 egg, beaten

1 cup flaked coconut
1¾ cups oatmeal
½ cup chopped nuts
About 6 squares white almond
  bark

Stir dry ingredients together. Add melted butter, beaten egg, coconut, oatmeal, and nuts. Drop by teaspoon on cookie sheet and press down with fork or roll into balls; flatten with a glass. Bake at 350º until light brown, about 10–12 minutes. Frost with melted white almond bark. Makes 70–80 small cookies.

Sharing Our Best/Bergen Lutheran Church

"C'mon," Barbara beckons. "Let's go see what's inside." Go see indeed! You could spend days discovering the 525 specialty stores, 50 restaurants, 14 movie theaters, Camp Snoopy's 30 rides, Nascar's Silicone Motor Speedway, a four-story Lego showplace, the World's Best Shark Encounter. . . . No wonder forty-two million people visit the Mall of America each year, more than Disney World, Graceland, and the Grand Canyon combined.

Wild Rice Hot Dish

1 pound Jimmy Dean sausage
1 medium onion, chopped
1 teaspoon chopped chives
½ cup slivered almonds
2 (4-ounce) cans mushrooms,
  drained

½ cup butter or margarine
1 cup wild rice (soaked
  overnight)
1½ cups water
1½ cups chicken broth
½ cup Parmesan cheese

Brown sausage till partially done, then add onion, chives, almonds, mushrooms, butter, and wild rice. Cook over low heat 15 minutes. Add water and broth, then boil slowly 45 minutes. Stir in cheese. May be served immediately or reheated in 325° oven for 35 minutes.

Sharing Our Best to Help the Rest

Turkey Soup

The perfect recipe to use for leftover holiday turkey.

1 meaty carcass from a
  (12- to 16-pound) turkey
1–2 bay leaves
5–6 whole cloves
Salt and pepper to taste
2 tablespoons butter
3 tablespoons flour
2 tablespoons chicken base
½ cup uncooked rice
¼ cup chopped onion

1 cup chopped celery
Salt and pepper to taste
1 cup leftover gravy and
  turkey dressing
¼ teaspoon curry powder
  (optional)
1 hard-cooked egg, minced
½ cup orange juice
½ cup port wine
6–8 orange slices

Cut meat from bones, and cover carcass with water. Add bay leaves, cloves, salt and pepper. Simmer for 3–4 hours.

Remove bones and drain stock through a colander. Make a roux by melting butter and adding flour and chicken base. Add this to drained liquid a little at a time. Bring to a boil, using a wire whisk to blend thoroughly. Add rice, onion, and celery, and season to taste. Cook about 25 minutes until rice is done.

Add diced turkey and about one cup of the leftover gravy and turkey dressing. If using curry, mix it with a little broth and add to the soup. Simmer until serving. Add minced egg, orange juice, and wine just before serving, and top bowls with orange slices. Makes 6–8 servings.

Minnesota Heritage Cookbook

Pasties
(Meat and Potato Turnovers)

6 cups sifted flour
3 teaspoons salt
1½ teaspoons baking powder
2 cups shortening or lard
1–1½ cups ice water
3 cups thinly sliced potatoes
1½ cups sliced carrots
  (optional)
1½ cups chopped rutabaga
  (optional)

3 cups chopped onion
Salt and pepper
2 pounds beef sirloin, round or
  flank steak, cut in ½-inch
  pieces
¾ pound pork butt, ground or
  chopped (optional)
½ cup butter, melted with
  ½ cup water

Mix flour, salt, and baking powder in large bowl. Add shortening and cut in with a pastry blender. Add ice water, a little at a time, until dough can be easily handled. Divide dough into 6 pieces, wrap in wax paper, and refrigerate for 30 minutes.

For each pasty: Roll out dough into a 9-inch circle. Layer potatoes, carrots, rutabaga, and onion; sprinkle with salt and pepper. Add beef, pork, and more salt and pepper, ending with a second layer of potatoes. Fold in half, moistening edge with cold water, and seal edges. Crimp edge with a fork. Place on greased cookie sheet. In the top of each pasty, cut a small hole with a sharp knife.

Bake pasties in 425° preheated oven for 15 minutes. Turn oven to 350° and bake 35–45 minutes or until they are nicely browned. After ½ hour of baking, remove from oven and spoon the butter-water mixture into the hole; return to oven and complete baking. Serve hot or cold. Pasties freeze and reheat well. Yields 6 large pasties.

Minnesota Heritage Cookbook I

Mississippi

CAPITAL: *Jackson*

NICKNAME: *The Magnolia State*

*W*elcome to our home sweet home, where cotton blossoms spread the fields white in the summer sun and magnolias fill the air with sweetness, where the soulful sound of the Delta blues makes you tilt your head and tap your feet, and the coastal beaches beckon you to the warm gulf waters. We're known for delicious southern cooking and good old southern hospitality, too, where food is synonymous with friendship and love. Feeding the senses evidently feeds the mind and the soul, because we have a long list of famous people too numerous to mention them all: authors (Grisham, Faulkner), musicians (B.B. King, Elvis), football legends (Walter Peyton, Brett Favre, Jerry Rice), entertainers (Oprah, Jim Henson, James Earl Jones), four Miss Americas, and a whole bunch of Sweet Potato Queens! . . . and a Teddy bear. When President Theodore Roosevelt refused to shoot a wounded bear on a hunt in Mississippi, it inspired a merchant to create a stuffed toy bear he named "Teddy's bear." Mississippi's people are the friendliest . . . y'all come.

Beer-Batter Catfish

1 cup flour
1 cup cornstarch
1 teaspoon baking powder
1 teaspoon sugar
1 teaspoon red pepper
1 (12-ounce) bottle beer
2 pounds catfish fillets
Oil for frying

Combine first 5 ingredients in a bowl. Add beer; mix well. Cut fish into strips. Dip in batter. Fry in hot oil until golden brown. Yields 6 servings.

Going Wild in Mississippi

Easy Chicken and Dumplings

4 chicken breasts, boiled (or
  equivalent canned chicken)
4 cups chicken broth
1 (10¾-ounce) can cream of
  mushroom soup
1 (10¾-ounce) can cream of
  chicken soup

12 (6-inch) flour tortillas, cut
  into 1-inch strips
All-purpose flour
Salt and pepper to taste
½ cup milk
¼ stick margarine

Save broth from boiling chicken and add canned chicken broth as needed to make 4 cups. Cut chicken into bite-size pieces and return to broth. Add both soups and bring to a boil. Add strips of tortillas which have been dusted with flour. Add salt and pepper to taste. Cover and cook for 12–15 minutes, stirring occasionally. Add milk and margarine just before removing from heat. Stir well and serve while hot. Yields 8 servings.

With Special Distinction

Mary Mahoney's Bread Pudding

From her famous restaurant in Biloxi . . .

6 slices day-old bread
1 teaspoon cinnamon
½ cup seedless raisins
2 tablespoons butter, melted

4 eggs
2 tablespoons plus ½ cup sugar
2 cups milk
1 teaspoon vanilla extract

Break bread in small pieces in 1½-quart baking dish. Sprinkle cinnamon over bread and add raisins and melted butter. Lightly toast bread mixture in oven at 350º. Then add mixture of eggs, sugar, milk, and vanilla after mixing well. Bake about 30 minutes or until solid. Traditionally served with rum sauce (whisk together butter, powdered sugar, and a little rum). Serves about 8.

Cooking on the Coast

Established in 1889, the Neshoba County Fair, billed Mississippi's Giant House Party, offers Neshoba County "families" an opportunity to gather from across the country every July for a week-long family reunion. The fair includes a flea market, exhibit halls, amusement rides, harness racing, livestock shows, political speaking, and the Miss Neshoba County Pageant.

Country Club Squash

6–8 tender, small squash
Salt and pepper to taste
2 tablespoons butter
1 chicken or beef bouillon cube,
   or 1 teaspoon granules
1 tablespoon grated onion

1 egg, well beaten
1 cup sour cream
¾ cup bread crumbs
½ cup grated cheese
Dash of paprika

Slice squash and cook in water to cover until tender; drain and mash. Add salt, pepper, butter, bouillon cube, and onion. Add well-beaten egg and sour cream. Pour into a 1-quart casserole dish. Combine bread crumbs, grated cheese, and paprika, and sprinkle on top of squash. Bake at 350° for 30 minutes. Serves 6.

The Mississippi Cookbook

PHOTO BY GREG CAMPBELL

Gwen and Barbara met on the golf course in Jackson, Mississippi, in 1973. Friends tease them because they play so much the same game that they often hit the ball to the same spot! On occasion they take their clubs with them when they travel in hopes of being able to find a breakaway time to play their favorite game.

Shrimp and Grits

1½ pounds unpeeled, medium-
   size fresh shrimp
1 teaspoon salt
2 cups cooked grits
1 (6-ounce) tube garlic cheese
1 teaspoon butter or margarine
Ground white pepper
6 bacon slices, diced

2 cups sliced fresh mushrooms
1 cup sliced scallions
2 garlic cloves, minced
2 tablespoons chopped fresh
   parsley
6–8 teaspoons lemon juice
Salt and ground black pepper
   to taste

Peel shrimp and devein, if desired. Combine next 5 ingredients in
the top of a double boiler; keep warm over simmering water. Sauté
bacon in a skillet over medium heat until done, but not crisp.
Remove bacon from skillet. Drain drippings, reserving 2 tablespoons
in skillet. Return bacon to skillet. Add shrimp, and sauté until
beginning to turn pink, turning once. Add mushrooms, and sauté
2–4 minutes or until shrimp are pink and firm. Add scallions and
garlic, stirring well. Add parsley, lemon juice, salt and pepper to
taste. Spoon grits evenly onto 4 serving plates. Spoon shrimp mixture over grits, and serve immediately. Yields 4 servings.

Worth Savoring

Spicy Catfish Amandine

¼ cup butter, melted
3 tablespoons lemon juice
6 (6-ounce) catfish fillets

1½ teaspoons Creole seasoning
½ cup sliced almonds

Combine butter and lemon juice; dip each fillet in butter mixture;
arrange in 9x13-inch baking dish. Sprinkle fish with Creole seasoning and almonds. Bake at 375° for 25–30 minutes or until fish flakes
easily when tested with fork. Serves 4–6.

Grits 'n Greens and Mississippi Things

Hush Puppies

2 cups self-rising cornmeal	1 egg
2 tablespoons flour	½ cup chopped bell pepper
1 teaspoon sugar	1 onion, chopped
1 teaspoon black pepper	4 ounces (½ cup) beer
2 cups buttermilk	Oil for frying

Mix all dry ingredients, then add buttermilk, egg, bell pepper, onion, and beer. Mix well. Let the mixture sit in the refrigerator for about one hour before cooking.

Have your oil ready—good and hot. Now drop in the cornmeal mix by the spoonful (don't overcrowd). Cook until you decide the hush puppies are done. Drain on paper towels.

Deke's BBQ Hush Yer Mouth! This is It!

Chicken Fried Steak and Cream Gravy

2 pounds boneless round steak	½ teaspoon garlic salt
1 cup all-purpose flour	2 eggs
1 teaspoon salt	¼ cup milk
1 teaspoon pepper	Vegetable oil

Trim excess fat from steak; pound steak to ¼-inch thickness, using a meat mallet. Cut into serving-size pieces. Combine flour, salt, pepper, and garlic salt. Combine eggs and milk; beat well. Dredge steak in flour mixture, dip in egg mixture, then dredge in flour mixture again. Lightly pound steak. Heat one inch of oil in a skillet to 375°. Fry steak in hot oil until browned, turning steak once. Drain steak on paper towels. Reserve ¼ cup pan drippings for gravy. Serve steak with Cream Gravy. Yields 6–8 servings.

CREAM GRAVY:

¼ cup all-purpose flour	½ teaspoon salt
¼ cup pan drippings	¼ teaspoon pepper
2–3 cups milk	

Add flour to pan drippings; cook over medium heat until bubbly, stirring constantly. Gradually add milk; cook until thickened and bubbly, stirring constantly. Stir in salt and pepper.

Golden Moments

Mama's Stuffed Bell Peppers

4 large green bell peppers
½ pound butter
2 cups chopped onions
½ cup chopped celery
½ cup chopped parsley
1 clove garlic, minced
½ pound ground beef

½ pound shrimp, peeled and
  deveined
½ loaf fresh bread
3 eggs, beaten
Salt and pepper to taste
½ cup bread crumbs
½ cup water

Cut peppers lengthwise, remove seeds and stems, and wash. Boil in salt water; do not overcook. Remove and drain. In a large sauté pan, melt butter. Add onions, celery, parsley, and garlic. Sauté for 15 minutes. Add ground beef and shrimp; cook for 20 minutes. Preheat oven to 350°.

Wet bread under faucet; squeeze out all liquid and add to sautéed ingredients. Add eggs, salt and pepper. Stir well to blend. Fill peppers with mixture. Top with bread crumbs. Place filled peppers in a baking dish; add ½ cup water in bottom of dish. Bake until brown, 20–25 minutes.

Great American Recipes from Southern 'n' Cajun Cook'n'

FROM GWEN'S ROAD DIARY:
It is understandable that we get lost, but sometimes Barbara and I embarrass ourselves. In our own state, driving south from Memphis into the heart of the Mississippi Delta, we made a wrong turn in search of a small community, and eventually ended up in a cotton field. I kid you not! We were talking and not paying enough attention, while the road kept getting narrower and narrower, and then it just simply ended. The bumper was practically touching the cotton! We laughed so hard that I could hardly turn that big van around to head back.

Missouri

CAPITAL: *Jefferson City*

NICKNAME: *The Show Me State*

*T*he Show Me State is right in the heart of America! Missouri's cooking heritage is—you guessed it—Mid-American. It is a wonderful mixture of simple country, a few dashes of barbecue, a touch of elegance, and lots of yummy desserts. It was here that the ice cream cone was first introduced at the 1904 World's Fair, where the Pony Express got its beginning in St. Joseph, and where in 1925, Charles Lindbergh heard that someone was offering a prize of $25,000 to the first pilot to cross the Atlantic nonstop from New York to Paris. That famous plane, now hanging in the Smithsonian Air and Space Museum in Washington D.C., was called the Spirit of St. Louis.

Ozark Pudding

This is well remembered as Mrs. Harry S. Truman's simple Missouri pudding during World War II.

1 egg	½ cup chopped nuts
¾ cup sugar	½ cup chopped apples
2 tablespoons flour	1 teaspoon vanilla
1¼ teaspoons baking powder	Whipped cream or ice cream
⅛ teaspoon salt	

Beat egg and sugar until creamy. Add dry ingredients to eggs and sugar. Mix well. Add nuts, apples, and vanilla. Bake in greased 9-inch-square baking dish at 350° for 35 minutes. Serve warm with whipped cream or ice cream.

Cooking on the Road

The "Show Me" nickname has been around for a long time, but it gained fame in 1899 when Congressman Willard Vandiver of Cape Girardeau County said in a Philadelphia speech: "Gentlemen, frothy eloquence neither convinces nor satisfies me. I'm from Missouri; you've got to show me."

Ham and Eggs 4th of July

8 frozen Pepperidge Farm
  Patty Shells
2 ounces sliced mushrooms
2 tablespoons butter
2 tablespoons flour
⅛ teaspoon thyme

1¼ cups milk, divided
⅓ can cream of chicken soup
1 cup cubed ham
4 eggs, slightly beaten
¼ teaspoon salt
Parsley sprigs

Prepare patty shells according to directions on package. Brown mushrooms in butter and stir in flour and thyme. Add 1 cup milk and soup; stir until smooth. Add ham. Heat, stirring occasionally.

Gently scramble eggs with salt and remaining ¼ cup milk. Put eggs into hot patty shells and top with ham mixture. Garnish with sprigs of parsley. Serves 6.

Bouquet Garni

Deb's Lip-Lickin' Chicken

4 chicken breasts
Seasoned salt to taste
Lemon pepper to taste

Minced garlic to taste
½ cup soy sauce
½ cup Worcestershire

Wash chicken breasts and pat dry. Rub with spices and place on the grill, meat-side-down, searing for 5 minutes. Flip to bone-side-down and sear for 5 more minutes. Lower firebox to ⅔ down position and, with heat deflector in place, cook for 1 hour and 15 minutes.

Put soy sauce and Worcestershire in a spray bottle and use to baste meat frequently (every 20 minutes). Serves 4–6.

Kansas City BBQ

Dippity Stix

1 (8-ounce) package cream
  cheese, softened
2 tablespoons orange juice

1 (7-ounce) jar marshmallow
  crème

Mix ingredients well and serve with fruit.

Lavender and Lace

St. Louis Favorite Salad

1 head romaine lettuce	1 red onion, thinly sliced
1 head iceberg lettuce	¼ cup grated Parmesan
1 (10-ounce) jar artichoke	cheese
hearts, drained	⅓ cup white vinegar
1 (4-ounce) jar chopped	½ cup oil
pimentos	Hearts of palm (optional)

Wash and tear lettuce into bite-size pieces. Cut artichoke hearts and pimentos into pieces. Combine with onion slices in a large salad bowl. Add cheese. In a separate container, combine vinegar and oil. Just before serving, add hearts of palm, if desired. Pour oil mixture over salad and toss until well coated. Serves 10–12.

From Generation to Generation

The Gateway Arch in St. Louis is one of the most recognizable structures in the country, if not the world. But what about inside? There's a Museum of Western Expansion on the bottom. The car to take you to the top is a trip in itself, since it has to follow the curve of the Arch. Once there, by leaning on the wall, you get a lovely panoramic view of the city's skyline on one side and the Mississippi River and beyond on the other.

Hickory-Smoked Brisket

1 (4- to 6-pound) whole brisket
Salt
Dampened hickory chips or
  liquid smoke
1½ cups ketchup
¾ cup brown sugar
¾ cup chili sauce
½ cup white wine vinegar
¾ cup water
½ cup lemon juice
¼ cup bottled steak sauce
¼ cup prepared mustard
1 tablespoon celery seed
2 tablespoons Worcestershire
1 clove garlic, minced
Dash Tabasco
Freshly ground pepper to taste

Salt brisket and place on grill away from hot coals. Add dampened hickory chips, or brush meat with liquid smoke, and close hood. Barbeque slowly for 4 hours, or until meat is tender.

Cool and slice very thin across grain. Line up slices in shallow pan. Combine remaining ingredients and simmer 30 minutes; pour over meat. Heat one hour on grill or in 200° oven. Serves 8–12.

Company's Coming

Missouri Upside Down Cake

3 tablespoons butter or
  margarine
¾ cup brown sugar
2 cooking apples, peeled and
  sliced
¼ teaspoon cinnamon
⅓ cup shortening
⅓ cup sugar
2 eggs
1 teaspoon vanilla
1½ cups flour
2 teaspoons baking powder
½ teaspoon salt
⅔ cup milk

Melt butter in 9-inch round pan. Add brown sugar and stir until melted. Arrange sliced apples on sugar/butter mixture. Sprinkle cinnamon over apples.

Cream shortening and sugar. Blend in eggs and vanilla, beating thoroughly. Add dry ingredients alternately with milk. Pour over apples in pan. Bake at 350° for 40–45 minutes, or until done. Turn out onto serving plate immediately. Serve with whipped cream or pistachio ice cream. Yields 6–8 servings.

From the Apple Orchard

Irish Lace Sandwich Cookies

½ cup (1 stick) butter,
  softened
1 cup sugar
1 egg

1 teaspoon almond extract
2 tablespoons flour
⅓ teaspoon salt
1 cup quick-cooking oats

Cream softened butter and sugar in a mixing bowl. Add egg and almond extract, mixing well. Add flour, salt, and oats. Line a baking sheet with aluminum foil. Use a melon baller or drop by ½ teaspoonfuls onto foil. (Use only this small amount; dough will spread to give a lacy effect in the finished cookie.) Place only 6 cookies at a time on an average-size baking sheet.

Bake in a 350° oven for 5–8 minutes, or until light brown. Slide foil off cookie sheet and completely cool cookies before removing from foil. (If they resist at all, they are not completely cool.)

FILLING:

4 ounces bittersweet or
  semisweet chocolate
1 tablespoon butter

2 tablespoons grated orange
  zest
1 tablespoon Grand Marnier

Melt chocolate and butter in the top of a double boiler or in a microwave at MEDIUM. Stir in orange zest and Grand Marnier. Cool slightly. Spread mixture on flat side of one cookie, and sandwich with a second. Let cool and serve. Makes 18 sandwich cookies.

Note: Serve these light treats with a scoop of vanilla ice cream or orange sherbet, and a cup of cinnamon-flavored coffee.

Above & Beyond Parsley

FROM GWEN'S ROAD DIARY:
Almost all of the hundreds and hundreds of TV and radio appearances we have made have been live. Once in Kansas City, we couldn't find the back entrance to the TV studio. How maddening to be right there and not be able to get in! When we finally did, we were literally miked as we came in the door, with the anchorperson welcoming us to her audience as we came onto the set! Phew! From mountaintop radio stations to fenced multi-complexes to busy downtown studios all over the country, Barbara and I are very proud of the fact that we have never missed a scheduled appearance.

Montana

CAPITAL: *Helena*

NICKNAMES: *The Treasure State*

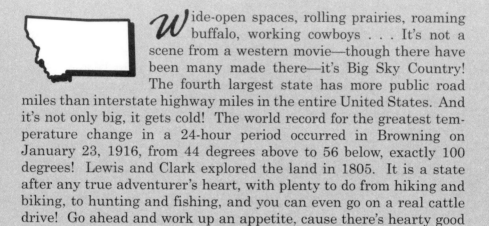

$\mathcal{W}$ide-open spaces, rolling prairies, roaming buffalo, working cowboys . . . It's not a scene from a western movie—though there have been many made there—it's Big Sky Country! The fourth largest state has more public road miles than interstate highway miles in the entire United States. And it's not only big, it gets cold! The world record for the greatest temperature change in a 24-hour period occurred in Browning on January 23, 1916, from 44 degrees above to 56 below, exactly 100 degrees! Lewis and Clark explored the land in 1805. It is a state after any true adventurer's heart, with plenty to do from hiking and biking, to hunting and fishing, and you can even go on a real cattle drive! Go ahead and work up an appetite, cause there's hearty good food waiting for you at the ranch.

Blodgett Lake Stuffed Trout

4 trout, cleaned
1 tablespoon butter
4 slices bacon, cooked and cut
  into 1-inch pieces
4 green onions, sliced thin
2 mushrooms, sliced

1 tablespoon lemon butter*
1 teaspoon cumin
1 teaspoon ground red pepper
2 tablespoons white wine
1 lemon, sliced thin

Preheat oven to 375°. Put trout in greased 9x13-inch baking dish; set aside. Melt butter in skillet and sauté bacon pieces, green onions, and mushrooms. Drain off fat. Stuff the trout with bacon mixture. Brush top of trout with lemon butter. Sprinkle cumin and red pepper on top of trout; pour wine on sides. Place lemon slices on top of trout and bake for 30 minutes. Serve hot with steamed rice. Makes 4 servings.

*To make lemon butter, mix ½ lemon juice and ½ melted butter.

Bitterroot Favorites & Montana Memories

Lemon Huckleberry Scones

Real huckleberries are not available commercially, but are very similar to the widely available blueberry.

2 cups flour
⅓ cup sugar plus 2 tablespoons, divided
2½ teaspoons baking powder
¼ teaspoon kosher salt
⅛ teaspoon ground nutmeg
½ cup (1 stick) cold butter, cut into chunks

1 egg
½ cup milk
2 teaspoons grated lemon zest
¾ cup fresh or frozen blueberries
1 tablespoon melted butter

Preheat oven to 400°. Stir together flour, ⅓ cup sugar, baking powder, salt, and nutmeg. Cut in the butter with pastry blender or by hand until mixture resembles coarse crumbs. Beat egg with milk and lemon zest. Pour egg mixture over flour mixture and stir once or twice, then add blueberries and stir just until moist.

Gather dough into a ball and place on greased baking sheet. Pat dough into a 9-inch circle, about ¾ inch thick. With a sharp, wet knife, and without cutting all the way through, score dough into 8 wedges. Do not separate the dough. Brush tops with melted butter and sprinkle with remaining 2 tablespoons sugar. Bake until golden brown, about 20–30 minutes. Remove from oven and cool 2 minutes. Separate scones into 8 pieces and serve. Makes 8 scones.

Recipe from Triple Creek Ranch, Darby
The Cool Mountain Cookbook

Editor's Extra: It helps to grease your hands, too, for easier patting down of dough. These are sooo good!

Beartooth Highway, a National Forest Scenic Byway, has been described by the late CBS correspondent Charles Kuralt as "the most beautiful road in America." From its beginning at the border of the Custer National Forest to its terminus near the northeast entrance to Yellowstone National Park, the 69-mile stretch of paradise will take you to the top of the world at 12,000 feet, and through the Custer, Shoshone, and Gallatin national forests. Glaciers are found on the north flank of nearly every mountain peak over 11,500 feet in these mountains.

Sinfully Chocolate Waffles

My craving for chocolate brings this absolutely fabulous recipe to my best of friends (and probably a few "unfriendlies," too). When I received the recipe from a friend, I thought chocolate waffles were going a bit far... wrong—they are the BEST waffles I have ever had the privilege to savor. Need I tell you more!!!?

2 cups all-purpose flour
4 teaspoons baking powder
1 teaspoon salt
3 tablespoons sugar
3 teaspoons cocoa

2 eggs, separated
1½ cups low-fat milk
1 teaspoon maple flavoring
4 tablespoons vegetable oil

In a large mixing bowl, add the dry ingredients and stir to mix well. Add egg yolks, milk, maple flavoring, and oil. Mix well. Beat egg whites until soft peaks form; add to batter mixture. Bake in waffle iron as you would any other waffle.

Serve with Mapeline Syrup or syrup of your choice. I spoon fresh fruit on top, then a little Mapeline Syrup on top of the fruit. Yields 6–8 waffles

MAPELINE SYRUP:
2 cups granulated sugar
1 cup water

½ teaspoon maple flavoring

Mix together and bring to a boil. Serve warm with waffles.

Best-of-Friends, Festive Occasions Cookbook

Ranch Beans

1 (16-ounce) can pork and beans
1 (16-ounce) can hot chili beans
1 (16-ounce) can dark kidney
  beans
1 cup ketchup

1 cup brown sugar
1 large onion, chopped
1 teaspoon mustard
2 pounds ground chuck,
  browned and drained

Mix all ingredients and cook in crockpot on LOW for 3–4 hours, or bake uncovered in oven at 400° for 1 hour.

Horse Prairie Favorites

Honeyed Onions

6 medium onions
2 tablespoons chili sauce
½ teaspoon salt
2 tablespoons butter or
  margarine, melted

2 tablespoons honey
⅛ teaspoon pepper
1 teaspoon paprika

Peel onions and cut in half crosswise. Place them in a 8x12x2-inch baking dish, cut-side-up. In a small bowl, stir together other ingredients and brush over onion halves. Bake covered for an hour at 350°, or until fork-tender.

Wolf Point, Montana 75th Jubilee Cookbook

Cherries in the Snow

This is our Christmas dessert.

1 (3-ounce) package cream
  cheese, softened
½ cup sugar
½ teaspoon vanilla

½ pint cream
Graham cracker crust
1 (21-ounce) can cherry pie
  filling

Blend cream cheese, sugar, and vanilla. In separate bowl, whip the cream. Mix whipped cream into cream cheese mixture. Pour into graham cracker crust. Top with cherry pie filling and chill overnight.

Note: This doubles nicely using an 8-ounce package of cream cheese.

Mountain Brook's Wacky Wonders of the Woods

Flathead Lake Monster Potatoes

2 pounds frozen hashbrown
  potatoes
1 (10¾-ounce) can cream of
  mushroom soup
2 cups grated Cheddar cheese

2 cups sour cream
½ cup chopped onion
½ stick butter, melted
1 cup cooked elk sausage or
  summer sausage

Combine hashbrowns, soup, cheese, sour cream, onion, melted butter, and elk meat. Turn into a greased 9x13-inch pan.

TOPPING:

2 cups crushed cornflakes

¼ cup butter, melted

Stir Topping ingredients together. Sprinkle over potato mixture. Bake at 350° for 30 minutes. (May add ½ cup green or red bell pepper for added zest.) Makes 8 side dishes.

Recipe from Outlook Inn B&B, Somers
A Taste of Montana

Yaak Trail Bars

1 cup brown sugar
⅔ cup peanut butter
½ cup light corn syrup
½ cup butter, melted
2 teaspoons vanilla
1½ cups quick oats
1½ cups crisp rice cereal
1 cup semisweet chocolate
  pieces

1 cup raisins
½ cup flaked coconut
½ cup raw, shelled sunflower
  seeds
⅓ cup wheat germ
2 tablespoons sesame seeds
Dash of cinnamon or more

Grease a 9x13x2-inch baking pan; set aside. Combine brown sugar, peanut butter, corn syrup, butter, and vanilla.

In another bowl, combine oats, cereal, chocolate pieces, raisins, coconut, sunflower seeds, wheat germ, sesame seeds, and cinnamon; stir in peanut butter mixture. Mix well. Press evenly into prepared pan. Bake in 350° oven for 25 minutes or until lightly browned. Cool. Cut into bars.

Yaak Cookbook

Nebraska

CAPITAL: *Lincoln*

NICKNAME: *The Cornhusker State*

*F*rom art museums to frontier military posts, from prehistoric elephants and rhinos to a world-class zoo, Nebraska has been called a 77,000-square-mile museum without walls. Nebraska's gold is its corn, but of course, cattle is huge, and therefore so is its beef production and meat packing. Once known as the Great American Desert, Nebraska has developed into a rich agricultural resource that helps feed the entire world. It is the birthplace of the Reuben sandwich and Kool-Aid. Campfire cooking at authentic covered wagon treks is just as likely to occur in the Cornhusker State as fine dining after the theater.

Smoked Deer Ham

1 (5- to 8-pound) deer ham,
  trimmed neatly
½ cup Worcestershire
1 cup Italian dressing
1 tablespoon cayenne pepper
1 tablespoon salt
1 tablespoon pepper
1 cup chopped onions
½ cup butter, softened

Put ham in large container; cover with mixture of all remaining ingredients. (You can slice holes in meat so it can marinate inside better.) Cover well; soak overnight or about 10 hours, turning over every 2 or 3 hours in marinade. Put on smoker and let smoke for 6 hours; turn and smoke 4 more hours or until tender.

The Oregon Trail Cookbook

Krunch Kone Koffee Pie

10 sugar ice cream cones,
  ground fine
¼ cup margarine, melted
½ cup hot fudge sauce
1 quart vanilla ice cream

1½ tablespoons instant coffee
1 teaspoon hot water
1 (8-ounce) tub whipped
  topping
½ chocolate bar, grated

Grind ice cream cones and combine with melted margarine. Press into 9-inch pie plate to form crust. Place in freezer. Microwave hot fudge sauce until pourable. Pour into prepared crust and return to freezer. Put ice cream in a medium bowl. Add instant coffee that has been stirred into hot water. Beat until blended and pour on top of fudge sauce. Return to freezer until solid. Top with whipped topping and grated chocolate bar. Freeze. Let set at room temperature for 5 minutes before serving.

Cooking with Iola

Holiday Pinwheels

2 (8-ounce) packages cream
  cheese, softened
1 (1-ounce) package Hidden
  Valley Ranch Salad Dressing
  Mix
3 green onions, finely minced
1 (4-ounce) jar pimento, diced

1 (4-ounce) can diced green
  chiles
1 (2¼-ounce) can chopped
  black olives
1 (3-ounce) package dried
  beef, finely cut
4 (12-inch) flour tortillas

Mix together all ingredients, except tortillas, and spread on flour tortillas. Roll tightly and wrap in Saran Wrap. Chill for at least 2 hours. Slice and place on serving tray.

Cooking with Iola

If you're fascinated with fossils, you'll really "dig" Ashfall Fossil Beds where paleontologists unearth the bones of prehistoric rhinosauruses, three-toed horses, and mastodons. Volcanic ash buried them there at a watering hole ten million years ago.

Chocolate Chip Cheesecake

2 cups crushed Oreos
2 tablespoons margarine,
  melted
3 eggs
2 (8-ounce) packages cream
  cheese, softened

¾ cup sugar
1 teaspoon vanilla
½ cup whipping cream
1¼ cups miniature semisweet
  chocolate chips, divided
1 teaspoon shortening

Combine crushed Oreos and melted margarine and press in bottom and up sides of 10-inch springform pan. In large bowl, beat eggs. Add cream cheese, sugar, and vanilla. Beat until smooth. Add whipping cream; blend well. Stir one cup chips in by hand. Pour into crust. Bake at 325° for about 60–75 minutes or until center is set. Edges will just begin to brown. Cool. Melt remaining chips and shortening in microwave. Drizzle over cooled cheesecake. Refrigerate several hours.

Hint: To minimize cracking, place shallow pan half full of hot water in oven while baking.

Kearney 125th Anniversary Community Cookbook

Beef Brisket

MARINADE:
2 tablespoons liquid smoke
1 teaspoon garlic salt
1 teaspoon onion salt

1 teaspoon black pepper
1 teaspoon celery salt
2 tablespoons Worcestershire

Combine Marinade ingredients.

1 (3½- to 4-pound) beef brisket   1 bottle barbeque sauce

Place brisket fat-side-down in 9x13-inch container 2 inches deep. Rub marinade into top and sides of meat. Cover and marinate overnight.

Next day, place meat fat-side-up, cover with foil, and bake 5 hours at 250°. Uncover; remove fat. Pour ½ of barbeque sauce on top. Bake one hour, uncovered. Let stand till cold to slice ¼ to ⅜ inch thick. Offer remaining barbeque sauce.

Heavenly Delights

Peppery T-Bone Steaks & Chili Corn

4 ears fresh sweet corn, in husks
1–2 garlic cloves, minced
½ teaspoon coarse-ground black pepper

2 well-trimmed beef T-bone steaks, cut 1–1½ inches thick
2 tablespoons butter
½ teaspoon chili powder
¼ teaspoon ground cumin

Pull back corn husks from each ear of corn, leaving husks attached to base. Remove corn silk. Fold husks back around corn; tie at the end of each ear with string or a strip of one of the outside corn leaves. Soak corn in cold water 3–4 hours. Remove from water and place on grill over medium coals. Cook 20 minutes, turning often.

Combine garlic and pepper; rub into both sides of beef T-bone steak. Place steaks on grill with corn; continue cooking, turning steaks once, and corn often. Grill 1-inch thick steaks 16–20 minutes for rare (140°) to medium (160°) or to desired doneness. Grill 1½-inch thick steaks 22–30 minutes (rare to medium) or to desired doneness. Remove corn when tender. Meanwhile, melt butter; add chili powder and cumin. Carve steaks into thick slices and serve with corn and seasoned butter.

Taste the Good Life! Nebraska Cookbook

Omaha's Rosenblatt Stadium hosts the annual College Baseball World Series.

Baked Earth Dried Apple Pie

Soak 2 cups dried apples in water overnight. Drain off water and mix apples with ½ cup sugar and 1 teaspoon each of allspice and cinnamon. Line an 8-inch pan with a crust. Add the apple mixture. Dot with 3 tablespoons butter and cover with a second crust. Make a few slashes in the top for ventilation and bake at 350° for about one hour or until the crust is golden brown.

The Mormon Trail Cookbook

Flint Ridge Pheasant

Those of us who cook for hunters always welcome a new recipe for fish or fowl. Here's one that we cheered for! This casserole is also wonderful for chicken.

2 cups cooked wild rice
  (from ⅔ cup dry)
1 cup julienned (matchstick)
  1-inch carrot strips, cooked
5 slices bacon
1–2 tablespoons oil, butter, or
  margarine
2 skinless, boneless pheasant
  breast halves, or 3 skinless,
  boneless chicken breast halves,
  cut in 2x2-inch pieces
Salt and pepper to taste

5 medium mushrooms, sliced
5 green onions, sliced
1 (10¾-ounce) can cream of
  chicken soup
¼ cup cream or milk
¼ cup sherry or dry, white
  wine
1 cup (4 ounces) shredded
  mozzarella cheese
1 (14-ounce) can artichoke
  hearts, drained, quartered
¼ cup grated Parmesan cheese

Put the wild rice in a 9x9x2-inch baking dish that has been sprayed with nonstick vegetable spray. Layer carrots over the wild rice.

In large skillet, cook bacon until crisp; drain and crumble over carrots. Pour off grease from skillet and add a tablespoon or two of oil. Sauté the pheasant until well browned on both sides (about 10 minutes). Transfer to baking dish.

In same skillet, sauté mushrooms and green onions until tender, adding additional oil if needed. Add soup, cream, and sherry, and mix well. Add mozzarella and gently stir in artichokes. Spread over the pheasant layer. Sprinkle with Parmesan. Cover dish with foil sprayed with nonstick vegetable spray. Bake at 350° for 30 minutes; remove foil and bake 15 more minutes until bubbly throughout. Serves 4–5.

Presentations

Nevada

CAPITAL: *Carson City*

NICKNAME: *The Silver State*

*R*ugged and wild, adventurous and fun, scenic and historic . . . Nevada is quite a study in contrasts! Most of the state is rural, with mountains, lakes, canyons, and desert that seems to stretch into infinity. And then there's Las Vegas, which definitely lights up the landscape. It's no surprise there are more and bigger and certainly brighter hotels there than anywhere else on earth. And of course there's lots of silver in the Silver State—but did you know that Nevada is the largest gold-producing state in the nation? It's second only to South Africa in the world! Dude ranches and cattle drives and real cowboys keep Western traditions alive. Food is everything from chuck wagon food to gourmet classics. Outdoorsmen love to slow cook food outdoors in Dutch ovens, a popular cooking style that they have most certainly perfected.

Nevada Heat Chili Fries

1 teaspoon chili powder
1 teaspoon cumin powder
1 teaspoon crushed red pepper
  flakes
½ teaspoon salt
6 large baking potatoes,
  scrubbed (about 3 pounds)

Preheat oven to 500°. In a bowl, combine chili powder, cumin powder, crushed red pepper flakes, and salt. Cut potatoes into sticks. Spray a baking sheet and place potatoes in a single layer. Sprinkle with spices. Bake 10 minutes, then turn potato slices over. Bake another 10–15 minutes, until potatoes are browned and fork-tender. Serves 6.

A Cowboy Cookin' Every Night

Roast, Dutch Oven Style

1 (4-pound) beef roast
3 onions
4–6 potatoes
3 bell peppers

6 carrots
1 clove garlic, minced
1 (18-ounce) bottle barbecue
   sauce

Prepare pit (see below). Lightly oil a large Dutch oven. Place roast in oven. Peel and quarter onion and potatoes, and place in the oven. Seed bell peppers, then cut into quarters and add with whole carrots and garlic. Pour entire bottle of barbecue sauce over the top. Place lid firmly on the oven and carefully lower it into the pit. Cook for about 2 hours.

TO PREPARE PIT:

Dig a hole about 2 feet deep and approximately 8 inches bigger around than your Dutch oven. About 2 hours before cooking, heat the hole by burning wood in it. You should use a wood that makes lots of ashes (sagebrush and smaller pine limbs are good). It takes a large fire to heat the ground. After heating the ground, take out the ashes, leaving 3 or 4 inches of ashes in the bottom of the hole. After setting the Dutch oven in the hole, put the ashes back in, surrounding the pan on all sides, and with 3 or 4 inches of ashes on top. Cover the ashes with 1 or 2 inches of dirt to hold the heat in, and you are cooking.

The Great Nevada Cookbook

PHOTO BY JAN MARIE ALBERT

"The Loneliest Road in America," Highway 50 between Ely and Fernley—there are few tourist stops in the 287-mile distance.

A Cowboy's "Real Chili Got No Beans in It, Ma'am" Chili

1 cup diced yellow onions
3 cloves garlic, minced
2 tablespoons oil
2 pounds beef sirloin, cubed
  into ¼-inch squares
2 cups chopped, peeled ripe
  tomatoes
1 cup tomato sauce
1 (12-ounce) bottle beer
1 cup strong brewed coffee
2 (6-ounce) cans tomato paste
½ cup low-salt beef broth

½ cup packed brown sugar
3 tablespoons chili powder
1 teaspoon cumin
1 teaspoon unsweetened cocoa
  powder
1 teaspoon dried oregano
1 teaspoon ground cayenne
  pepper
1 teaspoon salt
½ teaspoon black pepper
4 fresh jalapeño chile peppers,
  seeded and chopped

Sauté onions and garlic in oil. Add sirloin and lightly brown in oil for about 8–10 minutes. Mix tomatoes, tomato sauce, beer, coffee, tomato paste, beef broth, brown sugar, chili powder, cumin, cocoa powder, oregano, cayenne pepper, salt, and black pepper. Reduce heat to low and simmer for about 1½ hours. Stir in jalapeños and simmer for another 30 minutes. Authentic chili should not be thick. Serves 2 cowboys or about 6 tenderfoot sissies.

A Cowboy Cookin' Every Night

Nevada Ranchers' Cactus Salsa

2 cups chopped ripe tomatoes
1 cup chopped red onion
1 cup nopalitos (cactus meat)*,
  drained and rinsed

½ cup chopped fresh cilantro
¼ cup diced serrano chiles
½ teaspoon coarse salt
⅓ cup fresh lime juice

Combine all ingredients. Chill at least one hour before serving. Serves 4 rough-riding cowgirls or 6 city gals with sports cars.

*If you can't find nopalitos, substitute mild green chiles.

Authentic Cowboy Cookery Then & Now

Dancing Palomino Spice Cake

3 cups all-purpose flour
4 teaspoons ground ginger
2 teaspoons ground cinnamon
½ teaspoon ground cloves
½ teaspoon cardamom
2 sticks unsalted butter,
  softened

1 cup brown sugar
1 cup molasses
1 cup boiling water
2 teaspoons baking soda
2 large eggs, beaten

Preheat oven to 350°. Grease a 9x13-inch pan. Combine flour, ginger, cinnamon, cloves, and cardamom. In a separate bowl, beat together butter and brown sugar until fluffy, about 3 minutes. Whisk together molasses and boiling water in another bowl. Whisk baking soda into hot molasses. Combine dry ingredients and molasses, then fold in butter mixture until blended. Whisk eggs into mixture until smooth. Pour batter into cake pan and bake 55–60 minutes until toothpick inserted in center comes out clean. Cool before removing from pan. Prepare frosting.

CREAM CHEESE FROSTING:

2 (8-ounce) packages cream
  cheese, softened
1 stick unsalted butter,
  softened

1 teaspoon orange zest
2 cups powdered sugar

Beat together cream cheese, butter, and orange zest until fluffy. Slowly beat in powdered sugar. Chill frosting before spreading on cooled cake. Serves a couple of cowboys with a sweet tooth or 5 or 6 ranch kids.

Authentic Cowboy Cookery Then & Now

Chicken with Chocolate

You will be surprised at how truly delicious this chicken is. In the Basque region of Navarra, the use of chocolate, especially in game recipes, is popular.

1 (2½- to 3-pound) fryer, cut up
¼ cup cooking oil or olive oil
1 large onion, chopped
2 cloves garlic, minced
1 green bell pepper, chopped
  (1–1½ cups)
2 (8-ounce) cans tomato sauce

1–2 teaspoons crushed dried
  red pepper
1 teaspoon salt
¼ teaspoon Tabasco
2 cloves garlic, chopped
½ ounce unsweetened baking
  chocolate, finely grated

Soak chicken briefly (10–15 minutes) in cold, salted water. Trim off excess fat. Drain chicken pieces in colander. Pat dry with paper towels, if necessary. Heat oil in frying pan or electric skillet to a moderate 300° heat. Brown chicken pieces in oil. When nicely browned, remove pieces to a Dutch oven or casserole with cover.

In the skillet in which you browned the chicken pieces, sauté onion, garlic, and bell pepper for 10 or 15 minutes on low heat. Add remaining 6 ingredients, mixing well. Simmer about 5 minutes. Spoon sauce over chicken pieces in Dutch oven or casserole. Bake at 350° for one hour. Yields 5–6 servings.

Chorizos in an Iron Skillet

Spicy Avocado Salad

1 teaspoon salt
1 clove garlic, minced
1 teaspoon Worcestershire
½ teaspoon Tabasco
Juice of ⅓ lemon
3 tablespoons olive oil
3 ripe tomatoes, diced
2 ripe avocados, diced
Freshly ground pepper to taste

1 green chile, seeded, minced
3 tablespoons minced cilantro
3 tablespoons (heaping) diced
  Monterey Jack cheese
3 tablespoons (heaping)
  crumbled crisp-fried bacon
2 tablespoons (heaping) minced
  onion
½ green bell pepper, diced

Mash salt and garlic in bowl with fork until smooth paste forms. Whisk in Worcestershire, Tabasco, lemon juice, and olive oil until well blended. Pour over mixture of tomatoes, avocados, pepper, green chile, cilantro, cheese, bacon, onion, and green pepper in bowl; mix well. Marinate in refrigerator for 30 minutes. Serve on bed of mixed salad greens. Yields 4 servings.

Best Bets

Garlic Cream Cheese Mashed Potatoes

2 pounds unpeeled new
  potatoes, cut into 1-inch
  cubes
1¾ teaspoons salt, divided
½ cup (1 stick) butter, cut
  into pieces
4 ounces cream cheese, cut
  into pieces, softened
5 (or more) garlic cloves,
  minced

½ cup finely chopped fresh
  parsley
¼ cup grated Parmesan or
  Romano cheese
¼–½ teaspoon white pepper
2 ounces Monterey Jack cheese,
  shredded

Place potatoes in a saucepan. Add 1 teaspoon salt and enough water to cover the potatoes by 3 inches. Bring to a boil and boil until tender. Drain and place in a large bowl. Mash by hand for home-style potatoes or use an electric mixer for smoother potatoes.

Add butter, cream cheese, garlic, parsley, Parmesan cheese, remaining ¾ teaspoon salt, and white pepper to the potatoes and mix well. Spoon potatoes into a greased 12-inch baking dish. Top with Monterey Jack cheese. Bake at 450° for 10 minutes or until top is lightly browned. Yields 10–12 servings.

Variation: Use minced chives or green onions in place of parsley. Add ¼ cup sautéed onion.

Las Vegas Glitter to Gourmet

The Valley of Fire, not far from Las Vegas, has fascinating petroglyphs of animals and fish and birds and symbols. Gwen wonders: "Is there an early cookbook here?"

New Hampshire

CAPITAL: *Concord*

NICKNAME: *The Granite State*

*N*ew Hampshire is called the Granite State, the White Mountain State, the Mother of Rivers, and Switzerland of America, for its beautiful mountains and rivers. Of the thirteen original colonies, New Hampshire was the first to declare its independence from Mother England—a full six months before the Declaration of Independence was signed. Beyond its major cities, greenbelts of farming activity include dairy, vegetable and livestock products, and fruit orchards that produce a million bushels of apples annually. Indeed, apple cider has become a major product line for many orchard operations. Without farming, there would be no barns, silos, or sugar houses that give the state its special character.

New England Blueberry Pie

3½ cups blueberries
¾ cup sugar
⅛ teaspoon salt
¼ teaspoon cinnamon

3 tablespoons flour
Butter (1–2 tablespoons)
Pastry crust for a 2-crust
   (9-inch) pie

Mix blueberries and next 4 ingredients, in a large bowl. Line a shallow pie plate with bottom crust. Pour in berry mixture. Dot with 5–6 small pieces of butter. Moisten edge of crust with water.

Roll top crust to fit plate. Brush lightly with melted shortening and sprinkle with flour. Fold over and cut 3 or 4 small slits on the fold. Place over berries. Unfold and press down around the edge. Trim crust close to the edge of the plate and press again around the edge with floured tines of a fork. Hold pie over sink and pour about ¼ cup milk over crust, letting surplus drain off. Bake at 475° for 15 minutes. Reduce heat to 350° for 15 minutes longer. If frozen berries are used, increase last baking time to 30 minutes.

Homespun Cookery

Ham & Spinach Quiche

5–6 ounces spinach (about
  ½ bag)
¼ teaspoon salt
⅛ teaspoon pepper
1 tablespoon horseradish
4 tablespoons sour cream
4–6 ounces Swiss cheese, grated
  (part sharp Cheddar cheese
  may be used)

⅓ cup minced onion
4–6 ounces ham, cubed or cut
  into small pieces
4 eggs
1½–2 cups half-and-half
¼ teaspoon sugar
⅛ teaspoon cayenne pepper
⅛ teaspoon nutmeg
1 unbaked pastry shell

Cook spinach. Drain thoroughly, pressing out the water. Add salt, pepper, horseradish, and sour cream. Spread on pastry in 9-inch pie plate or regular quiche dish. Sprinkle with cheese and onion. Add ham.

Beat eggs with a whisk; add half-and-half, sugar, cayenne, and nutmeg. Mix well. Pour into pie shell. Bake at 425° for 15 minutes. Reduce heat to 300° for 30 minutes more or until a knife comes out clean. Cool on a rack 5–10 minutes before serving.

Homespun Cookery

Corned Beef Hash

1 large corned beef (raw)
4–6 potatoes, peeled
1 large onion, diced
4–5 stalks celery, diced
4 tablespoons butter

¼ cup flour
¼ cup Worcestershire
Salt and pepper to taste
1–1½ cups cooking liquid

Cook corned beef in a large pot, covered with water, for 6 hours or until tender. In the last hour of cooking, add the potatoes to pot and cook till soft. Drain, reserving 1½ cups cooking liquid. When cooled enough to handle, shred the corned beef into a large bowl. Mash potatoes and add to beef. Sauté the onion and celery in butter till tender. Add to the beef with flour and Worcestershire. Season with salt and pepper to taste. Add liquid as needed to hold the mixture together. Form into patties (approximately 5-ounce patties). Lightly brown in skillet in hot oil. Serves 16–20.

Note: Use leftover corned beef or smaller cuts of meat for fewer portions. You may substitute roast beef, turkey, or pork for a nice variation. These freeze well.

Washington Street Eatery Cook Book

Frosted Carrot Bars

4 eggs
2 cups sugar
2 cups flour, sifted
2 teaspoons baking powder
2 teaspoons cinnamon

1 teaspoon salt
1½ cups oil
3 cups grated carrots
1½ cups grated coconut
1½ cups chopped walnuts

Beat eggs until light. Gradually add sugar. Sift flour, baking powder, cinnamon, and salt. Add flour mixture alternately with oil. Fold in carrots, coconut, and walnuts. Spread in 2 (9x13-inch) pans. Bake at 350° for 25–30 minutes. Cool and frost.

CREAM CHEESE FROSTING:
1 (3-ounce) package cream
  cheese, softened
1 tablespoon light cream

2½ cups confectioners' sugar
1 teaspoon vanilla
⅛ teaspoon salt

Blend together cream cheese and cream. Add sugar and more cream, if necessary, to make frosting spreadable. Add vanilla and salt, and beat well.

A Hancock Community Collection

Cheesecake Supreme

This cheesecake is not too sweet. It stores well and maintains its texture. Easy to make and everyone loves it.

¼ pound butter, melted
1 pound cream cheese, softened
1 pint ricotta cheese
4 eggs
1½ cups sugar
3 tablespoons flour

3 tablespoons cornstarch
1½ teaspoons lemon juice
1 pint sour cream
1 teaspoon vanilla
1 (20-ounce) can crushed
  pineapple, well drained

Melt and cool butter. Mix all ingredients in order given, except pineapple. Lightly grease a 9-inch springform pan. Spread can of pineapple on bottom of pan. Pour in the cheese mixture and bake for one hour at 350°. Turn oven off and let cake stand for 2 hours before removing.

Do not open oven door during baking or cooling of cheesecake. Remove from pan and invert so pineapple is on top. Serves 16.

Great Island Cook Book

White Bean with Roasted Garlic Soup

2 cups navy or white beans,
  cleaned well
4–5 cups water or stock
1 bulb fresh garlic
2 tablespoons oil
2 carrots, peeled and diced

1 large onion, diced
1 bay leaf
1 tablespoon dried thyme
  leaves
Salt and pepper to taste

Soak beans overnight in water. Drain and rinse well in colander. Place in a soup pot with water or stock. Bring to a boil, then simmer for 1–1½ hours, skimming the surface from time to time. Separate the bulb of garlic into individual cloves, keeping skin on. Toss garlic in oil and wrap loosely in aluminum foil. Roast in a 450° oven for 10–15 minutes or until cloves become soft. Cool.

Add prepared vegetables, bay leaf, thyme, salt and pepper to the beans. Squeeze the garlic cloves out of their skins and mash with a fork. Stir into soup. Simmer until vegetables are tender. Add more liquid if too thick. Serve with unseasoned croutons. Yields 6–8 servings.

Washington Street Eatery Cook Book

Daniel Webster, one of this country's most famous statesmen, was born in Salisbury, New Hampshire, in 1782 and graduated from Dartmouth College in 1801. Webster served in the U.S. House and Senate, and was Secretary of State under Presidents Harrison and Fillmore.

Lemon Puffs

½ cup hot water
1 package active dry yeast
5 eggs, beaten
2 tablespoons powdered milk
¼ cup butter, melted
⅓ cup sugar, plus sugar for
  topping

Finely grated rind of 1 lemon
½ teaspoon salt
4½ cups flour
1 egg yolk, beaten
Finely chopped walnuts

Combine water and yeast and set aside to dissolve. In a large mixing bowl, combine eggs, powdered milk, melted butter, ⅓ cup sugar, lemon rind, and salt. Add dissolved yeast and mix well. Stir in flour. Allow dough to rise in a bowl, until it is doubled in volume. Punch down, remove from bowl, and knead lightly on floured board. Dough will be smooth and soft. Place in a clean bowl and set aside to rise again until doubled in volume. Punch down again and knead out the bubbles.

Preheat oven to 350°. Grease 2 baking sheets. Shape dough into 1-inch balls and place them 1 inch apart on prepared baking sheets. Brush tops with egg yolk and sprinkle with sugar and finely chopped walnuts. Bake 15 minutes and serve at once. Yields 30 rolls.

A recipe from Stafford's in the Field, Chocorua
Country Inns and Back Roads Cookbook

Sausage-Broccoli Bake

1 pound bulk sausage
1 cup sliced celery
1 (6-ounce) package long-grain
  and wild rice mix
1 (10-ounce) package frozen
  broccoli spears, thawed

1 (10¾-ounce) can cream of
  mushroom soup
⅔ cup milk
4 tablespoons grated Parmesan
  cheese, divided

Break up sausage and combine with celery in large skillet. Cook over medium-high heat until sausage is lightly browned. Remove from skillet, draining any fat, and place in a shallow, round 2-quart baking dish.

Preheat oven to 350°. Prepare rice mix with water as package directs, omitting butter or margarine in skillet. Stir into sausage mixture. Arrange thawed broccoli on top. Mix soup, milk, and half the cheese. Pour over broccoli. Sprinkle remaining cheese on top. Bake 30 minutes or until bubbly.

A Hancock Community Collection

New Jersey

CAPITAL: *Trenton*

NICKNAME: *The Garden State*

*N*ew Jersey is known as the Garden State for good reason. Over 150 types of fruits and vegetables are grown there, including blueberries, cranberries, peaches, spinach, bell pepper, and eggplant. Ocean Spray Cranberry Sauce started out as a tasty jar of jelly in New Egypt, and Campbell's Soup originated in Camden. New Jersey has the highest population density and most dense system of highways and railroads in the United States. It's always a treat to go to the Jersey Shore. Picturesque Cape May holds the distinction of being the oldest seashore resort in the United States and one of the most unique. We so enjoyed walking through neighborhoods of quaint gingerbread houses bedecked with colorful flowers. Atlantic City, where the Miss America Pageant is held and where the street names came from for the game Monopoly, has the longest boardwalk. Get your salt water taffy here!

Cape May French Toast Casserole

1 cup brown sugar
1 stick butter (½ cup)
2 tablespoons corn syrup
2 tart apples, peeled and sliced
1 loaf French bread, cut into
  ¾-inch slices

5 eggs, beaten
1½ cups milk
1 teaspoon vanilla

Cook sugar, butter, and corn syrup until syrupy. Pour into 9x13-inch dish. Spread apple slices on syrup. Place bread on apples. Whisk together eggs, milk, and vanilla. Pour over bread. Cover and refrigerate overnight.

Heat oven to 350°. Bake, uncovered, for 30–40 minutes. Serve with your choice of syrup. Makes 8 servings.

Cooking with the Allenhurst Garden Club

Jewish Apple Cake

3 cups flour
2 cups sugar
3 teaspoons baking powder
4 eggs, beaten
½ cup orange juice
1 cup vegetable oil

3 teaspoons vanilla
5 apples, peeled, cored, and
sliced
2 teaspoons cinnamon, mixed
with 5 tablespoons sugar

Combine the first 7 ingredients. Pour half the batter into a greased tube pan. Place a layer of apples and half the cinnamon mixture; pour remaining batter and apples on top with remaining cinnamon mixture. Bake in a 350° oven for 1 hour and 20 minutes. (The cake can be baked 1–2 days before serving because it keeps so well.)

The Happy Cooker 3

Chicken Pecan Fettuccine

This is a mouth-watering combination of ingredients.

1 pound chicken breasts,
skinned and boned
¾ cup butter, divided
3 cups sliced fresh mushrooms
1 cup sliced green onions
¾ teaspoon salt, divided
½ teaspoon freshly ground
black pepper, divided
½ teaspoon garlic powder,
divided

10 ounces fresh fettuccine
1 egg yolk
⅔ cup half-and-half
2 tablespoons freshly chopped
parsley
½ cup freshly grated
Parmesan cheese
1 cup chopped pecans, toasted

Cut chicken into ¾-inch pieces. Melt ¼ cup butter in a large skillet. Sauté chicken until lightly browned. Remove chicken from skillet and set aside. To drippings in skillet, add mushrooms, green onions, ½ teaspoon salt, ¼ teaspoon pepper, and ¼ teaspoon garlic powder. Sauté until mushrooms are tender. Return chicken to skillet and simmer for 20 minutes, or until chicken is done. Cook fettuccine in boiling salted water until al dente. Drain well.

Melt remaining ½ cup butter and combine with egg yolk, half-and-half, parsley, and remaining salt, pepper, and garlic powder. Stir butter sauce into fettuccine. Sprinkle with cheese, tossing until well mixed. Add chicken and mushroom mixture; toss until combined. To serve, arrange fettuccine on a warm platter and sprinkle with toasted pecans. Yields 6 servings.

A Matter of Taste

Tomato Flans

Canned tomatoes can be used here but, oh-boy, is it great made with fresh New Jersey tomatoes! Makes a great side dish.

3 cherry tomatoes, halved
2 tablespoons (¼ stick) butter
1 tablespoon olive oil
1 cup minced onion
1 pound tomatoes, peeled, seeded, and chopped
4 eggs

½ cup whipping cream
¼ cup grated Parmesan cheese
¼ cup grated Gruyère cheese
Salt and freshly ground pepper to taste

Generously butter 6 (½-cup) custard cups or ramekins. Place 1 cherry tomato half, skin-side-down, in each cup. Melt butter with oil in heavy large skillet over medium-low heat. Add onion and cook until translucent, stirring occasionally, about 10 minutes. Increase heat to high. Add tomatoes and cook until all liquid evaporates, stirring frequently. Cool slightly.

Preheat oven to 375°. Beat eggs and cream to blend. Stir in cheeses and tomato mixture. Season with salt and pepper. Carefully spoon mixture into prepared cups. Arrange cups in roasting pan. Pour enough water into pan to come halfway up sides of cups. Bake until tester inserted in centers comes out clean, 30–35 minutes. Let stand 10 minutes. Run knife around edge of cups to loosen flans. Invert onto plates and serve immediately. Makes 6 servings.

Why Not for Breakfast?

The drive into Princeton, New Jersey, in the snow is almost indescribable, sort of like you're inside a Courier and Ives painting. After a recommended local lunch, good research, and an invigorating walk around the beautiful campus, we left feeling much smarter.

Three Chocolate Fudge

⅔ cup evaporated milk
1⅔ cups sugar
½ teaspoon salt
2 tablespoons butter
1½ cups miniature
  marshmallows

½ cup white chocolate chips
½ cup milk chocolate chips
½ cup semisweet chocolate
  chips
1 teaspoon vanilla

In a 3-quart saucepan, combine milk, sugar, and salt; bring to a boil over medium heat. Cook for 5 minutes, stirring constantly (use a wooden spoon). Remove from heat and add butter, marshmallows, and chocolate chips. Stir until all are melted and blended well. Add vanilla; stir until blended. Spread mixture into a pie plate or pan (nonstick works well). When completely cooled, cut into squares.

Collected Recipes

Fish Chowder, Jersey Shore

1½–2 pounds Jersey Shore
  fish fillets
Cold salted water
2 ounces salted pork (or bacon)
1 large onion, chopped fine
8 medium potatoes, diced
2 cups boiling water

Salt and pepper to taste
1 quart milk, scalded
2 tablespoons butter
1 cup oyster or other crackers,
  crumbled
1 (12-ounce) can corn (optional)

Place fish in saucepan; cover with cold salty water. Bring to boil and boil for 5 minutes. Save stock. Remove any skin on the fish. Fry the salt pork (or bacon) until fat is rendered. Remove pork and drain on paper towels. Sauté onion in fat; add potatoes and boiling water. Boil for 5 minutes. Add fish and reserved stock. Simmer another 15 minutes. Check potatoes for doneness. Season with salt and pepper. Add milk, butter, and crackers. (In Belford, the cooks always added a small can of corn.) Makes 4 servings.

Atlantic Highlands

Italian Cheesecake
(Torta De Ricotta)

1 stick butter, melted
1 loaf pound cake, crumbled
3 pounds ricotta cheese
1 dozen eggs

1 cup sugar
2 cups milk
Rind of 1 lemon, grated

Mix butter and pound cake together to form crust on bottom and sides of a 10½-inch springform pan. Mix together ricotta cheese, eggs, sugar, milk, and lemon rind. Pour into crust. Bake in oven at 375° for 1 hour. Remove and let cool. Refrigerate.

La Cucina Casalinga

Sesame Chicken with Honey Dip

Served by popular request each year at an annual tailgate party.

CHICKEN:
½ cup mayonnaise
1½ teaspoons dry mustard
2 teaspoons instant minced
  onion

1 cup fine dry bread crumbs
½ cup sesame seeds
2 cups uncooked cubed chicken

Preheat oven to 400°. Mix mayonnaise, mustard, and minced onion in a shallow dish or pie pan; set aside. Mix crumbs and sesame seeds. Toss chicken in mayonnaise mixture, then roll in crumb mixture. Place on baking sheet. Bake at 400° for 12–15 minutes, or until lightly browned. Yields 2 dozen.

HONEY DIP:
2 tablespoons honey

1 cup mayonnaise

Combine honey with mayonnaise. Serve hot or at room temperature with dip.

A Matter of Taste

 A diner is defined as a small restaurant resembling a railroad dining car. New Jersey has the most diners in the world and is sometimes referred to as the Diner Capital of the World.

New Mexico

CAPITAL: *Santa Fe*

NICKNAME: *The Land of Enchantment*

Spice it up! New Mexico cooking sends your senses reeling with the pungent aroma of roasting chiles and simmering salsas. Southwestern is what this state is all about, and tortillas, pinto beans, cheese, and chiles are the most important ingredients. Chiles come in different sizes, degrees of hotness, and intensities of flavor and are used in everything from appetizers to desserts, and even wine! In New Mexico, there's actually a town called Pietown named for a merchant who made delicious homemade pies. Capitan Gap is the home of Smokey the Bear; Albuquerque has an awesome balloon festival every year; Roswell is the site of the International UFO Museum; and the state bird is the roadrunner! No wonder it's called the Land of Enchantment.

Southwestern Tamale Pie

1 pound ground beef
1 small onion, diced
1 (10¾-ounce) can cream of
  chicken soup
1 (10¾-ounce) can golden
  mushroom soup
1 cup evaporated milk
1 (4-ounce) can taco sauce
1½ cups chopped green chiles
1 dozen corn tortillas
1½ cups grated Cheddar or
  Monterey Jack cheese

Brown meat with onion in large skillet; drain excess fat. Add soups, milk, taco sauce, and green chiles. Simmer all ingredients together about 10 minutes. Cut corn tortillas into strips. (Tortillas do not need to be fried.) Layer on bottom of 2-quart casserole dish with meat mixture and cheese; continue alternating layers; top layer should end with cheese. Cover casserole and bake at 350° for one hour. Makes 5–6 servings.

Option: Use one cooked, boned, diced chicken in place of ground beef.

Comida Sabrosa

Green Chile Cream Chicken Enchiladas

CREAM CHEESE FILLING:

1–2 large onions, sliced thin
  or chopped
2 tablespoons butter
2 cups diced cooked chicken
½ cup roasted sweet pepper
  or red bell pepper or pimento

2 (3-ounce) packages cream
  cheese, diced
12 corn tortillas (blue
  preferred)

Sauté onions in large skillet in butter until limp and beginning to brown. Remove from heat and add chicken, red pepper, and cream cheese; mix well. Fry tortillas in small amount of oil in frying pan, or microwave. Spoon ⅓ cup filling in center of tortilla and roll up. Place seam-side down in a shortening-sprayed 9x13-inch baking dish. Fill all tortillas in this way.

GREEN CHILE SAUCE:

2 cloves garlic, minced
½ cup minced onion
¼ cup oil
1 tablespoon flour
1 cup chicken broth or water

1 cup diced green chiles
Salt and pepper to taste
½ cup chopped tomato
  (optional)
2 cups Jack cheese, shredded

Sauté garlic and onion in oil. Blend in flour and add broth and green chiles. Season to taste. Add chopped tomato, if desired. Bring to a boil and simmer 15–20 minutes. Pour Green Chile Sauce over filled tortillas. Sprinkle with shredded Jack cheese. Bake covered for 10 minutes at 375°. Uncover and bake another 10 minutes.

Bon Appétit de Las Sandias

Georgia O'Keeffe, renowned artist, fell in love with New Mexico on her first visit and remained there until her death at the age of 98. The Georgia O'Keeffe Museum in Santa Fe features the largest repository of her work in the world.

Mexican Pecan Candy

¾ cup milk
2 cups sugar
½ teaspoon baking soda

1½ teaspoons vanilla
1½ cups nuts
1 tablespoon butter

Mix milk, sugar, and baking soda in large saucepan. Cook until soft-ball stage. Add vanilla, nuts, and butter. (Will turn golden brown while cooking.) Beat until creamy. Drop to form patties on salted wax paper.

Recipes for Rain or Shine

Green Chile Muffins

These are moist and do not crumble. They go well with all New Mexican meals. Try the different cornmeals for variety.

¾ cup milk
1 (8-ounce) can cream-style
  corn
⅓ cup butter, melted or
  vegetable oil
2 eggs, beaten
1½ cups white, yellow, or
  blue cornmeal
1 teaspoon baking powder

½ teaspoon baking soda
1 teaspoon salt
1 teaspoon sugar
1½ cups mixed shredded
  Cheddar cheese and
  Monterey Jack cheese
1 (4-ounce) can chopped New
  Mexico chiles, drained

Preheat oven to 400°. Line 18 muffin cups with paper liners, or grease and flour each cup. In a medium-size bowl, stir together milk, corn, butter, and eggs. In a large bowl, whisk together cornmeal, baking powder, baking soda, salt, and sugar. Add mixture from medium-size bowl to dry ingredients and mix just until combined. Do not overmix.

Spoon a large spoonful of batter into each prepared muffin cup and top with a little cheese mixture and green chiles, dividing evenly and reserving a little for sprinkling on top. Top with remaining batter and reserved cheese and green chiles. Each cup should be ⅔ full. Bake 25–30 minutes, or until muffins are golden and a wooden pick inserted into the center comes out clean. Makes 18 muffins.

Sassy Southwest Cooking

Green Chile Pinwheels

8 ounces sharp Cheddar
  cheese, grated
8 ounces extra sharp Cheddar
  cheese, grated

2 cups flour
¼ pound butter, softened
3 tablespoons water
Chopped green chile to taste

Combine cheeses (room temperature) and flour, mixing thoroughly so cheese is coated with flour. Add butter and water and work mixture with hands until well blended. Divide cheese mixture into 4 parts and form each into a ball. Roll between 2 sheets of wax paper, like pie crust. Remove top sheet of wax paper and cover entire cheese surface with chile. Lift edge and roll as you would a jellyroll. Twist ends of wax paper and refrigerate for at least 30 minutes before slicing. At this point, they may be frozen for later baking, or stored in refrigerator for up to a week.

When ready to bake, preheat oven to 350°. Slice rolls about ¼ inch thick. Place on ungreased cookie sheet and bake 12–15 minutes or until golden. These freeze well.

Good Sam Celebrates 15 Years of Love

Northern New Mexico is among the richest places in the world when it comes to culture and tradition. The original Indian civilization was blended with the Spanish, and this distinctive civilization was, in turn, influenced by the impact of the Anglos in the 19th century. This cultural heritage of modern New Mexico is unique among the 50 states and is evident in their cuisine.

Mexican Cream with Strawberries

A delicious cooling dessert, not too sweet, after a hot spicy meal. It is the ideal choice for company, when you want something pretty and easy to prepare ahead.

1 tablespoon plain gelatin	2 cups sour cream
2 cups cream	1 teaspoon vanilla
½ cup sugar	Strawberries

Put gelatin, cream, and sugar in a saucepan. Cook over medium-low heat, stirring until gelatin and sugar are dissolved—don't let it boil. Place in a bowl, cover, and refrigerate an hour, or until thickened to the consistency of egg whites. Stir in sour cream and vanilla. Lightly oil a 1½-quart ring mold, add the cream mixture, cover, and chill until firm—about 6 hours.

To serve, run a knife around the mold, dip outside of mold in hot water a few seconds, and invert on a serving plate. Garnish with plenty of fresh strawberries in the center, and around the cream. Serves 8–10.

The Aficionado's Southwestern Cooking

Tequila-Lime-Grilled Chicken

⅔ cup olive oil	¼ cup minced fresh cilantro
½ cup fresh lime juice	6 skinned and boned chicken
1 jalapeño, seeded and minced	breast halves
¼ cup tequila	Salsa
2 tablespoons Triple Sec	

Combine first 6 ingredients; pour into a shallow pan. Add chicken, and turn to coat. Cover and chill chicken 4 hours, turning several times.

Prepare grill, or preheat broiler. Remove chicken from refrigerator 30 minutes before cooking, discarding marinade. Cook chicken 4 minutes per side on grill, or 4 inches from broiler. Serve with desired salsa. Makes 6 servings.

Savoring the Southwest Again

New Mexico Peanut Pie

½ cup sugar
¼ cup firmly packed brown
   sugar
¼ cup flour
2 tablespoons cornstarch
¼ teaspoon salt
3 cups milk
½ cup peanut butter chips

4 egg yolks
3 tablespoons butter or
   margarine
1½ teaspoons vanilla
1 (9-inch) pie shell, baked
1 (7¼-ounce) bag chocolate
   covered peanuts, chopped

Combine sugar, brown sugar, flour, cornstarch, and salt in saucepan. Add milk and peanut butter chips gradually. Cook and stir on medium heat until thick and bubbly. Reduce heat; cook and stir 2 minutes. Beat egg yolks lightly in small bowl. Gradually stir one cup hot mixture into yolks and return egg mixture to saucepan. Bring to gentle boil. Cook and stir on low heat 2 minutes. Remove from heat and stir in butter and vanilla. Pour mixture into baked pie shell and sprinkle with peanuts. Bake at 350° for 12 minutes. Cool to room temperature before serving.

Peanut Palate Pleasers from Portales

FROM GWEN'S ROAD DIARY:
Barbara and I have always made a good team because we are a lot alike, with differences that compliment each other. We both have two boys and a girl—in that order—numerous grandchildren, and have been married to the same husbands for more than 44 years. Having met on the golf course, we always talked about food during play, so it was a natural thing for us to get into a cookbook business together. We agreed from the start that if work ever interfered with our friendship, we would no longer work together. People think we are sisters, and though not biologically, we most definitely are.

New York

CAPITAL: *Albany*

NICKNAME: *The Empire State*

*S*tart spreading the news . . . New York is fabulous! The song is right; it is so much fun to be a part of it! Immigrants from all over the world have come here and many of them still call New York home, bringing with them the food traditions (and some apple seeds) from their native countries. In stark contrast to the skyscrapers of the Big Apple are the tranquil mountains, lakes, and streams of upstate New York. Adirondack Park is the largest state park in the United States—six million acres, which is about the size of Vermont! Central Park in Manhattan is another beautiful example of their reverence for their land. Though New York City usually takes the limelight (did you know it was the first capital of the United States in 1789?), the entire state is steeped in history. Hudson Valley is one of the country's principal producers of sweet corn. Rochester is known as both the Flour City and the Flower City. New York says, "Let us entertain you," and it does.

Cappuccino Parfaits

4 tablespoons instant coffee
1 tablespoon hot water
1½ cups cold milk (2% or skim)
1 (3-ounce) package vanilla
  or chocolate instant pudding
½ teaspoon cinnamon
1 cup Cool Whip, thawed
3 chocolate wafer cookies,
  crushed

Dissolve coffee in hot water in medium bowl. Add milk, pudding mix, and cinnamon. Beat with wire whisk for 1–2 minutes. Let stand 5 minutes or until thickened. Gently stir in whipped topping. Spoon ½ of pudding mixture in 5 dessert dishes. Sprinkle with crushed cookies. Garnish with whipped cream, if desired. Refrigerate until ready to serve.

Sharing Our Best

Blair's Bay Baked Brie

2 tablespoons unsalted butter
1 small onion, chopped (about
  ¾ cup)
½ tablespoon minced garlic
8 ounces Brie cheese
1 (8-ounce) package cream
  cheese, cut into pieces
½ cup sour cream
2 teaspoons lemon juice
2 teaspoons brown sugar
½ teaspoon Worcestershire
Salt and pepper
1 round sourdough loaf (about
  18 ounces)
Paprika for garnish
1 or 2 Granny Smith apples,
  cored and cut into ⅛-inch
  slices

Melt butter in medium skillet over medium to low heat. Add onion and sauté about 5 minutes. Add garlic and sauté until onions are golden brown (about 5 more minutes). Set aside.

Trim rind off Brie and cut into chunks. Place Brie and cream cheese in a large bowl and microwave on medium until just melted (about 2–3 minutes). Whisk onion mixture, sour cream, lemon juice, brown sugar, and Worcestershire into melted cheese mixture. Season to taste with salt and pepper.

Cut off top of sourdough bread loaf (save pieces) and scoop out interior of loaf, leaving about a ¾ inch shell. Spoon cheese mixture into loaf, replace bread lid, and wrap in aluminum foil. Bake in preheated 400° oven for 1½ hours or until cheese mixture bubbles. Unwrap and place on platter; remove bread lid. Sprinkle with paprika. Serve with apple slices and leftover sourdough bread pieces that have been cut up. Serves 8–10.

Simply...The Best

Iced Coffee

4 tablespoons instant coffee
¾ cup sugar
1 cup water
2 quarts milk
½ gallon vanilla or vanilla/
  chocolate ice cream
2 scoops vanilla sugar

In a pot, heat coffee, sugar, and water until boiling. Add milk. Add ice cream and vanilla sugar and combine with hand blender.

Optional: Ice chips may be used to keep coffee cold for longer periods of time.

Note: To make vanilla sugar, bury two vanilla beans in one pound of granulated (2¼ cups) or confectioners' (3½ cups) sugar. Store in airtight container for about a week.

Culinary Creations

Bavarian Apple Cheesecake

1⅓ cups sugar, divided
⅓ cup butter or margarine
1 tablespoon shortening
¾ teaspoon vanilla, divided
1 cup flour
⅛ teaspoon salt
4 cups peeled, cored, and sliced
  cooking apples (Golden
  Delicious or Granny Smith)

2 (8-ounce) packages cream
  cheese, softened
2 eggs
1 teaspoon ground cinnamon
¼ cup sliced almonds

In a medium mixer bowl, beat ½ cup sugar, butter or margarine, shortening, and ¼ teaspoon vanilla on medium speed with an electric mixer until combined. Blend in flour and salt until crumbly. Pat on the bottom of a 9-inch springform pan. Set aside.

Place apple slices in a single layer in a shallow baking pan. Cover with foil. Bake in a 400° oven for 15 minutes. Meanwhile, for filling, in a large mixer bowl, beat cream cheese, ½ cup sugar, and ½ teaspoon vanilla with an electric mixer until fluffy. Add eggs all at once, beating on low speed just until combined. Pour into dough-lined pan. Arrange warm apple slices atop filling. Combine remaining ⅓ cup sugar and cinnamon.

Sprinkle filling with sugar mixture and the almonds. Bake in a 400° oven for 40 minutes or until golden. Cool. Chill 4–24 hours before serving. Serves 12.

Hudson Valley German-American Society Cookbook

Buffalo Chicken Wings

20–25 chicken wings
Vegetable oil for deep-frying
¼ cup butter or margarine,
  melted

½ small bottle hot sauce
Bleu Cheese Dressing
Celery sticks

Disjoint chicken wings and discard tips. Rinse and pat dry. The wings must be completely dry to fry properly since there is no batter or breading. Preheat oil in a deep fryer or a large deep pan to 365°. Add chicken wings a few at a time to hot oil. Do not allow oil to cool as chicken is added. Deep fry for 6–10 minutes or until crisp and golden brown. Drain well by shaking in the fryer basket or a strainer. Blend butter with hot sauce for medium-hot wings. Add additional hot sauce for hotter wings, or additional butter for milder wings. Combine the wings and hot sauce in a large container. Let stand, covered. Serve with Bleu Cheese Dressing and celery sticks. Makes 20–25 chicken wings.

BLEU CHEESE DRESSING:
2 cups mayonnaise
3 tablespoons cider vinegar
½ teaspoon dry mustard
½ teaspoon white pepper

¼ teaspoon salt
8 ounces bleu cheese, crumbled
¼–½ cup cold water

Combine mayonnaise, vinegar, dry mustard, pepper, and salt in a large bowl and beat until well blended. Mix in bleu cheese. Gradually add enough cold water to make desired consistency, whisking constantly. Store in an airtight container in refrigerator. Makes 3½ cups.

Great Lake Effects

The Statue of Liberty was presented to America by the people of France on July 4, 1884, as an expression of friendship and the ideal of liberty shared by both peoples. It was shipped to America in 350 pieces, assembled, and officially accepted on October 28, 1886, by President Grover Cleveland. There are fascinating facts about Miss Liberty; she is 111 feet tall from heel to top of head, has a 4½-foot nose, a 42-foot right arm, and a 35-foot waist . . . and she weighs 450,000 pounds. There are 25 windows in her crown. The inscription on her tablet, in Roman numerals, reads "July 4, 1776." She remains a symbol of freedom.

Westside Bruschetta

1 baguette with sesame seeds
4–6 tablespoons extra virgin olive oil
1 tablespoon minced garlic
1 tablespoon Romano cheese
¼ teaspoon ground black pepper
1 red bell pepper, cut into ¼-inch pieces
1 yellow bell pepper, cut into ¼-inch pieces
2 plum tomatoes, cut into ¼-inch slices

3 green onions, cut into ¼-inch slices
½ cup shredded mozzarella, Asiago, or Gorgonzola cheese
4 ounces mushrooms, cut into ⅛-inch slices
4 ounces prosciutto or smoked ham, cut into ½-inch strips
Freshly grated pecorino Romano cheese

Slice baguette lengthwise into halves. Place cut-side-up on a baking sheet. Combine olive oil, garlic, 1 tablespoon Romano cheese, and pepper in a bowl and mix well. Spread over cut sides of bread halves. Arrange bell peppers, tomatoes, and green onions on each bread half. Sprinkle with mozzarella cheese. Top with mushrooms and prosciutto. Bake at 350° for 5–10 minutes or until cheese melts. Broil for 2–3 minutes or just until cheese begins to brown. Cut into 2-inch slices. Sprinkle with freshly grated Romano cheese. Serves 4–6.

Great Lake Effects

Central Park is 843 acres of winding paths through magnificent trees, tranquil lakes, historic statues, and welcoming benches. It provides a needed place for play and serenity . . . a soothing relief from the hustle and bustle of Manhattan.

Baked Shrimp Scampi

Everybody's favorite! This makes a great appetizer. It is so fast and easy.

1 pound shrimp, peeled and deveined
½ cup butter
3 cloves garlic, minced
2 tablespoons finely chopped fresh parsley
1 tablespoon lemon juice

½ teaspoon crushed red pepper flakes
1 teaspoon Worcestershire
½ teaspoon oregano
¼ teaspoon seasoned salt
½ cup bread or cracker crumbs

Arrange shrimp in a single layer in a shallow baking dish. In a small saucepan, combine all remaining ingredients except bread or cracker crumbs. Heat until butter has melted, stirring to mix seasonings. Pour evenly over shrimp, reserving 2 tablespoons.

Add reserved seasoned butter to bread or cracker crumbs; mix well. Sprinkle crumbs over shrimp. Bake at 450° for 8–10 minutes, or until browned. Serves 2–4.

Family & Company

Hazelnut Chocolate Chip Cookies

2 sticks unsalted butter, softened
¾ cup sugar
¾ cup brown sugar
1 tablespoon hazelnut liqueur
1 tablespoon coffee liqueur
2 eggs

2½ cups flour
1 teaspoon baking soda
½ teaspoon salt
4 cups milk chocolate chips
1 cup chopped walnuts
1 cup chopped pecans

In a large bowl, beat butter, sugars, and liqueurs until light and fluffy. Add eggs. Beat well. Mix flour, baking soda, and salt in a small bowl. Stir flour mixture into butter mixture. Mix in chocolate chips and nuts. Drop batter by rounded teaspoonfuls onto greased baking sheet, 1 inch apart. Bake at 325° for 16 minutes or until golden brown.

Beyond Chicken Soup

North Carolina

CAPITAL: *Raleigh*

NICKNAME: *The Tar Heel State*

 From the majestic peaks of the Smokey Mountains to the shorelines of Cape Hatteras, North Carolina is truly a beautiful state. There is a rich food heritage there, and a love to celebrate with food—clambakes, oyster roasts, pit-cooked barbecues, and hunt breakfasts. Funny how nicknames originate . . . Tar Heels is a nickname for North Carolinians that supposedly came from the days when they produced a lot of tar, and someone saw a set of footprints where someone had stepped. Babe Ruth hit his first professional home run in Fayetteville on March 7, 1914. America's largest home, Biltmore Estate in Asheville, includes a 250-room chateau, a world-class winery, and extensive gardens. And not far from there is Mount Mitchell, the highest peak (6,684 feet) east of the Mississippi. North Carolina leads the nation in furniture, tobacco, brick, and textile production, and is the largest producer of sweet potatoes in the nation.

Tryon Palace Ginger Crinkle Cookies

This recipe was provided in answer to many requests.

⅔ cup vegetable oil	2 teaspoons baking soda
1¼ cups sugar, divided	½ teaspoon salt
1 egg	1 teaspoon cinnamon
4 tablespoons molasses	1 teaspoon ginger
2 cups sifted flour	

Preheat oven to 350°. Mix oil and 1 cup sugar thoroughly. Add egg and beat well. Stir in molasses. Sift dry ingredients together and add to creamed mixture. Drop by teaspoonfuls into remaining sugar and form into balls coated with sugar. Place on ungreased cookie sheet 3 inches apart. Bake for 15 minutes. Cookies will flatten and crinkle. Remove to wire rack. Yields 5 dozen.

Pass the Plate

Tar Heel Crocks

½ pound sharp New York
   cheese (black rind)
2 hard-cooked eggs, mashed
¾ cup mayonnaise
1 teaspoon Worcestershire
8 stuffed green olives, chopped

½ teaspoon salt
¼ teaspoon paprika
1 teaspoon minced fresh
   parsley
¾ teaspoon grated onion

Allow cheese to soften (may want to grate cheese first). Combine all ingredients and blend together by hand. (Or use a food processor to purée the chopped ingredients.) Put in a crock and chill until ready to serve. Serve with crackers, Melba toast, or black bread rounds. Yields 1 large or 2 small cheese crocks.

Even More Special

Snow Cream

In the 1920s, teachers let kids make snow cream at school when it snowed. It all came under the heading of putting-first-things-first because it didn't snow that often and lessons could wait.

1 egg
½ cup sugar
1 cup milk

1 teaspoon vanilla
1 quart fluffy snow

Beat egg until fluffy; add sugar, milk, and vanilla. Keep cold while you run outside and get snow. Stir snow gently into milk mixture.

Korner's Folly Cookbook

North Carolina Chicken

8 ounces (2 sticks) butter or
  margarine
2 envelopes Italian Salad
  Dressing Mix

½ cup lime juice
1 teaspoon salt
5 pounds chicken pieces

Melt butter in saucepan. Stir in salad dressing mix, lime juice, and salt. Marinate chicken 3–4 hours or overnight. Bake at 350° for one hour or until done. Or cook on outdoor grill for one hour, turning and basting every 10–15 minutes. Serves 6.

Ship to Shore I

Best Baked Ham Ever

1 (10- to 15-pound) semi-
  boneless, fully cooked ham
2 cups sugar
1 cup cider vinegar
1 stick cinnamon
12 whole cloves

6 allspice berries
Additional cloves to stud ham
White pepper to taste
1½ cups brown sugar
1 cup sherry

Preheat oven to 350°. Wash ham and place in large roasting pan with lid. Add sugar, vinegar, cinnamon stick, cloves, and allspice berries. Half fill pan with water, cover, and place in oven. Cook 15 minutes per pound, turning ham often. Remove from oven and cool.

Lower oven temperature to 250°. Remove top skin, but leave fat on ham. Place ham in washed and dried roasting pan and stud at intervals with cloves. Sprinkle liberally with white pepper and spread brown sugar all over. Pour sherry into pan and bake, uncovered, for one hour. After 30 minutes of cooking time, baste every 10 minutes with pan juices. Remove from oven and keep covered and warm until serving time. Makes 20 servings.

MUSTARD SAUCE:
2 teaspoons dry mustard
¼ teaspoon salt
1 teaspoon sugar
2 tablespoons flour

¾ cup water
2 tablespoons vinegar, warmed
2 egg yolks, beaten
2 tablespoons butter, melted

Combine mustard, salt, sugar, and flour. Place in top of double boiler. Add water and vinegar, stirring until smooth and creamy. Add egg yolks and butter, stirring until thickened. Do not boil or eggs will curdle. Can be prepared one day ahead and reheated to serve.

Stirring Performances

Sweet Potato Cups

4–6 medium-size sweet potatoes
1 stick butter
1 (14-ounce) can crushed
  pineapple
3 eggs, beaten
½ cup dark rum
½ cup chopped walnuts
1 cup miniature marshmallows
Orange shells

Boil unpeeled potatoes until soft; drain, peel, and mash. To hot potatoes, add butter, undrained pineapple, eggs, rum, nuts, and marshmallows. Blend well. Mound into 6–8 orange shells. This can be done ahead of time. Heat in a 325° oven for 30 minutes or until heated through. Makes 6–8 servings.

Korner's Folly Cookbook

Green Beans and Zucchini Bundles

1½ pounds fresh green beans,
  stringed
2 zucchini squash, 2 inches
  in diameter
½ cup vegetable oil
¼ cup white wine vinegar
2 tablespoons Dijon mustard
2 tablespoons honey
2 cloves garlic, minced
2 teaspoons fresh basil

Cook beans in salted water until crisp-tender, about 7 minutes. Cool beans in ice water and drain. Set aside. Cut zucchini into 8 (1½-inch) slices. Carve out the centers so that you have rings with ¼-inch rims.

Steam zucchini rings for 2–3 minutes until crisp-tender. Immerse rings in ice water and drain well. Poke 8–12 beans through each zucchini ring. Arrange bundles in a 9x13-inch casserole dish.

Combine remaining ingredients in a blender and pour over the beans. Cover and refrigerate for 24 hours. Makes 8 servings.

Stirring Performances

The Blue Ridge Parkway was designed solely for vacation travel and no commercial vehicles are allowed. It skims the crest of the mountains between the North Carolina-Virginia line and the entrance to the Great Smoky Mountains National Park near Cherokee. With numerous scenic overlooks, trails, campgrounds, picnic areas, and recreation areas, it is considered America's most popular scenic parkway.

Banana Pudding

North Carolina natives think of banana pudding as a dessert served everywhere. It was not until I received a request for the recipe from New York City that I began to realize, it is distinctive to this section.

½ cup plus 6 tablespoons
  sugar, divided
Pinch of salt
3 tablespoons flour

4 eggs, divided
2 cups milk
Vanilla wafers
Bananas

Blend ½ cup sugar, salt, and flour. Add 1 whole egg and 3 yolks (reserve whites) and mix together. Stir in milk. Cook over boiling water, stirring, until thickened. Remove from heat and cool.

In a baking dish, arrange a layer of whole vanilla wafers, a layer of sliced bananas, and a layer of custard. Continue, making 3 layers of each.

Make a meringue of remaining egg whites and 6 tablespoons sugar. Spread over banana mixture and brown in 375° oven. Makes 8 servings. Serve cold.

North Carolina and Old Salem Cookery

Fresh Broccoli Salad

1 bunch fresh broccoli, chopped
½ cup raisins
½ cup Spanish peanuts
2 stalks celery, chopped
1 carrot, grated
1 tablespoon Parmesan cheese

½ jar real bacon bits
1 cup mayonnaise-type salad
  dressing
2 tablespoons sugar
1 tablespoon vinegar

Combine broccoli, raisins, peanuts, celery, carrot, Parmesan cheese, and bacon bits in bowl; toss to mix. Combine salad dressing, sugar, and vinegar in small bowl; mix until sugar dissolves. Pour over broccoli mixture. Marinate for 12 hours or longer before serving. Yields 6 servings.

Goodness Grows in North Carolina

North Dakota

CAPITAL: *Bismarck*

NICKNAME: *The Peace Garden State*

*I*f you threw a dart at a map of North America, landing in North Dakota would hit the bull's-eye! The geographical center of the continent is actually in Rugby, North Dakota. Widely considered a top birding destination, the Sioux State has more national wildlife refuges than any other state, as well as dozens of state wildlife management areas, several state forests, and two national grasslands. With all that land area, the state naturally produces an abundance of beef and dairy cattle, hogs, sheep, potatoes, sugar beets, corn, and so much grain that they lead the nation in the production of durum and other spring wheat. Fishing and hunting are big in the state, too, with abundant game birds such as duck, grouse, pheasant, and goose. It's a haven for golfers, as they have one of the highest number of golf courses per capita in the nation. And guess what the state beverage is . . . milk!

Hot Potato Skins

Bake potatoes until tender. Cool, and cut in quarters lengthwise, then in half crosswise, to form 8 sections. Scoop out potato pulp (save for another use), leaving about ¼ inch. Brush skins on both sides with melted butter and a little soy sauce. Bake at 500° until crisp, about 10–12 minutes. Serve with assorted dips, or add shredded cheese and crumbled, cooked bacon, then heat until cheese melts.

Red River Valley Potato Growers Auxiliary Cookbook

The International Peace Garden straddles the international boundary between North Dakota and the Canadian province of Manitoba. Reflecting pools, terraced walkways, and dazzling flowers adorn the 2,339-acre botanical garden. In addition to the Peace Towers, Peace Chapel, and 911 Memorial, there are several buildings that accommodate conventions and receptions. On seven Peace Polls, "May Peace Prevail" is inscribed in twenty-eight different languages.

Potato Pepperoni Hot Dish

This hot dish brings many compliments.

1½–2 pounds hamburger
1 small onion, diced
1 (10¾-ounce) can Cheddar
  cheese soup
1 (10¾-ounce) can tomato soup
1 cup milk
½ teaspoon oregano

¼ teaspoon pepper
1 teaspoon sugar
6–8 potatoes, peeled, sliced
1 package pepperoni slices
½ cup Parmesan cheese
1 cup shredded mozzarella
  cheese

Brown hamburger and onion. Mix the soups, milk, and seasonings.
Mix together the hamburger, potatoes, and soup mixture. Place in a
9x13-inch pan. Bake at 350° for one hour, or until potatoes are tender. Top with pepperoni slices. Bake for 5 minutes. Top with
Parmesan and mozzarella cheese. Bake until cheese melts.

North Dakota...Where Food is Love

Almond Bark Oatmeal Bars

CRUST:
1 cup butter
2 cups brown sugar
2 eggs
1 teaspoon vanilla

2½ cups flour
1 teaspoon baking soda
1 teaspoon salt
3 cups oatmeal

FILLING:
1 (14-ounce) package light
  almond bark, melted
1 (14-ounce) can sweetened
  condensed milk

3 tablespoons butter, softened
¾ cup chopped nuts
2 teaspoons vanilla

Cream butter and sugar; add rest of Crust ingredients and mix well.
Press two-thirds of the mixture into bottom of a 10x15-inch pan. Mix
and spread Filling over Crust and sprinkle with rest of Crust mixture. Bake in 350° oven for 25 minutes.

Norman Lutheran Church 125th Anniversary Cookbook

Wild Rice Salad

3 cups diced, cooked chicken
  breasts
4 cups cooked wild rice (or
  ½ white and ½ wild rice)
2 cups green grapes, cut
1 cup chopped cashews

1 cup sliced water chestnuts
2 cups mayonnaise
1 teaspoon soy sauce
¼ teaspoon curry powder
½ teaspoon Lawry's Seasoned
  Salt

Mix first 5 ingredients. Add mayonnaise, soy sauce, and seasonings. Toss and chill.

North Dakota...Where Food is Love

Hash Brown Quiche

3 cups frozen hash browns,
  thawed and pressed between
  paper towels
⅓ cup margarine, melted
4 ounces hot pepper cheese

4 ounces Swiss cheese
6 ounces ham
Salt to taste
2 eggs
½ cup cream

Put well-dried hash browns in 9-inch pie plate, pressing some up sides. Drizzle with melted margarine. Bake 10 minutes at 400°.

    Process balance of ingredients in food processor. Pour over hash brown crust. Bake 35–45 minutes at 350° or until knife comes out clean. Let stand 10 minutes before serving. Can be served hot, cold, or at room temperature for lunch, brunch, or as an appetizer.

If It Tastes Good, Who Cares? II

Roasted Potatoes

A must-try recipe! You can use this recipe as the base for many of your own creative variations.

4 pounds potatoes	2 teaspoons dried oregano
8 cloves garlic	Ground black pepper to taste
4 tablespoons chopped fresh parsley	8–12 tablespoons light olive or vegetable oil
2 teaspoons dried basil	Salt to taste

Preheat oven to 350°. Peel potatoes (or leave skins, if you wish), and cut each potato in 2-inch chunks. Mince garlic. In large bowl, combine all ingredients except salt, and toss so potatoes are covered with oil. Spread potatoes in single layer in 9x13-inch (or larger) pan. Bake uncovered for one hour, turning once, or until golden brown and cooked through. Season potatoes with salt before serving. Serves 4–6.

Hall's Potato Harvest Cookbook

FROM GWEN'S ROAD DIARY:
Driving through North Dakota in the early fall was a moving experience for us, especially since we were listening to a patriotic CD. "Oh beautiful, for spacious skies, for amber waves of grain . . ." We watched farm machinery, like tiny dots moving through the fields, cut darker ribbons into the golden wheat. Against a bright blue sky, it was like a painting! Then there were miles and miles of huge sunflowers. Near Fargo, a sudden rain shower left an unbelievable rainbow that stretched its brilliance across the sky. When we turned, it doubled, and we could see its "ends" rippling over cars, signs, fence posts as if it were following us! It was a phenonenon we will never forget. "America . . . God shed His grace on thee."

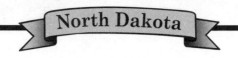
Chicken and Stuffing Casserole

4 cups stuffing mix
1 cup butter, melted
4 cups chopped cooked chicken
2 (10¾-ounce) cans cream of
  chicken soup
1 (13-ounce) can evaporated milk
1 (10-ounce) package frozen
  peas, thawed
¼ cup minced onion
1 (2-ounce) jar chopped
  pimento, drained

Combine stuffing mix with melted butter in bowl; mix well. Press half the mixture into a 9x13-inch baking dish. Combine chicken, soup, evaporated milk, peas, onion, and pimento in bowl; mix well. Spread in prepared dish; top with remaining stuffing mix. Bake at 350° for one hour. Yields 8 servings.

Y Cook?

Toffee Delight Muffins

BATTER:
2 cups flour
1 cup sugar
1 cup water
4 eggs
1 (3-ounce) package instant
  vanilla pudding
1 (3-ounce) package instant
  butterscotch pudding
2 teaspoons baking powder
1 teaspoon salt
¾ cup vegetable oil
1 teaspoon vanilla

TOPPING:
1 cup firmly packed brown
  sugar
¾ cup chopped pecans
1 teaspoon cinnamon

Mix together Batter ingredients. Beat 2 minutes. Using ½ the Batter, pour and fill greased muffin cups ⅓ full. Mix together Topping. Sprinkle ½ of Topping on muffins. Add remaining Batter to fill each muffin cup ⅔ full, then sprinkle rest of Topping. Bake 15–20 minutes at 350°.

Heavenly Recipes

In North Dakota, there is a stretch of the Great Plains known as the Missouri Plateau. Its topography is starkly varied. Many flat-topped buttes stand as high as 600 feet above the plains, and in the southwest, there is a strip of Badlands, which are spectacular formations produced by the erosion of soft sedimentary rocks.

Ohio

CAPITAL: *Columbus*

NICKNAME: *The Buckeye State*

*O*hio is a melting pot. Primarily settled by New Englanders, the Buckeye State soon became a destination for Hungarians, Polish, Czechs, Germans, Swiss, and Italians who were drawn to the state's large industrial cities. And, of course, with them came their old country recipes using sauerkraut, pork, tomatoes, potatoes, breads, fish, wine, beer . . . everything from fancy to homemade fare. And they are proud of their recipes. Ohio has one of the largest state fairs in the United States. It also has the largest Amish population in the world. Thomas Edison and Jack Nicklaus were born there, as were seven U.S. presidents: Ulysses S. Grant, Rutherford B. Hayes, James A. Garfield, Benjamin Harrison, William McKinley, William H. Taft, and Warren G. Harding. Ohioans seem to reach for the sky. Astronauts John Glenn and Neil Armstrong are from Ohio, and so was Orville Wright. And here's a real American footnote; Ohio claims to have given America its first hot dog in 1900.

Sauerkraut Balls

1 pound sausage
½ cup chopped onion
1 (8-ounce) package cream
  cheese, softened
4 tablespoons bread crumbs
4 tablespoons parsley
2 tablespoons garlic salt

2 teaspoons mustard
¼ teaspoon pepper
1 quart sauerkraut, drained
  and chopped
Flour
3 eggs, beaten
Bread crumbs

Fry sausage and onion; let drain. Cool. Add cooled sausage and onion to next 7 ingredients. Mix well. Make balls. Roll in flour, then in beaten eggs, then in bread crumbs. French-fry until brown.

Recipes & Remembrances

Fabulous Cream Cheese Squares

Simply elegant.

CRUST:

1 (8½-ounce) package chocolate
  wafer cookies (Nabisco only)
8 tablespoons unsalted butter,
  melted

1 tablespoon confectioners'
  sugar

Put cookies in food processor and pulse 6 times until cookies are crushed. Put in a bowl. Add melted butter and confectioners' sugar and mix well. Put in a 9x13-inch casserole dish and press firmly until pan is covered to form crust. Bake at 350° for 10–15 minutes until firm. Cool.

CHEESE FILLING:

3 (8-ounce) packages cream
  cheese, softened
2 eggs

1 teaspoon vanilla
2 teaspoons fresh lemon juice
¾ cup sugar

Cream until smooth the cream cheese, eggs, vanilla, lemon juice, and sugar. Pour into Crust; bake at 325° for 30 minutes. Remove from oven and cool one hour.

TOPPING:

1 pint sour cream (2 cups)
1 teaspoon fresh lemon juice

1 cup sugar

Combine all ingredients in a medium-size bowl and mix well. Pour on cheesecake. Bake at 350° for 15 minutes. Cool and refrigerate until serving time. Top square with cherries, fresh strawberries, or crushed red raspberries with a little sugar to sweeten.

Angels and Friends Cookbook II

Ohio Chicken Pot Pie

Chicken pot pies in the Midwest tend to be meaty, with just a few vegetables for color, and served with a gravy on top. They are substantial, heartwarming dishes, so it's no wonder they're making a comeback.

3 pounds chicken pieces, white
  or dark meat
1 large carrot, quartered
1 bay leaf
½ cup (1 stick) butter, divided
¼ cup chopped celery
¼ cup chopped onion
7 tablespoons all-purpose flour,
  divided

1 teaspoon poultry seasoning
2 cups milk, divided
½ teaspoon salt or to taste,
  divided
½ teaspoon freshly ground
  pepper or to taste, divided
¼ cup chopped parsley
Pastry for 2-crust pie
1 tablespoon fresh lemon juice

In a deep kettle, cover chicken with water (or chicken broth). Add carrot and bay leaf, bring to a boil, then reduce heat and simmer until very tender, about 30 minutes. When chicken is cool enough to handle, discard skin and bones and bay leaf, and cut meat into bite-size pieces—you should have 3½–4 cups of chicken. Chop 2 cooked carrot pieces very finely and combine with chicken in a greased 9x13-inch flat pan. Cover with plastic wrap and refrigerate. Chill broth until fat rises and can be discarded.

Preheat oven to 375°. In a large saucepan, melt ¼ cup butter over medium heat; add celery and onion and cook until tender, but not brown, about 4–5 minutes. Stir in 3 tablespoons flour and poultry seasoning and cook and stir until mixture bubbles up in middle of pan. Add 1 cup milk and 1 cup broth and whisk and cook over medium heat until mixture thickens; season with ¼ teaspoon salt, ¼ teaspoon pepper, and parsley.

Pour sauce over chicken and set aside. Roll out pastry to fit top of dish, crimping edges to the top of the dish; slash top so steam can escape. Bake for 45 minutes, or until top is golden brown and bubbling up in center.

While pot pie bakes, make gravy. In a medium saucepan, melt remaining ¼ cup butter and add remaining 4 tablespoons flour and ¼ teaspoon each of salt and pepper. Cook and stir until mixture bubbles, about 2 minutes; do not allow it to brown. Whisk in 1 cup broth, the remaining 1 cup milk, and lemon juice; cook and whisk gravy over medium heat until thickened, about 3 minutes. Serve with baked pot pie. Makes 10–12 servings.

Heartland

Crunch-Top Potatoes

⅓ cup margarine
3 or 4 large baking potatoes,
   peeled and sliced
¾ cup crushed cornflakes

1½ cups shredded sharp
   cheese
1½ teaspoons paprika
Salt (optional)

Melt margarine in 8x8-inch pan at 375°. Add single layer of potatoes; turn in the margarine. Mix remaining ingredients; sprinkle over. Bake ½ hour until done.

Tumm Yummies

Baked Sweet Sauerkraut with Tomatoes and Bacon

The Ohio Sauerkraut Festival is held in Waynesville, population 2,000, the second week of October and attracts thousands of people. Remember, this was settled by Germans; they flock to sample the food and buy crafts at the festival's five hundred booths. It is sort of like a krauty Mardi Gras. This old, old recipe is a real treasure. The few ingredients—all listed in the title—would have been in any Ohio kitchen at the turn of the century. The dish is baked quite a long time, until the top caramelizes, the liquid cooks away, and the kraut is nearly transparent.

1 (14-ounce) can tomatoes,
   coarsely chopped, undrained
1 (16-ounce) can sauerkraut,
   undrained
1 cup sugar

6 slices raw bacon, cut in
   ½-inch pieces
½ teaspoon freshly ground
   pepper

Preheat oven to 325°. Grease a flat, 2-quart glass baking dish (see Note). Place all the ingredients in the dish and combine thoroughly. (You may have to use your hands to distribute bacon evenly.) Bake uncovered for 2 hours and 15 minutes, or until the top begins to brown deeply and most of the liquid has cooked away.

Note: It is important to use a flat dish so the liquid evaporates as it cooks.

Heartland

 Ohio has the largest Amish population in the world; about 35,000 "plain people" live in the state. It is ironic that in their desire for a separate life, they make such an appealing picture that the rest of us can scarcely leave them alone.

Pork Roast with Mustard Sauce and Honey Apples

1 tablespoon rubbed sage
¼ teaspoon dried marjoram
2 tablespoons soy sauce
2 cloves garlic, minced

½ cup Dijon mustard
5 pounds rolled boneless pork
  loin roast

Combine first 5 ingredients in small bowl; mix well. Place roast, fat-side-up, in shallow roasting pan. Spread with mustard mixture. Insert thermometer, making sure it does not touch fat. Bake uncovered at 325° for 2–2½ hours or until thermometer registers 160°. Serve roast with Honey Apples.

HONEY APPLES:
4 Granny Smith apples
½ cup honey
¼ teaspoon salt

¼ teaspoon ground cinnamon
2 tablespoons vinegar

Peel, core, and slice apples into ½-inch thick slices; set aside. Combine remaining ingredients in large saucepan; bring to a boil. Add apples; reduce heat and simmer 10 minutes. Serves 10–12.

MDA Favorite Recipes

Seven-Layer Cookies

1 stick butter or margarine
1 cup graham cracker crumbs
1 cup chopped pecans
1 cup flaked coconut
1 (6-ounce) package
  butterscotch chips

1 (6-ounce) package chocolate
  chips
1 (14-ounce) can sweetened
  condensed milk

Melt butter in a 9x13-inch pan. Layer crumbs, nuts, coconut, butterscotch, and chocolate chips. Pour milk evenly over all. Bake at 300° until melted and light brown around edges (about 30 minutes). Cool and cut into squares.

Tumm Yummies

Oklahoma

CAPITAL: *Oklahoma City*

NICKNAME: *The Sooner State*

On April 22, 1889, the first day homesteading was permitted, 50,000 people swarmed into the Oklahoma area. Those who tried to beat the noon starting gun were called Sooners. Once known as Indian Territory, Oklahoma is home to 67 American Indian tribes. And being that Oklahoma is cow country, Sooners know how to cook up juicy beef dinners for barbecues and pot lucks, and chuck-wagon meals that can satisfy a crowd of hungry folks. In the old days, Route 66 went through Oklahoma, where travelers found neon-lit diners, drive-in theaters, mom-and-pop gas stations, and rustic trading posts along the route—maybe you still can if you can find remnants of the highway. The first Boy Scout Troop in the United States was founded here in 1909; the first passenger plane was built here; and Oklahoma had the first flowing commercial oil well in the world. The song says it all: "You're doin' fine, Oklahoma . . . Oklahoma, O.K." And we learned firsthand, the wind most certainly does sweep down the plain.

Prairie Schooners

4 large potatoes, baked
1 (15-ounce) can ranch-style
  beans
1 cup sour cream
1 stick butter, room
  temperature
Salt and pepper to taste
1 cup grated mild Cheddar
  cheese
1 onion, chopped
1 green pepper, chopped

Slice off top ⅓ of baked potato lengthwise. Scoop out potato with a teaspoon, leaving ¼ inch around potato skin. Mash scooped-out potato until free of lumps. Drain beans thoroughly, reserving sauce. Mash beans. Whip sour cream, butter, mashed beans, salt and pepper. Add to mashed potatoes, adding enough bean juice to moisten. Spoon mixture lightly into potato shells. Top with grated cheese, onion, and green pepper. Bake at 425° until browned. Serves 4.

Sooner Sampler

Stick-To-Your-Ribs Ribs

JASMEEN'S JAZZI BARBECUE SAUCE:

1 medium onion, finely
  chopped
½ cup chopped green pepper
1 tablespoon vegetable oil
1 (24-ounce) bottle ketchup
½ cup firmly packed brown
  sugar

½ cup honey
3 tablespoons prepared
  mustard
½ cup water

Sauté onion and green pepper in oil in a large saucepan until vegetables are tender. Add ketchup, brown sugar, honey, and mustard; bring mixture to a boil. Stir in water; reduce heat and simmer, uncovered, 15 minutes.

6½ pounds spareribs
1 onion, coarsely chopped
½ cup cider vinegar

12 black peppercorns
1 teaspoon salt

Cut ribs into serving-size pieces. Place ribs in a large Dutch oven; add water to cover. Add onion, vinegar, peppercorns, and salt. Bring to a boil; cover, reduce heat, and simmer one hour. Drain well. Grill ribs over low coals (275° to 300°) 15 minutes, turning after 8 minutes. Baste ribs generously with Jasmeen's Jazzi Barbecue Sauce and grill 8 minutes. Turn ribs; baste again with Sauce. Grill ribs an additional 7 minutes or to desired degree of doneness.

Kitchen Klatter Keepsakes

Once known as Indian Territory, Oklahoma is still home to more American Indians than any other state in the Union. Thirty-nine tribal headquarters and members of at least 65 tribes make their home here. Native American art galleries, museums, historic sites, powwows, dances, and festivals are part of life in Oklahoma.

Oklahoma Sandplum Jelly

*Earliest kitchen memories of many an Oklahoman include the pickin' of sand-
plums for jelly makin'. Each family watched for a plum thicket to get the pickin'
before everybody else discovered the plums were ripe (jelly the color of an
Oklahoma sunrise being the coveted reward for scratches gotten in the thicket).
Sandplum jelly is still a tradition on the Oklahoma Range...the tart red plums
make the sampling just as pleasurable as the memories.*

5½ cups prepared plum juice   7½ cups sugar
1 box fruit pectin

To prepare plum juice, wash plums, cover with cold water, and boil
until plums are soft and skins pop. Press through jelly bag, strain,
and measure. (At this point, juice may be frozen for later use.)

To prepare jelly, mix plum juice with pectin and bring to a boil,
stirring constantly. Add sugar, continue stirring, and boil hard for
one minute. Pour into sterile jars. Let set for one minute and skim
off top. Seal with new lids. Let jelly cool slowly as sudden temperature change can cause jar to explode. The foamy jelly skim makes a
fun treat for little helpers as well as a tasty memory of jelly-making
time.

Stir Ups

Black-Eyed Susans

½ cup butter or margarine,
  softened
½ cup sugar
½ cup firmly packed brown
  sugar
1 egg
1½ tablespoons warm water
1 teaspoon vanilla

1 cup creamy peanut butter
  (not crunchy)
1½ cups flour
½ teaspoon salt
½ teaspoon baking soda
½ cup semisweet chocolate
  chips

Combine butter and sugars, creaming until light and fluffy; add egg,
warm water, vanilla, and peanut butter. Beat, mixing well. Combine
dry ingredients. Add to creamed mixture, mixing well. Using a cookie press with a flower-shaped disc, press dough onto lightly greased
cookie sheet. Place a chocolate chip in the center of each flower.
Bake at 350° for 8 minutes or until lightly browned. Remove to wire
racks and cool. Chill 30 minutes to firm up centers. Yields about 10
dozen cookies.

Court Clerk's Bar and Grill

Cowboy Cookies

1 cup shortening
1 cup white sugar
1 cup brown sugar
2 eggs
2 cups sifted flour
½ teaspoon salt
1 teaspoon baking soda

½ teaspoon baking powder
1 teaspoon vanilla
1 (12-ounce) package semisweet
  chocolate chips or
  butterscotch chips
2 cups rolled oats (quick)

Cream shortening and sugars. Add eggs and beat. Sift flour, salt, baking soda, and baking powder together and add to creamed mixture. Add vanilla, chips, and oatmeal. Drop by teaspoons onto cookie sheets. Bake at 350° for 15 minutes.

Company Fare I

Cotton Eyed Joe's Baked Beans

On the south edge of Claremore, just across the railroad track from Route 66, is Cotton Eyed Joe's, a serious barbecue stop.

2 (16-ounce) cans pork and
  beans
⅛ teaspoon salt
3½ tablespoons brown sugar
2 tablespoons Worcestershire

¼ cup barbecue sauce
1 teaspoon dry mustard
3 drops liquid smoke
1 teaspoon onion powder

Combine all ingredients in a large container and bake at 300° for 1 hour. Makes 10 servings.

The Route 66 Cookbook

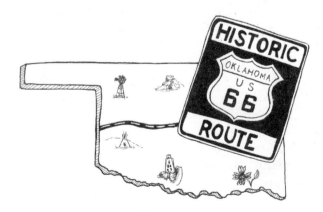

Beef and Potato Casserole

1 pound ground beef
1 medium onion, chopped
1 (4-ounce) can chopped
   mushrooms, drained
1 (10¾-ounce) can cream of
   mushroom soup
1 (15-ounce) can ranch-style
   beans, drained

1 (28-ounce) package frozen
   O'Brien potatoes (hash
   browns)
1 (8-ounce) package grated
   Cheddar cheese

Brown meat; drain and add onion; cook until done. Add mushrooms, soup, and beans. Pour O'Brien potatoes into a greased 9x13-inch pan and pour meat mixture over the potatoes. Top with grated cheese and bake 25–30 minutes in 375° oven until heated through or cheese is melted. Very good!

Seasoned with Love

Oklahoma Pecan Pie

On the outskirts of Vinita, the Little Cabin Creek Pecan Orchard Gift Shop makes a mouth-watering stop. Don and Michel Gray own forty acres of pecan trees that have supplied three generations of Highway 66 travelers. This is one of their favorite recipes.

3 eggs, lightly beaten
1 cup sugar
1 cup light corn syrup
1 tablespoon melted butter

1 teaspoon vanilla
1 cup pecan halves or pieces
1 unbaked (9-inch) pie shell

Beat eggs, then add sugar, corn syrup, and butter, and mix together until well blended. Stir in vanilla and pecans. Pour mixture into pie shell and bake in a preheated 350° oven for 45–55 minutes or until knife inserted halfway between center and edge comes out clean. Cool well on wire rack. Serve plain or with whipped cream. Makes 6–8 slices.

The Route 66 Cookbook

 Route 66, dubbed the Will Rogers Memorial Highway, rolls within a few blocks of the Will Rogers Memorial in Claremore. The Will Rogers birthplace is in nearby Oologah.

Taco Soup

2 pounds hamburger
1 large onion, finely chopped
2–3 cloves garlic, minced
1 (4-ounce) can green chiles
2 (14½-ounce) cans diced
  tomatoes, undrained
1 (15-ounce) can corn,
  undrained
1 (15-ounce) can kidney beans,
  undrained

1 (15-ounce) can pinto beans,
  undrained
1 (15-ounce) can black-eyed
  peas, undrained
1 package Old El Paso Taco
  Seasoning
1 package Hidden Valley
  Original Ranch Dressing Mix
2 cups water

Brown hamburger with onion and garlic; drain. Add remaining ingredients and bring to a boil; simmer at least 2 hours.

100 Years of Cooking

Editor's Extra: Crumble tostados or Fritos on top of each serving along with a sprinkling of grated cheese.

William F. "Buffalo Bill" Cody, in bronze at the National Cowboy Hall of Fame in Oklahoma City, seems to hide his head at the pitiful renditions Barbara and Gwen are doing of his pose.

Oregon

CAPITAL: *Salem*

NICKNAME: *The Beaver State*

*T*he Oregon Trail is the longest of the overland routes used in the westward expansion of the United States. The Cascade Mountains divide Oregon dramatically from rolling wheat fields in the east to mountains and forests in the west. We loved the coastline, looking down—way down—to the Pacific Ocean. Our favorite drive was probably the Fruit Loop in the fertile Hood River Valley, where dozens of orchards and vineyards and gardens yielded the sweetest fruits and tastiest nuts. Oregon is the only state that has an official state nut—the hazelnut—and accounts for 99% of total U.S. production. It has wonderful cheeses, too; Tillamook is its largest cheese factory. We saw a lot of logging there. No wonder Oregon's state flag pictures a beaver on its reverse side—the only state flag to carry two separate designs. Oregon has a lot of depth. At 7,000 feet deep, Hells Canyon is the deepest river gorge in North America. Crater Lake is the seventh deepest lake in the world and was formed in the remains of an ancient volcano some 7,700 years ago. Its crystal-blue waters are world renowned.

Baked Salmon Fillets

2 pounds salmon fillets	¼ cup chopped onion
Salt and pepper to taste	1 teaspoon dill weed
1 tablespoon lemon juice	Bread crumbs
½ cup sour cream	1 tablespoon butter

Place fillets, skin-side-down, in baking pan. Season with salt and pepper. Squeeze fresh lemon juice over salmon. Spread sour cream over fillets and sprinkle chopped onion and dill weed over the cream. Brown bread crumbs in butter, then scatter on dilled salmon. Cover and bake at 325° for 45 minutes or until fish flakes.

Our Favorite Recipes

Sweet and Sour Salmon

4 salmon steaks, cut about
   ¼ inch thick
Salt and pepper
Flour
2–3 tablespoons butter or
   margarine

1 large onion, chopped
½ cup red wine vinegar
2 tablespoons sugar

Sprinkle salmon on both sides with salt and pepper, then coat lightly with flour. Brown in heated butter in a large heavy frying pan until golden brown on each side. Remove salmon and keep warm. In the same pan, cook onion until lightly browned, adding more butter, if needed. Stir in vinegar and sugar and bring to a boil. Return salmon to pan; reduce heat and simmer for 3 minutes. Remove from heat and let stand, covered, for 10 minutes. To serve, spoon sauce over salmon.

Fresh-Water Fish Cookbook

Blackberry Dumplings

We are so blessed here in Oregon to have plentiful blackberries, and this is a good way to use them.

¾ cup sugar
½ cup water
1½ teaspoons lemon juice

⅛ teaspoon salt
1½ quarts blackberries
1 teaspoon vanilla

Use a saucepan of at least 4½-quart capacity with tight-fitting lid. Mix sugar, water, lemon juice, and salt, and heat over low heat 3 minutes. Add the blackberries; cover and simmer 10 minutes. Add vanilla.

DUMPLINGS:
2¼ cups flour
3 teaspoons baking powder
1½ teaspoons sugar
⅓ teaspoon salt

2½ tablespoons butter or
   margarine, softened
1 cup milk

Mix flour, baking powder, sugar, salt, butter, and milk and beat until smooth. Spoon batter on berries and simmer 25 minutes longer, keeping a tight cover in place. Serve berries ladled over dumplings while still warm.

Recipes and Remembering

Thai Chicken Fettuccine

A colorful warm summer day entrée. Serve with fruit and roll for a complete meal.

1 cup picante sauce
¼ cup peanut butter
2 tablespoons honey
¼ cup orange juice
1 teaspoon soy sauce
½ teaspoon ground ginger
12 ounces dry fettuccine,
  cooked and well drained
2 cups cooked chicken breast,
  cut in chunks (3 breasts)

Iceberg lettuce or savory
  cabbage leaves for garnish
¼ cup chopped cilantro
¼ cup chopped unsalted
  peanuts
¼ cup thinly sliced red bell
  pepper

Combine picante sauce, peanut butter, honey, orange juice, soy sauce, and ginger in small saucepan. Cook and stir over low heat until blended and smooth. Reserve ¼ cup picante sauce mixture; toss remaining mixture with hot cooked fettuccine. Mix reserved picante sauce mixture with cooked chicken pieces. Line large platter with lettuce leaves, if desired. Arrange fettuccine mixture over lettuce; top with chicken mixture. Sprinkle with cilantro, peanuts, and red bell pepper. Cool to room temperature before serving, or serve chilled. Serves 6.

Tastefully Oregon

Editor's Extra: Go heavy on the picante sauce and red bell pepper for an even bigger flavor!

The Oregon Trail is the longest of the overland routes used in the westward expansion of the United States. Used between 1840 and 1860, it was about 2,000 miles long, starting in Missouri and ending in Oregon.

Huckleberry-Cherry Pie

3 tablespoons quick-cooking
  tapioca
1 cup sugar
2 cups huckleberries
1 cup canned cherries

½ cup cherry juice
1 tablespoon lemon juice
2 (9-inch) pie shells
1 tablespoon butter

Combine tapioca, sugar, huckleberries, cherries, cherry juice, and lemon juice. Pour mixture into prepared 9-inch pie shell. Dot with butter and add top crust. Bake at 400° for 55 minutes.

Huckleberries and Crabmeat

Dungeness Crab Puffs

6 ounces Dungeness crab
1 cup mayonnaise
1 cup grated Swiss cheese
½ cup finely chopped onion

1 package frozen puff pastry
  (2 sheets), defrosted
1 whole egg beaten with
  1 teaspoon water

Preheat oven to 400°. Combine crab, mayonnaise, Swiss cheese, and onion in a medium bowl, blending well. Flatten sheets of puff pastry and lightly roll them out. Cut each of the sheets into thirds length-wise, and then into fourths along the short side, making a total of 12 squares per sheet. Brush lightly with beaten egg and water. Put a teaspoon of filling in center of each square. Fold squares in half diagonally, and seal by pressing tines of a fork around the edges. Brush tops with more of the beaten egg mixture. Place puffs on a baking sheet lined with baking parchment (or a nonstick baking sheet) and bake for 10–12 minutes, or until puffed and golden brown. Let cool for 4 minutes or so before serving. Makes 24 appetizers.

All About Crab

Dungeness crab is the world's standard for super-premium crab. It is unmatched for quality, texture, and taste. Dungeness is unique to the West Coast of the United States. The crab season on the Oregon coast begins on December 1st, and continues through August 15th. Peak harvest occurs during the first eight weeks, with up to 75% of the annual production landed during this period. Oregon fisherman land, on average, ten million pounds of Dungeness crab annually.

Northwest Cioppino

1½ pounds halibut, lingcod,
    rockfish, or sea bass (fresh or
    frozen)
2 cups sliced onions
2 cloves garlic, finely minced
¼ cup oil (olive or canola)
1 (1-pound 12-ounce) can Italian
    stewed tomatoes, undrained
1 (8-ounce) can tomato sauce

1 cup water
¼ cup chopped parsley
2 teaspoons salt
1 teaspoon basil
½ teaspoon oregano
¼ teaspoon pepper
1 dozen clams (in shells),
    washed
1 cup cooked, peeled shrimp

Cut fish into 1½-inch chunks. Cook onion and garlic in oil till onion
is tender but not brown. Add tomatoes, sauce, water, and all spices.
Cover and simmer 30 minutes. Add fish chunks; cover and simmer
10–20 minutes. Add clams in shell and shrimp; cover and cook 10
minutes longer or until fish flakes easily when tested with a fork.
Yields 6–8 servings.

Coastal Flavors

Chocolate Espresso Sorbet
with Fresh Berries

*The following recipe comes from Portland Farmers' Market, Chef in the Market
series, where every year chefs from local restaurants give cooking demonstrations
that include farm fresh produce.*

2 cups sugar
1 cup cocoa
1 teaspoon cinnamon
Pinch of salt
4 cups water
½ cup espresso or strong coffee

1 tablespoon coffee liqueur or
    hazelnut liqueur (optional)
Garnish: 1 cup mixed fresh
    berries or cherries, mint
    sprigs, and chopped toasted
    hazelnuts

In a large saucepan, stir together all ingredients and bring to a boil,
stirring constantly. Cool in the refrigerator until thoroughly cold.
Freeze in an ice cream machine according to manufacturer's instructions. To serve, scoop into a bowl and garnish with fruit, mint, and
toasted hazelnuts.

Recipe by Mark Gould, executive chef, Red Star Tavern & Roast House, Portland
Oregon Farmers' Markets Cookbook and Guide

Pennsylvania

CAPITAL: *Harrisburg*

NICKNAME: *The Keystone State*

 It is said in Pennsylvania that, "America starts here." No doubt about it, our country's heritage is alive here and much celebrated. Once the United States capital city, Philadelphia is where the Declaration of Independence was signed, and is home to the Liberty Bell. It is also home to the cheesesteak sandwich, TastyKakes, and the first commercial pretzel bakery in America. A delicious place to visit, Hershey is the Chocolate Capital of the United States, and the whole town smells like chocolate . . . even the light fixtures are designed like Silver Kisses. In Lancaster County, the lifestyle of the Amish intrigues and fascinates visitors. Farmers' markets with homemade goodies are truly a delightful taste of a step back in time. Speaking of steps, Pittsburgh has over 712 sets of city maintained steps. But the most famous are the "Rocky Steps" at the Philadelphia Museum of Art. Do it . . . the view is spectacular.

Apple Butter

The wonderful aroma while making this apple butter will bring back memories of years gone by. The flavor is the same, with much less work.

12 pounds tart cooking apples, peeled, cored, and quartered (in the fall, use Winesap apples)	2 cups water 3½ cups granulated sugar 1 cup cider vinegar 1 teaspoon cinnamon

Cook apples and water in a pan over low heat until soft, about 20 minutes. Rub through a food mill.

Add sugar, cider vinegar, and cinnamon, mixing well. Put mixture in heavy roaster pan, uncovered, and cook in preheated 375° oven for approximately 2½ hours, stirring every 15 minutes with a wooden spoon. The apple butter is thick enough when you can put 2 tablespoons of mixture on a saucer and turn it upside down without it dropping off. Ladle into hot sterilized pint or quart jars and seal. Makes about 3½ quarts, or 7 pints.

Betty Groff's Up-Home Down-Home Cookbook

Short-Cut Pepperoni Bread

1 loaf frozen bread dough
½ pound Swiss cheese, sliced
½ pound pepperoni, thinly
  sliced

1 egg
Grated Parmesan cheese

Thaw dough according to package directions and let rise. After dough has risen, cut in half; roll out each half as thin as possible. Layer with Swiss cheese and pepperoni. Beat egg and spread thinly over pepperoni and cheese. Sprinkle with Parmesan cheese. Roll into loaves. Bake at 350° for 30 minutes or until golden brown. Yields 15 slices.

Philadelphia Homestyle Cookbook

Zucchini Beef Skillet

1 pound ground beef
1 cup chopped onion
¾ cup chopped green pepper
1½ teaspoons salt
¼ teaspoon pepper
1 teaspoon chili powder

5 cups sliced zucchini
2 large tomatoes, chopped
½ cup water
2 cups corn
2 tablespoons chopped pimento
¼ cup chopped parsley

Sauté beef, onion, and pepper in large skillet until browned. Add remaining ingredients. Cover and simmer 15 minutes or until vegetables are tender.

River Brethren Recipes

The Liberty Bell weighs 2,080 pounds and is 12 feet in circumference at the lip. It bears the following inscription: "Proclaim Liberty Throughout All the Land unto All the Inhabitants Thereof. Lev. xxv:x."

Lady 'n' Amaretto

3–4 packages ladyfingers
Amaretto to taste
4 (8-ounce) packages cream
cheese, softened
2 eggs
1 cup sugar
⅓+ cup amaretto
2½ cups sliced strawberries

2 cups heavy cream
1 teaspoon vanilla
3 tablespoons confectioners'
sugar
10 whole strawberries
¼ cup toasted almonds

Layer bottom of trifle bowl with split ladyfingers; sprinkle lightly with amaretto.

Cream softened cream cheese with eggs, sugar, and ⅓ cup amaretto until smooth. Spread half the cream cheese mixture over ladyfingers. Top with half the sliced strawberries. Add another layer of ladyfingers; sprinkle with amaretto. Spread rest of cream cheese mixture over ladyfingers.

Whip cream with vanilla and confectioners' sugar; place in pastry bag and decorate top of torte. Garnish with whole strawberries and almonds. Serves 12.

Settings

Chicken Corn Rivel Soup

1 (3- to 4-pound) stewing
chicken
2 tablespoons salt
¼ teaspoon pepper
1½ cups chopped celery

1 medium onion, chopped
2 tablespoons minced parsley
1 quart corn (fresh, frozen, or
canned)
Rivels

In large kettle, cover chicken with water. Add salt and pepper. Cook until soft. Remove bones and skin from chicken and cut meat into small pieces. Heat broth to boiling point and add remaining ingredients. Cook about 15 minutes. Add meat. Heat thoroughly. Garnish with hard-boiled egg or parsley.

RIVELS:
1 cup flour
1 egg

¼ cup milk

Combine flour and egg. Add milk. Mix Rivels by cutting with two forks to make crumbs the size of cherry stones. Drop Rivels into boiling broth while stirring to prevent Rivels from packing together. Makes 8–10 servings.

From Amish and Mennonite Kitchens

Apple Danish Bars

2½ cups all-purpose flour	1 teaspoon lemon juice
1 teaspoon salt	¾ cup sugar
1 cup shortening	1 teaspoon cinnamon
1 egg, separated	1 cup confectioners' sugar
1 cup cornflakes	4–5 teaspoons milk
8 cups sliced peeled apples	

Mix flour and salt in bowl. Cut in shortening until crumbly. Combine egg yolk with water to measure ⅔ cup. Add to flour mixture; mix well. Roll half the dough to fit a 10x15-inch baking pan. Fit over bottom and sides of pan. Sprinkle with cornflakes. Layer apples over cornflakes. Sprinkle with lemon juice and mixture of sugar and cinnamon. Top with remaining pastry. Seal edges; slash top. Brush with slightly beaten egg white. Bake at 350° for 50 minutes. Mix confectioners' sugar and milk in a bowl. Drizzle over top while warm. Cool. Cut into bars. Yields 36 bars. Can do ahead; easy; can freeze.

Laurels to the Cook

FROM GWEN'S ROAD DIARY:
In Altoona, we had a taping at a TV studio with a tall, handsome young man who loved good food and was intrigued with our *Best of the Best from Pennsylvania Cookbook*. He was also taken with our *Best of the Best from North Carolina Cookbook* since that's his home state, so we gave him a copy. Little did we know we would be seeing lots of him in the future—on QVC. David Venable is one of QVC's hosts, and he delights in putting on his famous "yummy face" when tasting BEST OF THE BEST dishes. Like all the QVC hosts, he is as delightful as he appears . . . and a cherished friend.

Sweet Potato Snackers

Sweet potato skins   **Powdered Sugar**

Wash potato skins; dry them. Deep-fry skins in deep, hot oil (375°) till very crisp. Drain. Sprinkle with powdered sugar.

The Best of the Sweet Potato Recipes

Schnitz Pie

Since apple trees, which grow abundantly in eastern Pennsylvania, produced more apples than could be eaten fresh in most households, the German settlers dried much of their fruit. It was a home operation. The apples were peeled and cut into slices (schnitz means to cut into pieces), then laid on a roof or on racks above a heat source to dry.

Most apples dried in 24–48 hours, depending upon the thickness of the slices, the temperature of the heat source, and the temperature and humidity of the weather. Once dried, the sweet slices were stored in a dry container for use at any time of the year.

Today, schnitz pie is usually served at the lunch which follows the Sunday morning church service. It is traditionally part of the main course at the snack meal of the day when either potato soup or bean soup is on the menu. Schnitz pie is now prepared commercially in Pennsylvania, so it is available to those without their own source of fresh apples.

3 cups dried apples   **⅔ cup brown sugar**
2¼ cups warm water   **2 unbaked (9-inch) pie shells**
1 teaspoon lemon extract

Soak apples in warm water, then cook over low heat until soft. Mash apples and add lemon extract and sugar.

Pour into unbaked pie shell. Cover with top crust. Seal edges and cut slashes in top. Bake at 425° for 15 minutes; then at 350° for 30 minutes. Serve warm. Makes 1 (9-inch) pie.

The Best of Amish Cooking

Rhode Island

CAPITAL: *Providence*

NICKNAME: *The Ocean State*

*T*here's so much history here, that "Little Rhody" is virtually a living museum. For one so small, the state boasts one of the nation's largest concentrations of historic landmarks. The most famous, of course, are the palatial Gilded Age Newport mansions that were once the summer "cottages" of New York's wealthiest families. It is the smallest state with many fascinating firsts. It was home to the first open golf tournament (1895). In 1774, Newport hosted the first circus in the country. And also, Newport has one of the country's oldest tavern buildings (the White Horse Tavern, 1673). President John F. Kennedy and Jacqueline Bouvier were married at St. Mary's church in Newport. George M. Cohan, who wrote 40 Broadway plays and musicals, including the songs "I'm a Yankee Doodle Dandy" and "You're a Grand Old Flag." was born in Providence in 1878. And guess what the official state drink is . . . coffee milk!

Rhode Island Johnnycakes

. . . made with white cornmeal and cooked on a hot griddle. Some Rhode Island cooks would omit the sugar, others the eggs.

3 eggs
2 cups stone-ground white cornmeal
2 teaspoons baking powder
2 tablespoons flour
1 teaspoon salt
2 tablespoons sugar (optional)
1 tablespoon melted butter or shortening
1–2 cups milk

In medium bowl, beat eggs well. Add remaining ingredients, stirring in enough milk to make thin batter. Pour batter onto hot griddle (use ¼-cup measure to dip batter). Cook until brown on one side; flip and brown on other side. Serve with butter and maple syrup.

Variation: Break completely with tradition! Try serving johnnycakes topped with smoked salmon and crème fraîche or sour cream; sprinkle with plenty of fresh snipped dill. Yields about 12 (4-inch) cakes.

All Seasons Cookbook

Steamed Lobsters

2 lobsters (1¼–1½ pounds each)
2 cups water
1 teaspoon sea salt
¼ pound butter, melted
Lemon wedges

Select a pot with a tight-sealing lid large enough to hold the 2 lobsters. Put water and salt in the pot and bring to a boil. Set live lobsters in the pot, and cover. Cook lobsters 12 minutes. Add 5 minutes for each additional ½ pound of lobster.

Remove cover (be careful as the steam will be hot), and remove lobsters to heated plates. Serve with individual nut crackers and a bowl for the shells. Serve immediately with warm melted butter and lemon wedges.

Seafood Expressions

Vanilla Bread Pudding with Butter Rum Sauce

BUTTER RUM SAUCE:
½ cup butter, melted
¾ cup powdered sugar
¼ cup Meyer's rum

Combine all ingredients and cook over medium heat for 15 minutes.

6 eggs
2 cups milk
1¾ cups sugar
2 teaspoons ground cinnamon
½ cup raisins
2 teaspoons vanilla extract
1 loaf French bread
(approximately)
½ cup walnuts
½ cup brown sugar

In a large bowl, mix together eggs, milk, sugar, cinnamon, raisins, and vanilla. Cut up enough French bread in small cubes to absorb the mixture. Pour mixture into a greased deep baking pan and top with walnuts and brown sugar. Bake in oven for 45 minutes at 350°. To serve, cut bread pudding into squares and serve warm, topped with heated Butter Rum Sauce.

A recipe from Muriel's Restaurant, Newport
A Taste of Newport

Scallop Stuffed Shrooms

40 good fresh mushrooms
  (large, approximately 1¾–2
  inches in diameter)
⅓ stick butter or margarine
5 tablespoons Italian bread
  crumbs

40 good fresh sea scallops
  (approximately 2 pounds)
20 slices bacon, cut in halves
  to make 40 short slices
  (should be about 1 pound)

Wash mushrooms and pat dry. Remove stems with a sharp paring knife, hollowing out each mushroom slightly. (Save the stems for soup, stew, steaks, or omelets.) Melt butter in small saucepan and mix in bread crumbs. Remove from heat. Place a small amount of bread crumb mixture in each hollowed-out mushroom cap. Take the raw scallops and fit each one inside a mushroom cap. Large scallops go into large mushrooms; small scallops go into small mushrooms and so on. Fill in any gaps and top scallops with small amount of bread crumb mixture. Wrap each with bacon and secure with toothpick.

Place in a shallow baking dish and bake at 350° for 10–15 minutes. Remove from oven and place dish in broiler. Broil mushrooms, turning them over once or twice until bacon reaches desired doneness, approximately 5 minutes.

A Taste of Salt Air & Island Kitchens

Seldom Seen Farm
Lamb Chops in Foil

So easy, anyone will become the "Chef of the Day."

FOR EACH SERVING ALLOW:

2 lamb chops
1 zucchini, unpeeled, sliced
1 small onion, sliced
1 small tomato, quartered

Dash of basil
Salt and pepper
Garlic powder

Make a packet of foil with the above in each, wrapped tightly. Grill on low about 25–30 minutes. Be sure to turn several times. Another great way to use this recipe is to bake at 350° for 1¼–1½ hours.

A recipe from Seldom Seen Farm, Harmony
The Island Cookbook

Roasted Broccoli
with Sesame Dressing

1 pound large broccoli flowerets,
  including 3 inches of stem
3 tablespoons olive oil
4 tablespoons fresh lemon juice
2 teaspoons oriental sesame oil
4 teaspoons soy sauce

3 tablespoons vegetable oil
4 teaspoons sesame seeds,
  toasted
1 teaspoon ground ginger
½ teaspoon minced garlic
Pinch sugar

In a bowl, toss broccoli with olive oil until coated well, and roast in a jellyroll pan in a preheated 500° oven, turning it occasionally with tongs, for 10–12 minutes, or until crisp-tender.

While broccoli is roasting, in a blender or food processor, blend lemon juice, sesame oil, soy sauce, vegetable oil, sesame seeds, ginger, garlic, and sugar until dressing is smooth. Transfer broccoli to a serving dish and pour dressing over it. Serves 4.

Hasbro Children's Hospital Cookbook

Lobster Quiche

CRUST:

1½ cups flour
1 teaspoon salt
6 tablespoons butter or
  shortening

3–5 tablespoons ice water

Mix together flour and salt. Using a pastry fork or food processor, cut in shortening until the mixture resembles coarse meal. Mix in just enough ice water to form a ball. Wrap in plastic wrap and refrigerate for one hour.

Roll out chilled dough on a lightly floured board to ⅛-inch to ¼-inch thickness. Line a 9-inch quiche pan with the dough, cover with plastic wrap, and refrigerate until ready to use.

FILLING:

3 eggs
1½ cups half-and-half
1½ cups coarsely chopped
  cooked lobster meat
¾ cup grated Swiss cheese
¾ cup grated Cheddar cheese
1 small onion

1 tablespoon butter, melted
1 clove garlic
¼ teaspoon dry mustard
½ teaspoon tarragon
1 teaspoon chopped parsley
Salt and pepper to taste

Preheat oven to 350°. In a large bowl, beat eggs well. Add half-and-half and beat again. Stir in lobster meat and cheeses. Set aside. Finely chop the onion and sauté in a little butter. When the onion is almost done, crush the garlic and stir in; remove from heat. Add onion and garlic, dry mustard, herbs, salt and pepper to the lobster mixture and combine well. Pour into the Crust and bake at 350° for 45 minutes. Cool on a rack for 5 minutes before slicing.

A recipe from Murphy's Bed & Breakfast, Narragansett
The Bed & Breakfast Cookbook

The first street in America to be illuminated by gaslight was Pelham Street in Newport, Rhode Island, in 1806.

Cold Salmon Mousse

1 (16-ounce) can red salmon;
  drain, remove bones and flake
1 (8-ounce) package cream
  cheese (room temperature)
1 tablespoon lemon juice
¼ teaspoon salt
1 tablespoon horseradish,
  grated

2 tablespoons onion, grated
½ tablespoon liquid smoke
  (optional)
6 tablespoons chopped pecans
½ cup chopped fresh parsley

Blend all ingredients except pecans and parsley. Chill for at least 4 hours. Make 2 balls by dividing mixture in half. Roll each ball in 3 tablespoons chopped pecans mixed with ¼ cup chopped parsley just before serving. Serve with French bread. Garnish with small pickles, tomatoes, cucumbers, and whatever you have. Flavors improve if made the day before.

Note: This dish is also great molded in individual molds (line molds with plastic wrap) and used as a first course. Press pecans and parsley on molded salmon.

Seafood Expressions

FROM GWEN'S ROAD DIARY:
In Newport, we were blown away by the opulent mansions behind gated entries one after another on lovely tree-lined streets, many of them overlooking the ocean. The Cliff Walk was adventurous, and the town was fascinating, too. "Muriel's has the best chowder," people told us, so we set out to find it. "Just up the street," each person asked would say, and "up" was right. In the hot summer sun we walked much farther than we bargained for, but when we finally sat down to Muriel's award-winning chowder—and it was indeed—there came a slight breeze blowing the curtains in this charming little place, and once again, we knew our spirits had moved us in the right direction. What a lovely taste of Rhode Island.

South Carolina

CAPITAL: *Columbia*

NICKNAME: *The Palmetto State*

If you only had one word to describe South Carolina, it would have to be "charming." South Carolina's unmatched charm stretches from historic Charleston and the Grand Strand coastal beaches all the way to the beautiful upcountry mountain region. Upcountry is Blue Ridge and Piedmont—the Upper Whitewater Falls is the highest cascade in eastern America; it descends for nearly 411 feet. And Lowcountry starts with the sandhills and goes down a broad, even plain to the tidewater. A powerful symbol to both the South and the North, Fort Sumter was where the Civil War began on April 12, 1861. It is said rice was introduced to America around 1694 when a ship captain bartered a portion of his rice cargo for needed repairs—rice fields now line the swampy riverbanks. With quaint old buildings, islands and inlets, azaleas and irises, golf courses and thoroughbreds, it's no wonder the leading industry in the state is tourism. Better bring your appetite.

Frozen Chocolate Charlotte

½ cup white crème de menthe
Ladyfingers
1 (8-ounce) package semisweet
  chocolate
6 eggs, separated

½ cup sugar
3 tablespoons instant coffee
½ cup boiling water
1 teaspoon vanilla
1½ cups whipped cream

Brush surface of 9-inch springform mold with crème de menthe, then line mold with ladyfingers. Melt chocolate in top of double boiler. Beat egg yolks in bowl until foamy. Beat in sugar gradually and beat until thick. Dissolve coffee in boiling water. Add coffee, vanilla, and chocolate to egg yolks and sugar. Beat egg whites until stiff. Stir 1 cup egg whites into chocolate to lighten it. Fold in whipped cream which has been blended with rest of egg whites. Freeze. Serves 12.

Sea Island Seasons

Buttermilk Custard Pie

¾ cup butter
½ cup sugar (about)
3 eggs, separated
3 tablespoons flour

Grated rind of 1 lemon
2 cups buttermilk
Pastry for 2 pies

Cream butter and sugar and add well-beaten egg yolks. Add flour and grated lemon rind, then the buttermilk. Fold in stiffly beaten egg whites and turn into 2 pie pans lined with pastry. (The crust should be baked in a hot oven, about 400°, for 15 minutes before putting in the filling.)

Bake in a moderately hot oven (375°) for about 40 minutes. If the milk is very sour, add more sugar.

Two Hundred Years of Charleston Cooking

Crab Cakes

In South Carolina, Daufuskie Crab Cakes tend to be made with plenty of bread-ing and seasoning. This recipe, though, is lots of flaky crabmeat with just enough moistened bread crumbs added to simply hold the meat together.

3 slices white bread, day old
    works best
1 pound lump crabmeat
2 tablespoons mayonnaise

1 teaspoon dry mustard
1 teaspoon parsley
1 egg

Break bread into crumbs. Gently mix with all other ingredients until thoroughly combined. Shape into patties. Pan-fry in butter until brown and cooked through. Serves 2–4.

Hudson's Cookbook

Editor's Extra: Good with a spoon of your favorite sauce.

The Pee Dee area of the state lies almost entirely within South Carolina's coastal plain. It is drained by the Great and Little Pee Dee, Black, and Lynches rivers. Stephen Foster's original lyrics for his famous song read: "Way down upon the Pee Dee River . . . ."

Charleston Shrimp Bake

1 cup chopped onion
1 cup sliced celery
⅓ cup margarine
1 (14½-ounce) can tomato
  wedges, undrained
3 cups cooked rice

1 teaspoon dill weed or oregano
1 pound peeled, deveined, and
  cooked shrimp
4 ounces crumbled feta cheese
½ cup sliced black olives

Cook onion and celery in margarine until tender. Add tomato wedges and heat. Stir in rice, dill weed, shrimp, cheese, and olives. Bake at 350° for 25 minutes or until shrimp are cooked. Makes 6 servings.

Southeastern Wildlife Cookbook

The Greenhouse Restaurant's Fried Bananas

1 banana
½ cup self-rising flour
1 cup cooking oil
¼ cup honey

1 teaspoon mayonnaise
¼ teaspoon cinnamon
¼ cup finely chopped pecans

Peel the banana and cut lengthwise into 4 sections. Roll each section in flour. Fry in hot oil until golden brown; drain. Combine honey, mayonnaise, and cinnamon, mixing well so flavors are thoroughly blended. Pour honey sauce over bananas and sprinkle with pecans. Serves 1 or 2.

South Carolina's Historic Restaurants

Dixie Sweet Potato Pie

PIE:

1 cup cooked and mashed
  sweet potatoes
1 (12-ounce) can evaporated
  milk
½ cup margarine, melted
2 cups sugar

4 eggs
1 teaspoon nutmeg
1 teaspoon cinnamon
1 teaspoon vanilla
2 deep-dish pie shells, unbaked

TOPPING:

1 cup brown sugar
1 tablespoon margarine, melted

1 teaspoon vanilla
1 egg, well beaten

Preheat oven to 350°. With an electric mixer, combine all Pie ingredients. Mix well. Pour into pie shells, and bake 30 minutes or until lightly browned. Combine all Topping ingredients, and spread over pies. Return to oven until browned. Watch closely—Topping will burn easily. Serves 16.

Stir Crazy!

Dove Bog

3 medium onions, chopped
4 stalks celery, chopped
1 teaspoon salt
2 teaspoons pepper

10 dove breasts
5 pieces raw chicken
1½ pounds smoked sausage
2 cups raw rice

In a 7-quart pot, place onions, celery, salt, pepper, dove, and chicken. Cover with water and boil covered about 45 minutes. Cut sausage into thick slices and add to pot. Continue cooking an additional 15 minutes. Remove dove, chicken, and sausage; reserve broth. Debone chicken and dove. Cut into bite-size pieces. Measure broth, adding enough water, if necessary, to yield 4 cups. Return broth to pot, add rice, and bring to a boil. Cook on low 10 minutes. Add dove, chicken, and sausage. Cook 10–15 minutes on medium, stirring occasionally. Can prepare ahead to time. Serves 8.

Uptown Down South

Hopping John

Hopping John, made of cow peas and rice, is eaten in the stateliest of Charleston houses and in the humblest cabins and always on New Year's Day. "Hoppin' John eaten then will bring good luck" is an old tradition.

1 cup raw cow peas (dried field
  peas)
2 teaspoons salt
4 cups water

1 cup raw rice
4 slices bacon, fried with
  1 medium onion, chopped

Boil peas in salted water until tender. Add peas and 1 cup pea liquid to rice, bacon with grease and onion. Put in rice steamer or double boiler and cook for 1 hour or until rice is thoroughly done. Serves 8.

Charleston Receipts

Stuffed Crabs and Mushrooms

2 tablespoons butter
1 cup sliced mushrooms
1 tablespoon flour
½ cup cream
1 pound cooked crabmeat

Juice of ½ lemon
1 teaspoon capers
1 teaspoon chopped parsley
2 egg whites, beaten stiff

Melt butter and add mushrooms; cook until tender. Remove mushrooms or put them to one side of the pan and add flour. When well blended, add cream; stir until thick, remove from fire, and add other ingredients in order given. Put mixture back into crab shells, or if shells are not available, use a buttered casserole dish. Bake casserole in a moderate oven (350°) for about 20 minutes. Serves 8.

Two Hundred Years of Charleston Cooking

When you get close to Myrtle Beach, you just have to wiggle your toes in the water.

South Dakota

CAPITAL: *Pierre*

NICKNAME: *The Mount Rushmore State*

 *L*ewis and Clark, George Custer, and Sitting Bull lived out larger-than-life adventures in South Dakota. Four presidents are still there and are literally larger than life, their faces carved on Mount Rushmore. The Crazy Horse mountain carving nearby is in progress and will be the world's largest sculpture. It is the focal point of a memorial to and for the North American Indian. South Dakota is the home of the Dakota, Lakota, and Nakota Indian tribes, which make up the Sioux Nation. Even they avoided the Badlands. But it is fascinating to see this piece of the earth's architecture at Badlands National Park, consisting of 244,000 acres of sharply eroded buttes, pinnacles, and spires. Nearby Sturgis is home to the annual Black Hills Motor Classic, and historically preserved Deadwood takes you back to Wild Bill Hickok and Calamity Jane days. Oh, and you can still get 5¢ coffee at Wall Drugs. South Dakota . . . "Great Faces, Great Places."

Best in the West Sugar Cookies

These are the "melt-in-your-mouth" kind of cookies.

1 cup powdered sugar
1 cup white sugar
1 cup butter, softened
1 cup oil
2 eggs
1 teaspoon vanilla

4 cups plus 4 heaping
  tablespoons flour
1 teaspoon salt
2 teaspoons baking soda
1 teaspoon cream of tartar

Cream powdered sugar, white sugar, butter, and oil. Beat in eggs and vanilla. Sift and add remaining ingredients. Place walnut-size balls of dough on nonstick cookie sheet and flatten with fork. Bake 8–10 minutes at 375°.

The Best Little Cookbook in the West

Impossible Garden Pie

2 cups chopped or thinly sliced
  zucchini
1 cup chopped tomato
⅓ cup chopped onion
1 cup shredded Swiss or Jack
  cheese
2 cups milk
4 eggs, beaten
1 cup Bisquick
⅓ cup Parmesan cheese
¼ teaspoon salt
⅛ teaspoon pepper

Grease a 10-inch pie plate, or 7x11-inch glass casserole dish. Layer all vegetables in pan. Sprinkle cheese over vegetables. Beat milk, eggs, Bisquick, cheese, and spices. Pour over all and bake 35–40 minutes or until a knife inserted comes out clean. You may also add a layer of cooked ground beef and a few green pepper rings (use a slightly deeper casserole dish). Garnish with zucchini and tomato slices, if desired.

Rainbow's Roundup of Recipes

Hot Chicken Sandwich

1 loaf Pepperidge Farm Bread
½ cup butter, softened
3 cups chopped, cooked
  chicken
3 hard-boiled eggs, chopped
2 tablespoons chopped onions
1 (4-ounce) can mushrooms,
  drained
1 cup sliced ripe olives
⅔ cup mayonnaise
1 (10¾-ounce) can cream of
  mushroom soup
1 cup sour cream
Slivered almonds
Paprika

Remove crust from bread, and butter both sides. Put 8 slices of bread in 9x13-inch pan. Mix together chicken, eggs, onions, mushrooms, olives, and mayonnaise. Put on bread. Put 8 slices of bread on top. Mix soup and sour cream together. Put on top of bread. Sprinkle with slivered almonds and paprika. Bake at 325° for 30 minutes.

St. Joseph's Table

Every summer, a new castle rises from the plains of Mitchell, elaborately decorated with murals and onion domes. This annual construction is made up of 11 different types of corn, as well as various grains and grasses . . . the world's only Corn Palace.

Cow Punching Chili and Dumplings

CHILI:
1 pound ground beef, browned
1 cup chopped onion
1 (29-ounce) can tomatoes
2 (8-ounce) cans tomato sauce
1 tablespoon chili powder
2 teaspoons salt
1 (16-ounce) can chili beans
   (optional)

Make up Chili (cook all in pot) and simmer until right before serving time. Add Dumplings 15 minutes before serving.

DUMPLINGS:
1 cup flour
1 cup mashed potato flakes
2 teaspoons baking powder
½ teaspoon salt
1 cup milk
1 egg
2 tablespoons oil

For Dumplings, combine flour, flakes, baking powder, and salt. Mix milk with egg and oil and add to above. Stir to moisten. Let stand several minutes. Place spoonfuls on Chili, cover tightly, and cook 15 minutes.

The Best Little Cookbook in the West

Pineapple Cream French Toast

3 eggs
¾ cup half-and-half
¼ teaspoon ground nutmeg
1 (8-ounce) can crushed
   pineapple, with juice
½ cup brown sugar
⅔ loaf French bread, cut into
   ¾-inch slices
¼ cup butter, for frying
Powdered sugar

In a small bowl, beat eggs, half-and-half, nutmeg, pineapple, and brown sugar. Place bread in single layer in 9x13-inch glass baking dish (may need an extra dish). Pour egg mixture over bread, lifting to let liquid run under bread. Refrigerate overnight.

   In the morning, melt 2 tablespoons butter in frying pan. Add 3 or 4 slices bread and cook over moderate heat until golden brown on each side. Melt 2 more tablespoons butter and cook remaining slices. Dust with powdered sugar; serve with syrup. Makes 3–4 servings.

Recipe from Creekside Cottage Bed and Breakfast, Hill City
South Dakota Sunrise

Apple Dumplings

4-6 tablespoons butter or solid
  shortening
1¾ cups all-purpose flour
3 tablespoons sugar
½ teaspoon salt

3 teaspoons baking powder
¾ cup milk
4 medium apples, peeled and
  sliced

Preheat oven to 375°. Cut shortening into dry ingredients with pastry blender or knives until mixture is consistency of coarse cornmeal. Make well in the center of these ingredients. Pour in milk. Stir lightly until all ingredients are moistened and dough cleans the sides of the bowl; not more than ½ minute. Turn dough onto lightly floured surface. Knead 10 times. With floured rolling pin, roll dough into 9x12-inch rectangle about ½ inch thick. Cover with apples. Starting on the long end, roll up jellyroll style. Pinch side edge together. Cut tube into 10–12 slices and place in greased 9x13-inch cake pan. Pour Sauce over slices and bake for 45 minutes or until apple are tender.

SAUCE:
1 cup white sugar
1 cup packed brown sugar
1 cup margarine

2 cups water
1 teaspoon cinnamon

Combine all ingredients in saucepan; bring to a full boil. Boil one minute. Pour over sliced apple roll.

St. Joseph's Table

Mount Rushmore is a national treasure. The sixty-feet tall faces of Presidents Washington, Jefferson, Theodore Roosevelt, and Lincoln were originally carved at a cost of slightly less than one million dollars. The sculptor, Gutzon Borglum, worked on the memorial fourteen years, from 1927 until his death in 1941. These amazing faces are 500 feet up, with the changing sky creating interesting backgrounds and shadows. Awesome and inspiring to behold, they are "the most famous men in rock."

Hidden Pear Salad

1 (16-ounce) can pears, reserve
  liquid
1 (3-ounce) package
  lime-flavored gelatin
1 (3-ounce) package cream
  cheese, softened

¼ teaspoon lemon juice
1 envelope whipped topping
  mix
Lettuce leaves

In a saucepan, bring pear liquid to a boil. Stir in gelatin until dissolved. Remove from heat and cool at room temperature until syrupy. Meanwhile, purée pears in a blender. In a mixing bowl, beat cream cheese and lemon juice until fluffy and smooth. Add puréed pears and mix well. Prepare whipped topping according to package directions; fold into pear mixture. Fold in cooled gelatin. Pour into an oiled 4½-cup mold. Chill overnight. Just before serving, unmold salad onto a lettuce-lined platter. Yields 6–8 servings.

Rainbow's Roundup of Recipes

Deviled Egg Bake

8 hard-boiled eggs, peeled
¼ cup butter, melted
½ teaspoon Worcestershire
1 teaspoon dried parsley

1 tablespoon grated onion
¼ teaspoon dry mustard
1 cup shredded Cheddar cheese

Cut hard-boiled eggs in half; remove yolks. To the yolks, add melted butter, Worcestershire, parsley, onion, and dry mustard. Mash and mix together. Fill egg whites and put into greased baking dish.

WHITE SAUCE:
2 tablespoons butter
¼ cup flour
1 cup hot water

Salt and pepper to taste
¾ cup cream

Melt butter and blend in flour. Add hot water to flour mixture. Season with salt and pepper. Add cream. Mix well and cook over low heat until thick. Pour White Sauce over eggs and sprinkle with cheese. Cover dish and bake at 350º for 25 minutes. Makes 4–6 servings.

Recipe from Willow Springs Cabins Bed & Breakfast, Rapid City

South Dakota Sunrise

Tennessee

CAPITAL: *Nashville*

NICKNAME: *The Volunteer State*

*T*ennesseans are down-home country folks who take pride in their state, their heritage, and their cooking, too. It's a lively state with so much happening! Sports, good food, and entertainment are everywhere. The Grand Ole Opry went on the air in 1925 and is the longest continuously running live radio program in the world. Check out the replica of the Parthenon in Nashville's Centennial Park. And there's skiing in the Volunteer State, too—all year round! At the Ober Gatlinburg Ski Resort in Gatlinburg, a five-acre artificial ski surface permits skiing in any type of weather. Davy Crockett was not born on a mountaintop, but on the banks of the Nolichucky River in east Tennessee in 1786, where a replica of the Crockett's log cabin stands today. Elvis loved Tennessee—his home, Graceland, is located in Memphis, and is the second most visited house in the country (after the White House). Better get some Memphis barbecue while you're in town—yum!

Bourbon and Chocolate Pecan Pie

This pie is labeled Jackson Pie on Miss Daisy's Menu. Pierre Franey, former food columnist for the New York Times, *while at a luncheon, described this as one of the best pecan pies he had ever eaten.*

1 cup sugar
¼ cup butter, melted
3 eggs, slightly beaten
¾ cup light corn syrup
¼ teaspoon salt

2 tablespoons bourbon
1 teaspoon vanilla
½ cup chopped pecans
½ cup chocolate chips
1 (9-inch) pie shell

Cream sugar and butter. Add eggs, syrup, salt, bourbon, and vanilla. Mix until blended. Spread pecans and chocolate chips in bottom of pie shell. Pour filling into shell. Bake in a 375° oven for 40–50 minutes. Yields 6–8 servings.

The Original Tennessee Homecoming Cookbook

Garlic Cheese Grits

1 cup quick-cooking grits
1 (6-ounce) roll garlic cheese
1 stick butter

2 eggs, beaten
¾ cup milk

Cook grits as package directs. Add cheese and butter. Cool. Combine eggs and milk. Put grits in 2-quart buttered casserole and pour egg-milk mixture over grits. Bake uncovered for 1 hour in 375° oven. Can be made ahead. Serves 8.

Note: Egg-milk mixture can be stirred into the cooled grits, if desired, and top dusted with paprika.

Party Potpourri

Sweet 'n Sour Chops

6 butterfly (boneless) pork
  chops
1 (10½-ounce) can beef
  consommé
½ cup drained pineapple
  chunks

¼ cup chopped green pepper
¼ cup ketchup
2 tablespoons wine vinegar
1 tablespoon brown sugar
1 teaspoon soy sauce
½ teaspoon dry mustard

Brown chops in frying pan; pour off excess fat. Arrange chops in 9x13x2-inch casserole. Combine consommé, pineapple, chopped pepper, ketchup, wine vinegar, brown sugar, soy sauce, and dry mustard. Pour over chops and bake uncovered in 400° oven for 45 minutes. Serves 6.

Southern Secrets

Hot and Spicy Barbequed Shrimp

½ teaspoon cayenne pepper	½ teaspoon salt
1 tablespoon thyme	3 tablespoons olive oil
½ teaspoon celery salt	1 teaspoon crushed rosemary
1 tablespoon chopped parsley	½ pound butter
⅔ cup Worcestershire	3–4 pounds raw shrimp in
½ teaspoon black pepper	shells, rinsed and drained

Combine all ingredients except shrimp in saucepan. Heat until butter is melted and all ingredients are well blended. Cool marinade slightly before pouring over unpeeled shrimp in 9x13-inch glass baking dish. Marinate at room temperature 45 minutes, then refrigerate for at least 4 hours. Turn shrimp occasionally.

Bake, uncovered, at 350° for about 30 minutes, until shrimp are pink and firm. This is MESSY, but super. Serve with lots of French bread to absorb the butter sauce.

Grand Tour Collection

Carrot Casserole

2 cups mashed cooked carrots	3 tablespoons flour
(8–12, depending on size)	1 teaspoon baking powder
½ cup margarine	3 eggs, beaten
1 cup sugar	1 teaspoon pumpkin pie spice

Add margarine to hot carrots and stir until melted. Stir in remaining ingredients. Bake in a buttered casserole dish for 15 minutes at 400°. Reduce heat to 350° and bake an additional 30–45 minutes or until slightly browned.

I usually make ⅓ of this recipe and it takes only 20 minutes at 350° after 15 minutes at 400°. Serves 6.

St. Paul Cooks

Tennessee is "Musicland." Elvis Presley, the King of Rock and Roll, and W.C. Handy, the Father of the Blues, both chose Memphis as their home. Presley, Johnny Cash, Jerry Lee Lewis, Carl Perkins, Roy Orbison, Charlie Rich, and Conway Twitty all recorded at Sun Records in Memphis and grew to international fame. And, of course, Nashville is Music City—home to the Grand Ole Opry and hundreds of country music stars.

Pluto Pups

12 frankfurters
12 wooden skewers
½ cup flour
½ teaspoon sage
½ cup cornmeal

1 teaspoon salt
2 teaspoons sugar
1 tablespoon baking powder
1 cup milk
2 eggs

Insert skewer in end of each frankfurter. Steam for 7 minutes. Cool. Sift dry ingredients together. Beat milk and eggs together and blend well into dry ingredients. Dip franks in batter and fry in deep fat at 350° until brown. Wrap handle in paper napkin. Serve at once.

Kountry Kooking

Smoky Barbecued Meatloaf

MEATLOAF:
1 pound ground lean beef
1 egg
1 cup low-sodium bread crumbs

1 medium onion, chopped
Pepper to taste

SAUCE:
½ cup unsalted tomato purée
3 tablespoons firmly packed
  brown sugar
1 tablespoon low-sodium
  prepared mustard

½ cup vinegar
1 teaspoon liquid smoke
1 teaspoon Mrs. Dash Original
  Blend

Mix ingredients for Meatloaf with half the Sauce mixture. Shape into 2 loaves and place in a 12-inch iron skillet. Pour remaining Sauce over meatloaves and bake at 325° for 1 hour. Yields 6 servings.

Tip: Cooking in iron utensils increases iron content of food. Iron is a nutrient often deficient in our diet.

Change of Seasons

More than 900 miles of hiking trails meander through the 500,000 acres of wilderness in the Great Smoky Mountains National Park. The Cherokee Indians called this land Shaconage—"Place of the Blue Smoke."

Barbecued Roast

1 (3- to 4-pound) beef roast	2 cloves garlic, minced
2 teaspoons salt	2 tablespoons brown sugar
¼ teaspoon pepper	½ teaspoon mustard
3 tablespoons fat	¼ cup lemon juice
½ cup water	¼ cup ketchup
1 (8-ounce) can tomato sauce	¼ cup vinegar
3 medium onions, sliced thin	1 tablespoon Worcestershire

Rub meat with salt and pepper, and brown in fat; add water, tomato sauce, onions, and garlic. Cover and cook over low heat on top of stove for 1½ hours. Combine remaining ingredients and pour over meat. Cover and continue cooking about one hour or until tender.

Note: Let your roast stand at room temperature about one hour before cooking.

Parties & Pleasures

FROM GWEN'S ROAD DIARY:
Coming from Kentucky in January of 1987, when we were scheduled to be in Knoxville the next morning, we opted to take the map's shortest distance to try to beat the upcoming snow storm. But that short distance was over Jellico Mountain! (Two Deep South girls are not experienced in driving in snow *or* mountains.) When we saw a truck starting up the mountain, that triggered our decision . . . "If he can do it, we can do it," and we rationalized that it was only 24 miles. We were barely into our ascent when the snow began to come down heavily. Our visibility was totally white, and our headlights made spiraling funnels of the blinding snow. We were on the edge of our seats knowing we couldn't stop, praying so hard . . . when suddenly we could see the faint red tail lights of that miraculous truck! Staying within sight of him and utilizing his ruts to feel the road, we somehow made it! God bless you, man-in-truck, wherever you are. We'd like to see Jellico Mountain on a clear day . . . it's no doubt beautiful.

Texas

CAPITAL: *Austin*

NICKNAME: *The Lone Star State*

*T*he Lone Star State has it all, from tall sky-scrapers to wide-open prairie land, from rugged cowboys to delicate debutantes, from haute cuisine to open-pit barbecue. With their own brand of cooking, Texans are particularly famous for Tex-Mex and for chili, which is their state dish. Austin is considered the "eat, drink, and be merry" city because it has the most restaurants and bars per capita than any other city in America. The "bigger-thans" of Texas could go on for pages. It has more farms than any other state, and the King Ranch is bigger than Rhode Island! You can drive for miles and miles and miles and still be in Texas. In fact, El Paso is closer to California than it is to Dallas. Texans are big on letting food liven up their taste buds . . . for goodness sakes, spice it up with some sweet Texas onions and a few peppers! Yee haw!

Brisket Rub

This recipe comes from Fritz's Capitol City Catering of Austin. When these people cook, they really cook. The following recipe makes enough rub for 21 briskets. Don't despair, though; the leftover rub stores well.

1 cup sugar
1 cup salt
½ cup chili powder

¼ cup garlic powder
½ cup black pepper

Combine all ingredients and store in a tightly covered container. Rub 2½ tablespoons of mixture onto brisket prior to cooking. Makes about 3½ cups.

Texas Barbecue

Taco Salad

A great and relatively thinning luncheon dish—a nice change from chef's salad.

1 pound lean ground beef
1 tablespoon chili powder
½ teaspoon cumin
1 clove garlic, pressed
½ teaspoon oregano
¼ teaspoon dry red pepper

2 tomatoes, chopped
½ cup onion, chopped
1 cup grated sharp cheese
1½ heads iceberg lettuce
1½ cups crushed Fritos
2 avocados, peeled and sliced

DRESSING:
2 tablespoons lemon juice

½ cup mayonnaise

Sauté beef with seasonings until done. Drain very well. Keep at room temperature. Combine and toss all ingredients with Dressing.

It's a Long Way to Guacamole

King Ranch or Mexican Chicken

1 dozen tortillas
Chicken broth (about ¼ cup)
1 cup diced onions
1 (4-ounce) can diced green chiles
1 (10¾-ounce) can cream of mushroom soup
1 (10¾-ounce) can cream of chicken soup

1 tablespoon chili powder
1 (2- to 3-pound) fryer, cooked and diced
¾ pound Cheddar cheese, grated
1 (10-ounce) can Ro-Tel tomatoes and green chiles, or 1 can tomato soup mixed with 1 tablespoon chili powder

Line a large baking dish with a layer of tortillas. Sprinkle with chicken broth. Sauté onions and green chiles and add soups and chili powder. Pour a layer of soup mixture over tortillas, then a layer of chicken, then a layer of cheese. Repeat layers. Pour Ro-Tel tomatoes (or tomato soup) over top and sprinkle with chili powder. If a milder taste is desired, you may use ½ can Ro-Tel tomatoes and ½ can plain tomatoes. Bake 1 hour in 350° oven. Serve with vegetable salad and Mexican rice or beans.

Decades of Mason County Cooking

 With over 825,000 acres, the King Ranch is one of the largest in the United States and covers all of one, and part of three Texas counties.

Easy Nacho Spread

1 (8-ounce) carton avocado dip
1 bunch green onions, chopped,
  tops included, or 1 (4-ounce)
  can chopped green chiles
3 peeled and chopped tomatoes
1 (8-ounce) jar picante sauce
1 (8-ounce) carton sour cream

1½ cups shredded Monterey
  Jack or Cheddar cheese
1 (10½-ounce) can bean dip
  (optional)
1 (4½-ounce) can chopped
  ripe olives (optional)

Layer ingredients in bowl or 8x8-inch dish in order listed. Serve with tortilla chips.

    If you want to make your own avocado dip, mash 4 or 5 avocados with ⅛ teaspoon garlic powder, ⅛ teaspoon garlic salt, 1 tablespoon lemon juice, and 2 tablespoons mayonnaise.

Easy Does It Cookbook

Carmelitas

32 light candy caramel squares
¼ cup half-and-half and/or
  or evaporated milk
1 (16-ounce) roll chocolate chip
  refrigerator cookies

1 (6-ounce) package milk or
  semisweet chocolate pieces
½ cup chopped pecans

Melt caramels and cream in top of double boiler. Slice cookie dough ¼ inch thick and place in greased 8 or 9-inch square pan. Bake at 375° for 20–25 minutes. They will be puffy when removed from oven. Cool slightly. Sprinkle chocolate pieces over warm cookies. Carefully spread caramel mixture over top of chocolate, then sprinkle with chopped pecans. Refrigerate 1–2 hours. Yields 36 squares.

Ready to Serve

After many years of Spain and then Mexico's rule, some Texans demanded independence—and the Texas Revolution began, leading to the Battle of the Alamo. There on March 6, 1836, a small band of Texans held out for 13 days before falling to Mexico's forces. Among the casualties were non-Texans, Davy Crockett and Jim Bowie. That defeat inspired others to "Remember the Alamo" and win Texas independence.

Peach Cobbler

A true West Texas version. Ranch cooks, usually cooking with canned fruit, could not get along without this recipe and the variations listed below.

2 cups fresh sliced peaches
2 cups sugar, divided
6 tablespoons margarine
¼ teaspoon salt

1 teaspoon baking powder
¾ cup flour
¾ cup milk

Mix peaches and 1 cup sugar together and let stand while making batter. Melt margarine in a 2-quart casserole. In a bowl, mix remaining 1 cup sugar, salt, baking powder, and flour. Beat in milk until lumps are gone. Pour batter on melted margarine. Do not stir. Spoon peaches over top of batter. Again, do not stir. Bake at 350° for 45 minutes or until golden brown.

Almost any canned, frozen, or fresh fruit may be used. If canned or presweetened fruit is used, omit the cup of sugar that fruit stands in. Also, be sure to drain the juice. Serves 6.

San Angelo Junior League Cookbook

Barbara Harris' Chicken Fried Steak

2½ pounds round steak,
  tenderized and cut into 6
  equal pieces
2 cups buttermilk (in a pie
  plate)

2 cups flour, seasoned to taste
  (in separate plate)
Vegetable shortening, for frying

Dip each steak in buttermilk; dredge in flour; repeat process. Cook in deep fryer at 350° until golden brown, about 4–5 minutes. Serve immediately, drowned in wonderful creamy gravy! Serves 6.

Great Flavors of Texas

Tortilla Crisps

These little crisps may be used with soups and salads or made into a wonderful appetizer when spread with a cheese topping and reheated.

6 flour tortillas (10-ounce package)
½ cup corn oil

½ cup butter or margarine, melted

Cut each tortilla into 8 pie-shaped pieces. Place in a medium mixing bowl. Combine oil and butter or margarine, pour over tortilla pieces, and soak for 20–30 minutes. Place pieces on a cookie sheet and bake at 400° for 10–12 minutes.

CHEESE TOPPING
3 ounces shredded Cheddar cheese
3 tablespoons chopped ripe olives

¼ cup finely chopped green onions
½ cup mayonnaise

Combine ingredients, spread on Tortilla Crisps, and bake at 400° for 3–4 minutes. Yields 48 pieces.

More Tastes & Tales

Gourmet Chili

Excellent and very easy.

1½ pounds ground beef, salted
1 large onion, chopped
4 strips bacon, fried crisp and diced
2 (4-ounce) cans mushroom stems and pieces
1 (1-pound) can tomatoes
1 (8-ounce) can tomato juice

1 (1-pound) can pinto beans
1 (1-pound) can red beans
1 (1-pound) can chili beans
1 package Williams Chili Seasoning
¼ cup parsley flakes
¼ cup chopped chives

Brown beef with onion and bacon. Add mushrooms. Add remaining ingredients. Cook slowly for 1½ hours. Serves 8–10.

Amarillo Junior League Cookbook

Chile Rellenos Quiche

Add Egg Topping for puffy effect for a special "fiesta."

1 (9-inch) pastry shell
2 cups grated Monterey Jack
cheese, divided
1 (4-ounce) can diced green
chiles

4 eggs
1 cup half-and-half
¼ teaspoon pepper
Taco sauce

Bake frozen or prepared pastry shell at 475° for 5 minutes. Sprinkle one cup cheese in the partially baked crust. Layer with half the chiles. Sprinkle with remaining one cup cheese. Add remaining chiles, more if you like it hot. Mix together eggs, half-and-half, and pepper and pour over chiles. Bake in a preheated 375° oven for 30 minutes. Serve with taco sauce. Or, add Egg Topping, bake, and serve. Yields 6 servings.

EGG TOPPING:

In small bowl, beat until very stiff 2 egg whites. Fold in 2 egg yolks, slightly beaten, just until blended. Spoon over baked quiche. Be sure to seal topping to edge of crust. Return to oven and bake at 375° for 15 minutes or until golden brown.

Calf Fries to Caviar

FROM GWEN'S ROAD DIARY:
In January of '85, snow was coming down lightly in San Antonio—a rarity—but we simply couldn't leave without seeing the Alamo. The snow got heavier by the minute. There wasn't much traffic because anybody with any sense was staying home. We were able to park right across from the whitening Alamo. But when we stepped out into the empty cold setting, we took one look, got right back into the van, and said, "Forget the Alamo," and then laughed about the irony of that statement for a lot of careful miles.

Utah

CAPITAL: *Salt Lake City*

NICKNAME: *The Beehive State*

Utah is a land like no other. There are so many fun-to-explore national and state parks. Called "the rooftop of the United States," the average elevation of the tallest peaks in each of Utah's counties is 11,222 feet—higher than any other state. Amazing that you can be trekking in snow on Snow Bird Mountain in the morning, and that afternoon wade in the Great Salt Lake—and you'll burn your feet on the sand getting to it (we did!). At the Bonneville Salt Flats, you can see the curvature of the earth over dry land. And though it is mostly rocky, there are lots of trees. The Jardine Juniper tree in Logan Canyon is said to be the oldest living tree in the Rocky Mountains—about 1,500 years old! The Mormons settled in Utah in 1847 and brought their strong family values—and that always includes good cooking. Now world-renowned, the Mormon Tabernacle Choir began as a small choir that sang on what is now Temple Square in Salt Lake City. Utahns have a strong sense of state pride and desire to preserve the past . . . all the way back to dinosaur bones.

Great Salt Lake Taffy

Grandma used to say, "Cook it on a dry day, use a heavy pan, do not stir while cooking, don't undercook, and butter your hands."

1½ cups white vinegar
3 cups white sugar
¼ teaspoon baking soda

1 tablespoon butter or
   margarine

Combine vinegar and sugar in a heavy pan until sugar is dissolved. Cook over medium heat to soft-crack stage (between 270° and 290° on candy thermometer). Do not undercook. Remove from heat and add baking soda and butter. Pour onto greased platter to cool. When cool enough to handle, grease or butter hands, and pull until white. Cut into pieces and wrap in wax paper.

Recipes Thru Time

Meat Loaf in an Onion

4 large onions, peeled
1 pound lean ground beef
1 egg
¼ cup cracker crumbs
¼ cup tomato sauce
½ teaspoon salt
⅛ teaspoon pepper
½ teaspoon dry mustard

Cut off root at the bottom end of the onion so that removal of the center is easy. Cut onions in half horizontally and remove center part of onion, leaving a ¾-inch thick shell. The removed center of the onion can be diced and combined with ingredients or used later.

In a 1-gallon plastic zipper bag, combine ground beef, egg, cracker crumbs, tomato sauce, salt, pepper, and dry mustard, and mix by squeezing. Divide meat mixture into 4 portions and roll into balls. Place in the center of the 4 onion halves. Put onions back together. Wrap each onion in foil. Cook over a bed of hot coals for 15–20 minutes per side or in 350° oven for 45–50 minutes, or until ground beef and onions are cooked. Serves 4 as lunch or dinner.

Recipes for Roughing It Easy

Quilter's Potato Salad

Served frequently in women's homes when they came to quilt or sew carpet rags.

3 large potatoes
3 hard-cooked eggs, chopped
¼ cup minced onion
Salt and pepper

Cook potatoes in their jackets until tender, then cool, peel, and dice into ½-inch squares. Add eggs, onion, salt and pepper to taste.

DRESSING:
1 teaspoon dry mustard
1 teaspoon salt
3 tablespoons sugar
2 eggs
3 tablespoons melted butter
½ cup hot vinegar
1 cup heavy cream, whipped

Combine mustard, salt, and sugar. Add freshly beaten eggs with melted butter and hot vinegar. Cook in double boiler until thick. Chill. Combine with whipped cream and fold gently into remaining ingredients. Makes 6 servings.

Recipes Thru Time

Ken's Apricot Almond Chicken

This is a delicious recipe.

1 pound bacon, ¼ inch sliced
2 cups diced onions
3 cloves garlic, diced
6–8 skinless, boneless chicken
  breasts
1 teaspoon mustard powder
1 (48-ounce) jar apricot or
  orange marmalade
1 (6-ounce) container frozen
  orange juice concentrate

1 (6-ounce) package sliced
  almonds
2 tablespoons Worcestershire
  (optional)
2 tablespoons onion powder
1 tablespoon garlic powder
Pinch of chili powder

With 12 coals on the bottom and 12 on top of a 12-inch Dutch oven, cook bacon. (Coals are usually ready to use when they are mostly gray in color.) Remove grease and sauté onions and garlic for 3 minutes. Add chicken and brown. Add all other ingredients, stirring from the bottom to mix bacon, garlic, and onion. Cover and cook until done. Stir occasionally to keep ingredients mixed. Cook for approximately 30 minutes.

A Complete Guide to Dutch Oven Cooking

Utah's Famous Green Jell-O with Cheese

Mormons, for some unknown reason, have long been known for their consumption of Jell-O, especially green Jell-O. It has become such a tradition in the state, that Utah has named it their official food.

½ cup crushed pineapple
1½ cups water, divided
⅔ cup sugar

1 (3-ounce) package lime Jell-O
1 cup grated cheese
1 cup whipped cream

Mix pineapple, ½ cup water, and sugar. Boil remaining 1 cup water; add lime Jell-O to dissolve. Add pineapple mixture to Jell-O; chill and let set until wobbly. Add grated cheese and whipped cream and mix. Chill until set.

A Mormon Cookbook

Chicken Flips

FILLING:

¼ cup chopped onion
¼ cup sliced celery
2 tablespoons margarine
1 (10¾-ounce) can cream of
  chicken soup

¼ cup milk
2 cups diced chicken

In a small saucepan, cook onion and celery in margarine until tender. Add soup and milk. Stir in chicken. Heat through.

BATTER:

2 eggs, beaten
¼ cup flour
2 tablespoons Parmesan cheese
1 teaspoon chives

1 teaspoon parsley flakes
Dash salt and pepper
2 cups shredded zucchini,
  drained

In medium bowl, combine eggs, flour, cheese, chives, parsley, salt and pepper. Add zucchini and mix well. Drop Batter on griddle in large spoonfuls; flatten slightly. Cook on both sides until brown. Spoon on Filling and fold over.

How to Enjoy Zucchini

Roasted Leg of Lamb with Raspberry Glaze

1 (5- to 6-pound) leg of lamb
2 cloves garlic, slivered
⅓ cup seedless red raspberry jam (reserve 2 tablespoons for sauce)
3 tablespoons dry white wine

2 teaspoons Dijon mustard
¼ teaspoon rosemary leaves
¼ teaspoon crushed black pepper
1 cup beef broth
1 tablespoon cornstarch

Using the tip of a knife, make small slits evenly over leg of lamb and insert garlic slivers into each. In small bowl, mix together jam, wine, mustard, rosemary leaves, and pepper. Brush lamb with ¼ cup sauce mixture and place fat-side-up in roasting pan. Bake at 350° for 20–25 minutes per pound for medium rare (160° internal temperature). For more well-done meat, add 5 minutes per pound. Pour remaining sauce over lamb during last 40 minutes of cooking time. Remove lamb to warm platter and let stand 15 minutes.

Meanwhile, pour lamb drippings into saucepan. Remove excess grease. Mix broth, cornstarch, and reserved 2 tablespoons red raspberry jam, and whisk into drippings. Cook over medium heat, continuing to whisk until sauce thickens. Serve gravy hot with sliced lamb. Makes 6–8 servings.

Favorite Recipes from Utah Farm Bureau Women

Strawberries Divine

1 (8-ounce) package cream cheese, softened
3 tablespoons powdered sugar
2 tablespoons orange juice

1 quart fresh strawberries, washed, dried, stems on
Strawberry or mint leaves for garnish

Beat cream cheese until fluffy. Add powdered sugar and orange juice. Fill a cake decorator tube with mixture. From the point, slit each berry into quarters (do not cut through the stem bottom of the berry). Pipe cream cheese mixture into each berry. Arrange on a serving tray and garnish with strawberry or mint leaves.

A Pinch of Salt Lake

Vermont

CAPITAL: *Montpelier*

NICKNAME: *The Green Mountain State*

Though small in total area, picturesque Vermont is big on culture and community values. Montpelier, its capital city, is the smallest in the United States. Driving in and out of small townships separated by countless shades of nature's greenery in between gave us a feeling of calm and peace. The true-to-life paintings at the Norman Rockwell Museum of Vermont in Rutland enhanced our vision of small town America. Vermont's roadside farms—we stopped at several—are so much a part of the landscape that they provide a sense of place and an important connection to the land and heritage. America's largest producer of maple syrup, and known for its dairy industry—especially its wonderful cheeses Vermont also produces substantial crops of Macintosh apples, potatoes, eggs, honey, and lots of other vegetables. No wonder the New England Culinary Institute chose to locate there!

Amaretto Cheesecake Cookies

1 cup all-purpose flour	¼ cup granulated sugar
⅓ cup packed brown sugar	1 egg
6 tablespoons butter, softened	4 tablespoons amaretto
1 (8-ounce) package cream	½ teaspoon vanilla
cheese, softened	4 tablespoons chopped almonds

In a large mixing bowl, combine flour and brown sugar. Cut in butter until mixture forms fine crumbs. Reserve one cup crumb mixture for topping. Press remainder over bottom of ungreased 8-inch-square baking pan. Bake for 12–15 minutes at 350° or until lightly browned.

In mixer bowl, thoroughly cream together cream cheese and granulated sugar. Add egg, amaretto, and vanilla; beat well. Spread batter over partially baked crust. Combine almonds with reserved crumb mixture; sprinkle over batter. Bake for 20–25 minutes. Cool and cut into squares. Yields 16 cookies.

Dining on Deck

Buttery Waffles

So delicious with Vermont maple syrup.

4 eggs
2 cups all-purpose flour
1 teaspoon salt
1 teaspoon baking soda

1 teaspoon baking powder
1 cup milk
1 cup sour cream
1 cup butter, melted

Preheat waffle iron. Beat eggs until light. Sift together flour, salt, baking soda, and baking powder. Mix milk and sour cream. Add flour mixture and milk mixture alternately to beaten eggs, beginning and ending with flour mixture. Add melted butter and blend thoroughly.

For each waffle, pour batter into center of lower half of waffle iron until it spreads to one inch from edge—about ½ cup. Lower iron cover on batter; cook as manufacturer directs, or until waffle iron stops steaming. Carefully loosen edge of waffle with fork; remove.

Cool. Place wax paper between waffles. Freeze in airtight container. To serve, remove from freezer and toast until heated through.

Dining on Deck

Vermont's sugar maple trees yield their harvest in late winter when the days are warmer, but the nights are still cold. Four maple trees will yield 30–40 gallons of sweet, water-like sap that boils down to make one gallon of maple syrup.

Vermont Turkey and Broccoli Puff

SHERRY CHEDDAR SAUCE:

¼ cup butter
¼ cup flour
1 cup light cream
½ cup sherry

1 teaspoon salt
½ teaspoon basil
1 cup grated Vermont sharp
   Cheddar cheese

Melt butter in saucepan, add flour, and stir to combine. Stir in cream, sherry, salt, and basil, and cook over low heat, stirring, until thick. Stir in cheese until melted.

1 head broccoli, flowerets and
  stems
6 baked puff pastry squares
Fresh spinach leaves

Sliced turkey
12 slices Vermont sharp
  Cheddar cheese

Steam broccoli flowerets and stems (cut into diagonal slices ¼ inch thick) until tender. Mix the broccoli into the sauce and keep warm over low heat.

Split baked puff pastry squares and layer on the bottom half of each, in order: fresh spinach leaves, sliced turkey, ½ cup broccoli in sauce, 2 slices Vermont sharp Cheddar cheese. Heat under a broiler or in a hot oven to melt cheese. Cover with top of puff and serve immediately. Serves 6.

Peter Christian's Favorites

Stuffed Acorn Squash

4 medium acorn squash
1 pound mushrooms, chopped
2 cups chopped onions
2 garlic cloves, mashed
½ cup minced fresh parsley

1 teaspoon dried basil
4 tablespoons dry white wine
1½ cups wild brown rice
  blend, cooked
Pepper, paprika, parsley

Cut squash in half lengthwise. Remove seeds and bake for 30–35 minutes at 350°. Meanwhile, sauté mushrooms, onions, and garlic in a lightly oiled skillet until ingredients are lightly browned. Combine with herbs, wine, and cooked rice. Set aside.

Remove pulp from cooked squash and transfer to a large mixing bowl. Blend in the vegetable-rice mixture and spoon into each squash shell. Sprinkle with freshly ground black pepper, paprika, and a little more parsley. Bake at 350° for 25–30 minutes, or until heated through. Makes 8 servings.

The Chef's Palate Cookbook

Pumpkin-Lentil Soup

In the early 1960s, I introduced Pumpkin Soup to our family at the Thanksgiving table. I brought it to the table in a scooped-out pumpkin used as a tureen. The children loved the idea and everyone enjoyed the soup. The lentils in combination with the pumpkin add another dimension for taste and nutrition.

2–4 tablespoons unsalted butter
  or olive oil
2 large onions, diced
1 rib celery, sliced
1 carrot, sliced
½ cup lentils, rinsed in water
5 cups chicken stock
1½ cups cooked or canned
  pumpkin

¼ teaspoon marjoram
⅛ teaspoon thyme
¼ teaspoon freshly ground
  pepper
Dash of Tabasco
1 cup half-and-half (optional)
Salt to taste

Melt butter or heat oil in a soup kettle. Add onions and cook until lightly colored but not browned. Add celery and carrot; cook for another minute. Stir in lentils and chicken stock. Add pumpkin, herbs, pepper, and Tabasco. Simmer about one hour.

Allow to cool, then purée in food processor. At this time, the soup can be refrigerated for up to 3 days or frozen for up to 2 months. Add half-and-half and reheat the soup before serving. Adjust seasoning. Serves 8–10.

Variations: To use the pumpkin as a tureen, cut across 2 inches below the top. Scoop out seeds and pulp. Warm pumpkin in a 300° oven for 5 minutes before filling with soup. Use pumpkin top as a cover.

The Best from Libby Hillman's Kitchen

Cider Rice Pilaf

3 tablespoons butter
1 cup white or brown rice
Salt and pepper, to taste
½ cup chopped onion
¾ cup chopped celery

1 teaspoon grated orange peel
¼ cup minced parsley, divided
¼ teaspoon dried rosemary or
  ¾ teaspoon fresh
1¾ cups apple cider

Melt butter in skillet. Add rice and stir until golden. Add salt, pepper, onion, celery, and orange peel. Sauté for 5 minutes. Add half the parsley and all the rosemary.

In a separate pan, bring cider to a boil, then stir into rice. Cover skillet and cook over low heat about ½ hour for white rice, or an hour for brown rice. Serve sprinkled with remaining parsley. Serves 4.

Vermont Kitchens Revisited

Charlie's Cuckoo's Nest

Named by one of our guests...is one of Charlie's big breakfast favorites!

French bread (thinly sliced)	**Vermont Cheddar cheese,**
2 eggs	**shredded**
⅓ cup milk	**Butter**

Butter an 8-ounce round ramekin. Fan thin slices of yesterday's French bread (overlapping slightly) on bottom of ramekin. Pour over the bread a mixture of eggs and milk. Sprinkle generously with cheese and dot with butter. Cover tightly with clear wrap and refrigerate overnight.

Bake at 375° for 20–25 minutes. Serve with cooked bacon criscrossed on top of "nest." Serves one. Adjust the recipe to serve as many as you wish.

From the Inn's Kitchen

Potage de Vermont

This smooth and creamy soup does justice to our wonderful Vermont Cheddar cheese. Although I always served it as a first course, it would make a delicious dinner of its own, accompanied by a loaf of crusty bread and a simple salad.

½ cup chopped carrots	**3 cups grated Vermont Cheddar**
½ cup chopped onion	**cheese**
½ cup chopped fresh dill weed	**2 cups half-and-half**
½ cup chopped celery	**Salt and freshly ground white**
2 tablespoons sweet butter	**pepper to taste**
5 tablespoons unbleached	**Toasted sesame seeds for**
white flour	**garnish**
5 cups chicken stock	

Sauté carrots, onion, dill, and celery in butter in a large saucepan. Sprinkle in flour one tablespoon at a time, stirring after each addition.

Add stock. Bring to a boil over medium heat, and cook for about 5 minutes. Strain out the vegetables, purée them in a food processor fitted with a steel blade, then return puréed vegetables to stock. Continue to cook over medium heat until soup boils, then reduce heat and let it simmer slowly for 15 minutes. Add grated cheese, stirring constantly with a large wire whisk until it is melted. Slowly add half-and-half and stir until well blended. Add salt and pepper to taste. Serve at once garnished with toasted sesame seeds. Serves 8.

Tony Clark's New Blueberry Hill Cookbook

Virginia

CAPITAL: *Richmond*

NICKNAME: *The Old Dominion State*

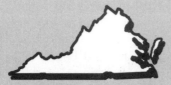

*V*irginia is for lovers—for lovers of nature, history, mountains, beaches . . . and most definitely, for lovers of good food. The history of the Old Dominion is so well preserved that one seems to walk around with an almost overwhelming pride that here is where our country began . . . the land our forefathers lived on, planted on, fought on, and died on. And meanwhile, our foremothers were feeding, clothing, birthing, and generally doing whatever needed to be done. Fortunately, they recorded things. *The Virginia House-wife* is considered by many to be the first regional American cookbook published in America. Jamestown was the first English settlement in America and was also the first capital of Virginia. In this "birthplace of a nation," eight presidents were born: Washington, Jefferson, Madison, Monroe, Harrison, Tyler, Taylor, and Wilson, and all but Harrison are buried there.

Spicy Raisin Sauce for Ham

1 cup sugar
½ cup water
1 cup raisins
2 tablespoons butter or
  margarine
3 tablespoons vinegar
½ tablespoon Worcestershire

½ teaspoon salt
¼ teaspoon ground cloves
Ground mace (few grains)
Black pepper (few dashes)
1 (10-ounce) jar apple currant
  jelly

Cook sugar and water together 5 minutes, stirring. Add remaining ingredients. Serve in sauce boat with your holiday ham.

The Enlightened Titan

Strawberry Soufflé

Take one quart of fresh strawberries, mash them through a colander, and add one cup sugar and beaten egg whites of five eggs; place in buttered dish. Sprinkle sugar over top; bake slowly (325°) for ½ hour. Serve with cream sauce.

Chesapeake Bay Country

Microwave Squash and Pepper Toss

½ teaspoon dried whole basil	2 pounds yellow squash,
¼ teaspoon dried oregano	cut into slices
¼ teaspoon thyme	1 large onion, chopped
½ teaspoon salt	1 clove garlic, minced
¼ teaspoon pepper	1 sweet red pepper, cut into
1 tablespoon red wine vinegar	strips
2 tablespoons water	2 tablespoons olive oil

Combine first 7 ingredients in a shallow 2½-quart casserole. Add squash. Cover with heavy plastic wrap. Microwave on HIGH for 3–4 minutes. Let stand, covered, 3–4 minutes. Add onion, garlic, sweet pepper, and olive oil; toss gently. Cover and microwave on HIGH for 3 minutes. Yields 6–8 servings.

Think Healthy

The world-famous Smithfield Hams are cut from peanut-fed hogs, then dry salt smoked, a technique learned from the Indians. In 1902, P. D. Gwaltney, Jr., insured a 20-year-old cured ham against fire or theft for $1,000. It is still edible, though it has never been refrigerated. It sports a brass collar that says, "Mr. Gwaltney's Pet Ham." You can view the ham at the Isle of Wight Museum in Smithfield.

Apple Blueberry Crisp

3 cups sliced tart apples
3 cups blueberries
Brown sugar to taste
1 cup flour
¾ cup sugar

1 teaspoon baking powder
¾ teaspoon salt
1 egg
⅓ cup butter, melted
½ teaspoon cinnamon

Grease baking dish and add apples, blueberries, and brown sugar to taste. Mix flour, sugar, baking powder, salt, and unbeaten egg with fork until mixture becomes crumbly. Sprinkle over fruit. Top with cooled, melted butter and sprinkle with cinnamon. Bake at 350° for ½ hour or until top is golden brown. Serve warm with cream. Serves 8.

Culinary Contentment

Ladyfinger Layer Cake

1 cup butter or margarine,
  softened
2 cups powdered sugar
4 eggs
1 (13½-ounce) can crushed
  pineapple, drained

1 cup chopped pecans
2 dozen ladyfingers, split
½ pint whipped cream or
  frozen whipped topping

Cream butter and sugar until light and fluffy. Beat in eggs one at a time. Add pineapple and nuts. Mix well. Line a loaf pan with wax paper. Pack the bottom of pan with split ladyfingers; fill in holes with broken pieces. Make a layer of pineapple filling. Continue until pan is full. Cover and refrigerate 6–8 hours or overnight.

Unmold onto cake plate and ice with whipped cream or thawed topping. Garnish with mint leaves and additional chopped pecans. Serves 8.

THE What In The World Are We Going To Have For Dinner?
COOKBOOK

Steeplechase racing in Virginia began when gentlemen in "pinks," after the fox hunt was over, had a friendly chase "to yon steeple." They cleared shrubbery and downed fences on their "natural course." Today steeplechasing is a spring family picnic affair surrounded by other outdoor activities.

Sweet Sour Baked Beans

8 bacon slices (or hamburger
  meat)
4 large onions
½–1 cup brown sugar
1 teaspoon dry mustard
½ teaspoon garlic powder
1 teaspoon salt
½ cup vinegar

2 (15-ounce) cans butter beans
1 (1-pound) can green lima
  beans
1 (1-pound) can dark red
  kidney beans
1 (1-pound 11-ounce) can New
  England-style baked beans

Pan-fry bacon until crisp; drain and crumble. Cut onions into rings. Put onions in skillet; add sugar, mustard, garlic powder, salt, and vinegar. Cook 20 minutes, covered. Add drained beans to onion mixture. Add bacon. Pour into 3-quart casserole. Bake at 350° for one hour.

Happy Times with Home Cooking

Charlotte

Stew any desired fruit until soft. Sweeten to taste and put in any spices you may wish. There should be 2 cups. Trim the crusts of slices of bread and cut bread to about the width of two fingers. Dip in butter and fry until a golden brown. Powder with sugar. Butter a round baking pan or glass dish and line with fried bread. Pour fruit in and set in a moderate oven (350°) for half an hour. Turn out on a platter. Set under broiler a moment to glaze the sugar.

Thomas Jefferson's Cook Book

Atlantic Stuffed Flounder Supreme

TOPPING:

24 Ritz Crackers
4 tablespoons butter

Tabasco to taste
Garlic powder to taste

Crumble crackers by hand or with food processor. Melt butter and stir into crackers. Season well with Tabasco and garlic powder; stir.

STUFFING:

3 onions
1 bell pepper
6 mushrooms
½ cup water
2 tablespoons vegetable oil

1 (8-ounce) package cream
  cheese, softened
8 slices toast
2 pounds flounder fillets
1 lemon

Slice onions, bell pepper, and mushrooms and place in a skillet. Add water and boil until most of the water is gone and vegetables begin to stick to surface of pan. Reduce heat, add vegetable oil, and stir-fry until vegetables have browned. Turn off heat, add cream cheese, and stir until well mixed. Slice or tear toast into pieces, add to pan, and stir until well mixed.

Preheat oven to 425°. Grease an 8x12-inch pan and spread Stuffing evenly in it. Layer flounder fillets over Stuffing. Sprinkle Topping evenly over fillets. Bake for 20 minutes or until Topping begins to brown. Putting the pan under the broiler very briefly will result in a nicely browned top. Serve with lemon wedges as an entrée or as a meal-in-itself. Other fish may be substituted for flounder. Do not overcook! Yields 4 servings.

The Great Taste of Virginia Seafood

Hospitable Grapes 'N Cheese Spread

16 ounces cream cheese,
  softened
3 tablespoons brandy
⅓ cup finely chopped chutney
¼ cup finely chopped green
  onions
¼ cup chopped toasted
  almonds

¼ teaspoon curry powder
1 cup green seedless grapes,
  halved
Green onion tops
Grapes in clusters

In large bowl, mix first 6 ingredients until well blended. Chill. When firm, mound in oval shape on serving tray, covering surface with grape halves, cut-side-down, to resemble a pineapple. Insert green onion tops at top of cheese mound. Surround with grape clusters and serve with crisp crackers. Yields 2½ cups.

Note: After cheese has been mounded, it can be refrigerated for up to 2 days before completing.

Tidewater on the Half Shell

FROM GWEN'S ROAD DIARY:
Over the years, we had a few flat tires, lost a few fan belts, had the air conditioning go out in steamy Florida, and once waited practically a precious day for an alternator in Virginia, but for all the miles we traveled, our car problems were remarkably few. Only once was our van broken into, or I should say attempted to be broken into. We got to the van in the hotel parking lot to find the entire lock had been pried out of the driver-side door. But the would-be robbers still couldn't get in! Problem was, neither could we. For the rest of that trip, we both had to get in on the passenger side and the driver had to crawl over the captain's seat. But we were so proud of our "fortress" van that we didn't mind at all.

Washington

CAPITAL: *Olympia*

NICKNAME: *The Evergreen State*

*W*hen you think of Washington food, you probably envision delicious, juicy apples—and with good reason. More than half of all apples grown in the United States for fresh eating comes from the seemingly endless acres of orchards in the foothills of the Cascade Mountains. The Evergreen State is also known for those wonderfully sweet Walla Walla onions. You can see most everything they produce displayed beautifully at Pike Place Market in Seattle. And the biggest coffee chain in the world, Starbucks, was founded right across the street. The Space Needle, built for the 1962 World's Fair, has a revolving restaurant at the top that was the first of its kind . . . the view is so incredible. Did you realize that Washington is the only state named after a president?

Puget Sound Oyster Bisque

The distinctive taste of oysters is a favorite of many Whidbey Island residents. This bisque makes the perfect starter to any entrée. It is equally suitable as a meal in itself when accompanied by a warm loaf of freshly baked bread.

¼ cup flour
¼ cup water
2 teaspoons salt
4 teaspoons Worcestershire
3 (10-ounce) jars shucked
  oysters

6 cups half-and-half
3 tablespoons margarine
Snipped parsley for garnish

In a large saucepan, whisk together flour, water, salt, and Worcestershire. Add oysters and their liquid. Depending on the size of the oysters, you may want to cut them into bite-size pieces. Cook over medium heat for 10 minutes, stirring constantly. The centers will be firm and the edge of oysters will curl a bit when cooked.

Add half-and-half and margarine and heat to boiling. Let the bisque stand at least 15 minutes to blend flavors. Garnish with snipped parsley if so desired. Makes 6 servings.

Simply Whidbey

Huckleberry Cream Tart

Wild huckleberries are full of flavor and combine well with cream cheese.

TART SHELL:

⅓ cup butter, softened
¼ cup granulated sugar

1 egg yolk
1 cup all-purpose flour

Preheat oven to 375°. Make tart shell by beating butter with sugar until light and fluffy. Add egg yolk and combine. Gradually beat in flour until just blended. Form dough into ball and press into bottom and sides of an ungreased 9- to 10-inch tart pan with removable bottom. Bake in oven for 10–12 minutes. Cool on rack.

FILLING:

3 cups huckleberries (fresh or
  frozen)
1 cup granulated sugar, mixed
  with ¼ cup all-purpose flour
1 tablespoon lemon juice
1 (3-ounce) package cream
  cheese, regular or light,
  softened

½ cup confectioners' sugar
½ teaspoon vanilla
½ cup heavy (whipping) cream

Combine huckleberries, sugar/flour mixture, and lemon juice in a medium saucepan and cook over medium or medium-high heat just long enough to thicken, 12–15 minutes, stirring frequently. (Turn down heat if mixture boils rapidly.) Berries should remain nearly whole. Let cool.

Beat cream cheese, confectioners' sugar, and vanilla in a medium bowl until light. Whip cream stiff in separate bowl and fold into cream cheese mixture. Spread evenly into baked Tart Shell and top with cooled huckleberry mixture. Chill in refrigerator for 2 hours or longer before serving. Serves 6–8.

Wandering & Feasting

Washington's Grand Coulee Dam on the Columbia River is four times larger than the Great Pyramid of Giza, one of the original seven wonders of the world. It is second only to the Great Wall of China as the largest man-made structure in the world. Washington leads the nation in production of hydroelectricity, tapping the waters of the Grand Coulee, Chief Joseph and John Day dams, along with additional dams on the Columbia River, the Snake River, and other rivers.

Salmon Dip

16 ounces smoked salmon
2 tablespoons lemon juice
1 bunch green onions, chopped
½ teaspoon liquid smoke
2–3 teaspoons horseradish

2 (8-ounce) packages cream
   cheese, softened
Pepper to taste
1–2 tablespoons mayonnaise
Red food coloring (optional)

Mix all ingredients in order given. Cover and refrigerate for 1–2 hours before serving. May be served with your favorite crackers or vegetables.

From Our Kitchen to Yours

Lopez Lamb Curry

Lopez Island offers serene, pastoral views of sheep grazing on gently sloping fields. Chicken or prawns can be substitutes for lamb in this aromatic, spicy dish. Serve on scented jasmine rice for additional flavor.

2 tablespoons extra virgin
   olive oil
½ cup chopped onion
2 cloves garlic, minced
1 tablespoon minced fresh
   ginger
1 tablespoon ground coriander
1 teaspoon ground cumin
½ teaspoon ground cardamom
½ teaspoon turmeric
¼ teaspoon cayenne pepper
1½ pounds lamb shoulder,
   cut into 1-inch pieces

1½ cups chicken stock
½ cup tomato purée
1 cinnamon stick
1 teaspoon salt
¼ teaspoon freshly ground
   pepper
6 cups cooked jasmine rice
½ cup yogurt
Toasted coconut, golden raisins,
   chutney, and peanuts for
   condiments

In a large frying pan, heat oil over medium heat. Sauté onion, garlic, and spices until onions are tender, about 5 minutes. Add lamb and sauté until lightly browned on all sides, 10–15 minutes. Add remaining ingredients, except rice, yogurt, and condiments. Cover pan with lid ajar and simmer curry for 30–40 minutes. While curry is cooking, prepare rice.

   Discard cinnamon stick. Just before serving, remove pan from heat and stir in yogurt. Serve curry over rice and offer bowls of condiments at the table. Serves 4.

San Juan Classics II Cookbook

Apple Blackberry Crisp

FILLING:

6 Golden Delicious apples

2 cups blackberries (fresh or
frozen)

½ cup sugar

2 tablespoons flour

Preheat oven to 350°. Butter a 9x13-inch baking dish. Peel and core apples. Cut into thin slices. Place apples in prepared dish. Top with blackberries. (If using frozen berries, do not thaw first.) Sprinkle with sugar and flour.

TOPPING:

½ cup rolled oats

½ cup flour

½ cup chopped nuts (optional)

⅓ cup butter, melted

⅓ cup brown sugar

1 teaspoon cinnamon

Combine oats, flour, nuts, butter, sugar, and cinnamon in a bowl till crumbly. Sprinkle Topping evenly over Filling. Bake till fruit is soft and bubbly and Topping is browned, 35–40 minutes. Serve warm, topped with ice cream or whipped cream. Serves 6.

Favorite Recipes from Our Best Cooks

Coming upon this huge troll unaware was quite a shock. The Fremont Troll has been lurking under the north end of the Aurora Bridge since 1990. He was sculpted by four Seattle area artists for the Fremont Arts Council. The 18-foot-high shaggy-haired troll glares southward with his shiny metal eye—possibly a hubcap—and in his left hand, he crushes an old-style Volkswagen beetle.

Roasting Walla Walla Sweets & Potatoes

3 large Walla Walla sweet onions
3–4 medium russet potatoes
2 tablespoons vegetable oil
Salt to taste
⅛ teaspoon black pepper

Halve each onion lengthwise through the top and root, then skin, peeling away any slippery membrane. Dig into center of each half with a metal spoon, and scoop out flesh, leaving a ½-inch-thick shell. Chop enough of the inner flesh to measure 2 cups and set aside. Scrub potatoes, peel, and cut enough of the potatoes into ¼- to ½-inch dices to make 4 cups. Heat oil in large skillet, adding chopped onion, and potatoes, salt and pepper. Sauté over medium-high heat, stirring occasionally, about 5 minutes until onion begins to soften.

Arrange 6 scooped-out halves in large greased baking dish. Spoon about ½ cup potato mixture into each onion shell, then arrange remaining potato mixture all around them in a layer no deeper than 1 inch. Bake in 375° oven for 1 hour, until potatoes are thoroughly cooked and deeply browned. Serves 6.

Washington Cook Book

Only onions grown in the Walla Walla Valley of southeast Washington and northeast Oregon can be called Walla Walla Sweet Onions, as protected by a Federal marketing order designating Walla Walla Sweet Onions as a unique variety and establishing a specific growing area for the crop.

Disgustingly Rich Potatoes

6 large Idaho potatoes
¾ cup butter or margarine,
  softened
2 teaspoons salt
1 teaspoon pepper

1 cup heavy cream
4 tablespoons butter or
  margarine
1 cup grated Cheddar or
  Gruyère cheese

Bake potatoes until soft. Split and scoop pulp into mixing bowl. (Leave as is—do not mash or chop.) Add softened butter, salt, pepper, and cream, mixing lightly. Transfer to flat baking dish. Dot with butter and sprinkle with cheese. Bake at 375° for at least 20 minutes.

Note: Half-and-half can be substituted for heavy cream.

Recipes from Our Friends

Halibut Amontillado

Halibut, being a more expensive fish, should be treated well! The crunchy texture of the hazelnuts is a perfect counterpoint to the smoothness of the mildly flavored cream sauce. Be sure to seek out "Amontillado" sherry as it retains its distinctive flavor even in the cooking.

½ cup flour
½ cup roasted and finely
  chopped hazelnuts
Salt and pepper to taste
2 (7-ounce) fresh halibut fillets
¼ cup olive oil

2 tablespoons diced shallots
½ cup Amontillado sherry
3 tablespoons heavy cream
¼ pound unsalted butter,
  cubed

Preheat oven to 375°. In a bowl, combine flour, hazelnuts, salt and pepper. Lightly moisten halibut fillets with cold water and press both sides of each fillet into flour/hazelnut mixture. Heat olive oil in skillet and brown fillets. After browning, transfer fillets to baking dish and bake in preheated oven for 10 minutes. While fillets are baking, prepare butter sauce.

In a small saucepan, combine shallots, sherry, and cream. Cook sauce, stirring constantly, and reduce by half. Remove from heat and whisk in cold butter. Remove fillets from oven, plate up, spoon sauce over halibut, and serve. Bon appétit! Serves 2.

La Conner Palates

West Virginia

CAPITAL: *Charleston*

NICKNAME: *The Mountain State*

On a trek through the Mountain State, you'll discover glistening lakes, towering mountains, rolling farmlands, historic battlegrounds, and coal mines in between. West Virginia is considered the southernmost northern state, and the northernmost southern state. They do a lot of home cookin'—you're as likely to get Poke Pickles and Pawpaw Pudding as Chicken Veronique! The first spa open to the public was at Berkeley Springs in 1756 (then, Bath, Virginia). The state was originally named Kanawha in 1861. Did you know that West Virginia has the most irregular boundary of any state? Or that the famous Hatfields and McCoys feuded here? Wild and wonderful—that's West Virginia!

Mom-Mom's Corn Fritters

1½ cups flour
2 tablespoons sugar
2 teaspoons baking powder
½ teaspoon salt
¼ cup milk

2 eggs
1 (16-ounce) can whole-kernel
  corn
1 tablespoon butter
Vegetable oil for frying

Place all ingredients, except oil, in medium bowl. With mixer, beat for 30 seconds. Stop and scrape bowl, then beat for 30 more seconds. Heat about 1½–2 inches of oil in a deep skillet to about 375°. Drop batter in hot oil one tablespoon at a time. Turn fritters once after they start to bubble and they are golden brown; continue frying on the other side. Drain on brown paper bag. Serve immediately with maple syrup. Yields 24 fritters.

Mom-Mom's Cookbook

Cranberry Apple Salad

Good for Thanksgiving and Christmas.

2 (1-pound) cans whole
  cranberries in sauce
2 cups boiling water
2 (3-ounce) packages
  strawberry gelatin
2 tablespoons lemon juice
½ teaspoon salt
1 cup mayonnaise
½ cup chopped walnuts
2 cups diced apples

Melt cranberry sauce over medium heat. Drain, saving the juice and berries separately. Mix together cranberry juice, boiling water, and gelatin. Stir until dissolved. Add lemon juice and salt. Chill until mixture mounds slightly on a spoon. Add mayonnaise; beat until fluffy and smooth. Fold in berries, nuts, and apples, and pour into a gelatin mold. Chill overnight. Makes 10–12 servings.

The Way Pocahontas County Cooks

Mountain Momma Mudslide

1 stick butter, softened
1 cup flour
1 cup chopped nuts
1 (8-ounce) package cream
  cheese, softened
1 cup powdered sugar
1 (12-ounce) carton Cool Whip,
  thawed, divided
1 (4-ounce) package chocolate
  instant pudding
1 (4-ounce) package
  butterscotch instant pudding
2 cups milk

Combine butter, flour, and nuts. Press into 9x13-inch pan. Bake 20 minutes at 350°; cool about 30 minutes. Combine cream cheese and powdered sugar, and beat till fluffy. Fold in ½ of Cool Whip; spread over crust. Combine puddings and milk; beat until stiff. Pour over cheese mixture; spread evenly. Spread remaining Cool Whip on top. Chill about 30 minutes. Serve.

Dutch Pantry Cookin'

West Virginia leads the nation in coal production. Coal occurs in 53 of its 55 counties. In West Virginia, 99% of the electricity comes from coal. More than 56% of the nation's electricity is generated from coal.

Luella's Blueberry Cake with Lemon Butter Sauce

This old-timey (sauce) recipe originally called for one cup butter and vinegar instead of lemon juice. If you're watching your fat intake, the cake tastes good by itself.

CAKE:

1 tablespoon butter	2 teaspoons baking powder
1 cup sugar	½ teaspoon salt
1 egg, beaten	1 cup milk
2 cups flour	2 cups fresh blueberries

Grease and flour a 9-inch-square cake pan. Cream butter and sugar. Add beaten egg into creamed mixture. Combine dry ingredients and add to egg mixture alternately with milk. Coat berries with a small amount of flour, then add to mixture. Bake at 375° for about 30 minutes.

LEMON BUTTER SAUCE:

2–4 tablespoons butter	Juice of 2 lemons
¾ cup sugar	Grated lemon rind
3 tablespoons cornstarch	1 teaspoon vanilla
1 cup water, divided	

Melt butter and stir in sugar. Mix cornstarch in with ½ cup cold water until dissolved. Add remaining water, lemon juice, and rind to melted butter mixture. Boil until clear. Take off heat and add vanilla. Pour over cake as you serve.

Take Two & Butter 'Em While They're Hot!

Mom's Shortcake

Prepare biscuit dough as suggested on Bisquick box, adding about ¼ cup sugar to every 2 cups of dough; knead, and divide in half. Generously butter a cookie sheet and your hands; spread half the dough very thinly on the cookie sheet, then spread on more butter. Butter your hands again and spread out the remaining dough on top of the first. Bake 8–10 minutes at 450°. Serve with sliced, sweetened strawberries, and whipped cream or milk.

Cakes...Cakes...and more Cakes

Shepherd's Pie

2½ pounds potatoes, peeled
and cooked
1–1½ cups sour cream
1 teaspoon salt
¼ teaspoon pepper
1 package frozen mixed
vegetables (may use frozen
vegetables of your choice)
2 pounds ground beef (chuck)

½ cup chopped onion
1 medium green pepper (or
red pepper), chopped
1 teaspoon garlic powder
1 (10¾-ounce) can cream of
mushroom soup, undiluted
½ cup milk
½ cup shredded Cheddar
cheese (or more)

Mash potatoes, adding sour cream, salt, and pepper. Set aside. Cook frozen vegetables according to directions on package. In a large skillet, cook beef, onion, and pepper until meat is brown and onion and pepper are tender. Drain mixture. Stir garlic powder into meat mixture. Add cream of mushroom soup, milk, and drained vegetables to meat. Mix well. Spread meat mixture into a 9x13x2-inch baking dish. Spread mashed potatoes over mixture. Bake for 30–35 minutes or until heated through. In the last 5 minutes of baking, sprinkle shredded cheese over potatoes and return to oven until cheese is melted. Serves 8–10.

Just Plain Country

Approximately 250,000 whitewater rafting enthusiasts raft West Virginia waters each year. It is no wonder that the first time the World Rafting Championships were held in North America, West Virginia was chosen as the location. The events were held on the New and Gauley rivers in Fayette and Nicholas counties in 2001.

Chocolate Cherry Bombs

1 cup margarine, softened
2 cups sugar
2 eggs
1 tablespoon vanilla extract
3 cups flour
½ teaspoon baking soda
½ teaspoon salt
½ teaspoon baking powder

1 cup baking cocoa
48 maraschino cherry halves
  (reserve juice)
1 (14-ounce) can sweetened
  condensed milk
2 cups chocolate chips
1 tablespoon maraschino
  cherry juice

Cream margarine, sugar, eggs, and vanilla in mixer bowl until light and fluffy. Add mixture of flour, baking soda, salt, baking powder, and cocoa; mix well. Shape into 1-inch balls. Place on ungreased cookie sheet. Bake at 350° for 12 minutes. Press cherry half into center of each cookie. Remove to wire rack.

Combine condensed milk, chocolate chips, and cherry juice in double boiler. Cook over hot water until smooth, stirring constantly. Frost warm cookies with chocolate mixture. Yields 48 cookies.

The Best of Wheeling

Ham Loaf

BASTING SAUCE:
½ cup brown sugar
½ cup hot water

1½ tablespoons mustard
2½ tablespoons vinegar

Combine all ingredients until brown sugar is dissolved.

HAM LOAF:
1 pound ground, smoked ham
1 pound ground pork
3 cups bread crumbs

1 cup milk
⅛ teaspoon pepper
2 eggs, beaten

Combine all ingredients; form into loaf and place in loaf pan or oblong baking pan. Baste Ham Loaf with Basting Sauce before and 2 or 3 times during baking. Bake in 350° oven for 1½ hours.

Our Best Home Cooking

West Virginia Apple
Black Walnut Cake

4 cups coarsely chopped raw apples	2 cups sifted all-purpose flour
2 cups sugar	1 teaspoon salt
3 eggs	2 teaspoons baking soda
¾ cup vegetable oil	1 teaspoon cinnamon
2 teaspoons vanilla	½ teaspoon nutmeg
	1 cup chopped black walnuts

Combine apples and sugar; let stand. Beat eggs slightly, then beat in oil and vanilla. Sift together flour, salt, baking soda, and spices. Stir in alternately apple mixture and dry ingredients. Add walnuts. Pour into greased and floured 9x13x2-inch baking pan. Bake at 350° for about an hour or until done. Cool, then cover with Lemon Butter Frosting.

LEMON BUTTER FROSTING:

4 tablespoons butter or margarine, softened	1 teaspoon lemon extract
3 cups confectioners' sugar	Few grains of salt
2 tablespoons lemon juice	1 or 2 tablespoons cold water

Cream butter; add sugar gradually, creaming thoroughly. Beat in lemon juice, lemon extract, salt, and enough water to make spreading consistency. Spread on cool cake. Makes 3½ cups frosting.

More than Beans and Cornbread

Wisconsin

CAPITAL: *Madison*

NICKNAME: *The Badger State*

Wisconsin is America's Dairyland. Some 79,000 farms produce millions of diary products. Known for its cheeses the world over, it is also known for its breweries. No surprise they have created some pretty tasty dishes with cheese and beer. Bring on the bratwurst and sauerbraten! The first ice cream sundae is said to have been concocted in Two Rivers in 1881, and two years later, the malted milk shake was created in Racine. Wisconsin has nearly 15,000 lakes. According to Native American legend, the Wisconsin Dells were formed by a giant serpent (or maybe glaciers). Their beloved Green Bay Packers have been NFL champions twelve times and have won three Super Bowl championships. The famous House on the Rock, built in the early 1940s, is perched on a 60-foot chimney of rock. Over 100 circuses originated in the Badger State. As we were told, "All you can imagine begins in Wisconsin."

Cheese Soup

1 cup finely chopped carrots
¼ cup finely chopped celery
¼ cup chopped onion
1¾ cups chicken broth
2 cups milk
¼ cup flour
Dash of paprika
1 cup shredded American or
   Cheddar cheese

In medium saucepan, combine carrots, celery, and onion. Add chicken broth; heat to boiling. Reduce heat; cover and simmer for 15 minutes. In a medium bowl, combine milk, flour, and paprika. Stir into broth mixture. Cook and stir until thickened and bubbly. Add cheese, stirring until melted.

A Taste of Christ Lutheran

Classic German Chocolate Pie

1 (9-inch) pie crust

FILLING:

4 ounces (1 bar) sweet cooking chocolate, chopped	¾ cup sugar
	2 tablespoons flour
⅓ cup butter, softened (no margarine please)	3 eggs, separated
	1 teaspoon vanilla extract

Preheat oven to 375°. In a large saucepan over low heat, melt chocolate and butter, stirring until smooth. Remove from heat. Add sugar, flour, egg yolks, and vanilla; stir until well blended. In small bowl, beat egg whites until stiff peaks form. Fold into chocolate mixture. Pour into pie crust-lined pan. Bake 24–30 minutes or until Filling is set. Remove from oven; cool while preparing Topping.

TOPPING:

½ cup sweetened condensed milk (not evaporated)	1 cup flaked coconut
	½ cup chopped pecans
1 egg	1 teaspoon vanilla extract

In small bowl, combine all Topping ingredients; blend well. Drop by teaspoonfuls over baked Filling; spread very carefully. Broil 6–8 inches from heat for 2–3 minutes or until coconut begins to brown. Watch carefully; do not burn crust. Cool on wire rack 30 minutes. Refrigerate for 2–3 hours before serving.

Cooking with Pride

Football Stew

This is a great company dish, because the oven does the cooking while you visit with your guests, and there are no dirty dishes in the sink.

2 cups tomato juice	1 onion, diced
2 tablespoons sugar	4 carrots, sliced
3 tablespoons tapioca	1 stalk celery, chopped
2 teaspoons salt	4 potatoes, cubed
1 pound beef stew meat	

Combine tomato juice, sugar, tapioca, and salt. Combine meat (do not brown) and vegetables. Top with tomato mixture, seal with aluminum foil, and bake 4 hours at 250°. Serves 4.

Note: I usually double or triple the recipe and use a broiler pan or large cake pan. Serve with fruit salad and rolls.

Foxy Ladies

Italian Tortoni

2 egg whites	¼ teaspoon almond extract
¼ teaspoon salt	½ cup blanched, toasted
4 tablespoons sugar	almonds, finely chopped, or
2 cups whipping cream	¼ cup almonds plus ¼ cup
½ cup sugar	macaroon crumbs
2 teaspoons vanilla	

Beat egg whites and salt. Beat 4 tablespoons sugar in gradually. Set aside. Whip cream; add ½ cup sugar, vanilla, and almond extract. Fold in egg white mixture and almonds or almond/macaroon mixture. Put into individual custard cup-size serving dishes and freeze. Let sit out of freezer about 15 minutes before serving. Makes 8 rich, elegant servings.

Marquette University High School Mother's Guild Cookbook

 Known as America's Dairyland, Wisconsin is the largest producer of milk, butter, and cheese in the nation. Monroe is called the Swiss Cheese Capital of the World. Area factories produce more than 55 million pounds of cheese each year.

Corned Beef in Round Rye

2 tablespoons minced onion
1 teaspoon dill weed
1¼ cups sour cream
1¼ cups mayonnaise
3 packages corned beef,
  snipped into small pieces
1 teaspoon Beau Monde
  seasoning
1 small round rye loaf

Mix and refrigerate all ingredients, except rye loaf, for 24 hours. Scoop out rye loaf and cut center into serving-size bites for the dip. Fill center of loaf with dip just before serving.

Picnics on the Square

Beer & Cheese Spread

Since the 1960s when it was brought to Kavanaughs', Madison, by a member of the staff, this spread has been featured at the restaurant and is a favorite of our guests.

2 cups shredded sharp
  Wisconsin Cheddar cheese
2 cups shredded Wisconsin
  Swiss cheese
1 teaspoon Worcestershire
½ teaspoon dry mustard
1 small clove garlic, minced
½–⅔ cup beer

Combine cheese, Worcestershire, mustard, and garlic. Beat in enough beer to make of spreading consistency. Serve on assorted crackers or rye bread. Yields 2 cups.

Our Best Cookbook 2

Wisconsin Whoppers

These are great high-energy cookies for trips or after skiing, skating, or other fun winter activities.

1¼ cups packed light brown
  sugar
¾ cup granulated sugar
⅔ cup butter, softened
1½ cups chunky peanut butter
3 eggs
6 cups rolled oats (not quick
  cooking)

2 teaspoons baking soda
1½ cups raisins or craisins
  (optional)
1 cup semisweet chocolate
  chips
4 ounces semisweet chocolate
  squares
½ teaspoon vanilla

With a mixer, cream sugars and butters about 3 minutes. Add eggs, one at a time. Beat one minute more. Add oats and baking soda. Mix in raisins, if desired, and chips. Shred the chocolate squares with a knife and mix into cookie batter. Add vanilla. Drop by ¼ measuring cup (or any desired size) onto cookie sheets. Flatten cookies with bottom of a glass tumbler that is dipped frequently in water. Bake at 350° about 15 minutes.

A Collection of Recipes

Chocolate Mousse Pie

At the Norske Nook, Osseo, owner Jerry Bechard and his staff enjoy trying new things, especially creating new pie varieties. This recipe is one of their creations that is now a favorite of customers, too.

5 cups heavy Wisconsin
  whipping cream
1½ teaspoons vanilla
2 cups powdered sugar
¾ cup dry chocolate pudding
  mix

3 tablespoons cocoa
3½ cups whipped topping,
  divided
1 (10-inch) crust, baked
1 tablespoon shaved semisweet
  chocolate

Mix cream and vanilla together in large bowl of electric mixer. Beat one minute. Add powdered sugar and beat another minute. Add pudding mix and cocoa; beat until firm. Fold in 1½ cups whipped topping and pour into crust. Chill until very firm. Top with remaining whipped topping and garnish with shaved chocolate. Yields 8 servings.

Our Best Cookbook 2

Wyoming

CAPITAL: *Cheyenne*

NICKNAME: *The Equality State*

*W*hen you think of Wyoming, Yellowstone is the first thing that comes to mind. Once you have been there, the beauty and performances of nature are forever emblazoned in your mind. In 1872, it was designated the first official National Park (there are now 388). In 1906, Devils Tower became the first National Monument. The Bucking Horse and Rider image, boasting a rich tradition for both the state of Wyoming and the University of Wyoming, has become an icon for the entire state and is now a registered trademark. Wyoming has interesting contrasts: Wyoming's state image projects a tough man on a bucking bronco, but it was the first state to give women the right to vote. Another contrast is that Wyoming has the lowest population of all fifty states, less than 500,000 residents, but more than three million people visit Yellowstone National Park each year.

Snow Flurries

These are my favorite holiday roll-out cookies. They are tasty and very tender.

1½ cups sugar
⅞ cup butter
⅔ cup shortening
1⅓ tablespoons lemon zest
3 eggs

1 teaspoon vanilla extract
½ teaspoon almond extract
½ teaspoon salt
½ teaspoon baking powder
4½ cups unbleached flour

Thoroughly cream sugar, butter, shortening, and lemon zest. Add eggs, one at a time, and stir. Beat batter until it becomes light. Add vanilla and almond extracts, and stir. Mix in salt and baking powder with the first cup of flour. Add the rest of flour one cup at a time, stirring after each addition.

Roll out on floured counter. Cut with floured cutters. Transfer to papered trays with metal spatula. Bake at 350° for about 10 minutes, until they barely start to brown. Makes 6–7 dozen.

Get Your Buns in Here

Chocolate Mousse Cheesecake

CRUST:

2½ cups crushed graham crackers

6 ounces butter or margarine, melted

Combine graham cracker crumbs and butter and press into a 9½ x 2½-inch springform cake pan, lining sides and bottom. Place in refrigerator to chill and set.

FILLING:

2 large tablespoons cream cheese, softened

1 teaspoon vanilla extract

1 egg, lightly beaten

4 tablespoons powdered sugar

1½ cups chocolate syrup

1 pint whipping cream

1 ounce unflavored gelatin

½ cup hot water

In a bowl, beat cream cheese until smooth with electric mixer. Add vanilla, egg, and powdered sugar. Beat until smooth. Add chocolate syrup and mix thoroughly. Set aside.

Place whipping cream in a bowl and beat with electric mixer until soft peaks form. Fold into cream cheese mixture. Heat the gelatin and ½ cup hot water in microwave for 30 seconds or until all of the gelatin granules have dissolved. While slowly stirring cream cheese mixture, add the gelatin a little at a time. Pour all into graham cracker crust. Chill until set (about 2½ hours). Serves 10.

Wyoming Cook Book

Prime Rib Roast

Standing prime rib, any size. Let meat stand at room temperature for 1 hour before cooking. Preheat oven to 375°. Rub meat well with salt and sprinkle with pepper. Place meat, fat-side-up, in shallow roasting pan, uncovered. (Do not add water.) Cook for 1 hour. Turn off heat. DO NOT OPEN OVEN DOOR! Leave for minimum time of 5–6 hours. Before serving, turn oven on again to 375° and cook for the following times: 30 minutes for rare, 40 minutes for medium, 50 minutes for well done. Works every time!

Home at/on the Range with Wyoming BILS

Sunrise Enchiladas

8 whole green chiles
  [about 2 (4-ounce) cans]
8 (7-inch) flour tortillas
2 cups cooked sausage,
  crumbled, or chopped ham
  or bacon
½ cup sliced green onions
½ cup finely chopped green
  bell pepper
2½ cups shredded Cheddar,
  divided

4 eggs
2 cups light cream
1 tablespoon flour
¼ teaspoon salt
1 clove garlic, minced
Tabasco
Avocado slices (optional)
Salsa for garnish
Sour cream for garnish
Cilantro for garnish

Place opened green chile on one end of tortilla. Combine meat, green onions, pepper, and ⅓ cup plus 3 tablespoons cheese. Spoon over green chiles. Roll up and arrange in greased casserole, seam-side-down. Combine eggs, cream, flour, salt, garlic, and Tabasco, and pour over tortillas. Cover and refrigerate overnight.

Preheat oven to 350°. Uncover and bake 45–50 minutes. Sprinkle with remaining cheese and bake 3 minutes. Serve with avocado, salsa, sour cream, and cilantro. Makes 8 enchiladas.

Breakfast and More

Old Faithful is the most recognized geyser in Yellowstone National Park, Wyoming. It erupts 18 to 21 times a day, usually reaching its average height of 130 feet, but has gone as high as 184 feet in 15 to 20 seconds. On average, about 5,000 to 8,000 gallons of water are discharged during each eruption.

Buffalo Stew

Flavor improves if stew is kept a day in refrigerator.

6 pounds buffalo steak, cut in
  2-inch chunks
10 tablespoons butter or
  margarine, divided
4 large onions, thinly sliced
½ cup flour
1 (12-ounce) can beer
1 (10½-ounce) can beef broth,
  undiluted

1 teaspoon chopped garlic
1 tablespoon vinegar
1 teaspoon sugar
1 teaspoon thyme
1 bay leaf
Salt and pepper to taste

Brown buffalo on all sides in 4 tablespoons butter in a large, preferably cast-iron, casserole. It may be easier to do in 3 or 4 batches,
since meat browns best in a single layer. Remove meat, and sauté
onions in 2 tablespoons butter until lightly browned. Set onions
aside.

Add remaining butter to the pan along with flour and mix to a
paste. Add beer and broth gradually, beating with a whisk until
sauce is thick and smooth. Add remaining ingredients and the meat
and onions. Mix gently together. Bring to a boil. Cover and bake at
275° for 3–8 hours, until tender. Serves 6–8.

The Great Entertainer Cookbook

Editor's Extra: Beef or venison steaks can be substituted for buffalo.

Shoe Peg Corn Dip

1 (15-ounce) can shoe peg corn,
  drained
1 tomato, peeled, seeded, and
  diced
½ green bell pepper, diced
½ red pepper, diced
10–15 ripe olives, sliced
½ cup diced red onion
Juice of 1 lime

½ cucumber, chopped
3 green onions, chopped
1 jalapeño, chopped
2 tablespoons sour cream
1½ tablespoons chopped
  cilantro
Seasoned salt and pepper to
  taste

Combine all ingredients and mix well. Refrigerate until well chilled.
Serve with crackers or chips. Best prepared a day ahead.

From the High Country of Wyoming

Festive Cranberry Torte

CRUST:

1½ cups graham cracker
  crumbs
½ cup chopped pecans

¼ cup sugar
6 tablespoons butter or
  margarine, melted

In mixing bowl, combine graham cracker crumbs, pecans, sugar, and melted margarine. Press onto bottom and up sides of 8-inch spring-form pan. Chill.

FILLING:

2 cups ground fresh cranberries
1 cup sugar
1 tablespoon frozen orange
  juice concentrate, thawed

2 egg whites
1 teaspoon vanilla
⅛ teaspoon salt
1 cup whipping cream

In large mixing bowl, combine cranberries and sugar; let stand 5 minutes. Add orange juice concentrate, unbeaten egg whites, vanilla, and salt. Beat on low speed of electric mixer till frothy. Then beat at high speed 6–8 minutes or till stiff peaks form. Whip cream to soft peaks; fold into cranberry mixture. Turn into Crust; freeze. Serve with Cranberry Glaze.

CRANBERRY GLAZE:

½ cup sugar
1 tablespoon cornstarch

¾ cup fresh cranberries
⅔ cup water

In saucepan, stir together sugar and cornstarch; stir in cranberries and water. Cook and stir till bubbly. Cook, stirring occasionally, just till cranberry skins pop. Cool to room temperature. (Do not chill.) Makes 1 cup.

To serve, remove torte from pan. Place on serving plate. Spoon Cranberry Glaze in center. Makes 10 servings.

Home at/on the Range with Wyoming BILS

Black Forest Cake

Chocolate cake mix
1 (21-ounce) can cherry pie
    filling
3 cups whipping cream
¼ cup powdered sugar

1 tablespoon instant vanilla
    pudding
1 (4-ounce) chocolate bar (or
    chocolate chips)

Make cake according to package directions; bake in 3 (8-inch-round) cake pans or in a springform pan and cut into 3 layers. Have cake layers ready and cooled.

Transfer one layer to cake platter and spread with cherry pie filling. Beat whipping cream until thick; sift powdered sugar and instant pudding over cream and continue beating until cream makes stiff peaks. Put second layer of cake on top of cherries and spread with ⅓ of the whipped cream. Leave enough cream to frost remainder of cake. Add third layer and frost entire cake with remaining whipped cream. Use potato peeler to make curls on top of cake from chocolate bar, or grate semisweet chocolate chips on top.

With Lots of Love

Shorty's Succulent Salsa Steak

½ cup salsa (medium or hot)
½ cup fresh lime juice
2 tablespoons hoisin sauce
    (available in oriental section
    of your supermarket)

2–4 cloves garlic, minced
1 pound sirloin steak (or
    individual filets, if preferred)
Thinly sliced green onions for
    garnish

Combine salsa, lime juice, hoisin sauce, and garlic. Place steak in glass pan. Pour marinade over meat. Cover and refrigerate at least 6 hours (overnight is better), turning occasionally.

Drain steak, reserving marinade. Broil or grill, brushing often with marinade. Garnish with thinly sliced green onions. Makes 4 servings.

You're Hot Stuff, Flo!

List of Contributing Cookbooks

PHOTO BY GREG CAMPBELL

*Twenty-two years, fifty states, outstanding recipes, and priceless memories
tucked inside each and every book...Gwen and Barbara congratulate themselves:
"We really did it!"*

Listed below are the cookbooks that have contributed recipes to the *Best of the Best from America Cookbook,* along with copyright, author, publisher, city, and state. The information in parentheses indicates the BEST OF THE BEST cookbook in which the recipe originally appeared.

Above & Beyond Parsley ©1992 Junior League of Kansas City, MO (Missouri)

The Aficionado's Southwestern Cookbook ©1985 by Ronald Johnson, Albuquerque, NM (New Mexico)

All About Crab ©2000 by Nancy Brannon, ConAmore Publishing, Florence, OR (Oregon)

All Seasons Cookbook ©1988 Mystic Seaport Museum Stores, Inc., Connie Colom, Mystic Seaport Stores, Mystic, CT (New England)

All-Maine Cooking ©1967 Courier-Gazette, Inc., Edited by Ruth Wiggin and Loana Shibles, Down East Books, Camden, ME (New England)

Amarillo Junior League Cookbook ©1979 Amarillo Junior League Publications, Amarillo, TX (Texas)

Amish Country Cookbook II ©1986 Bethel Publishing, Evangel Publishing House, Nappannee, IN (Indiana)

Angels and Friends Cookbook II ©1981 Angels of Easter Seal, Youngstown, OH (Ohio)

Angiporto, Inc. ©1991 Angiporto, Inc., Barbara McCormack and Deedee Borland, Lake Forest, IL (Illinois)

Anniversary Collection of Delectable Dishes, The Woman's Club of Jackson, AL (Alabama)

Another Cookbook, Kay Rose, Idaho Falls, ID (Idaho)

Applause Applause, Standing Ovation Cooks, Coggon, IA (Iowa)

Arkansas Celebration Cookbook ©1990 by Zoe Medlin Caywood, Zoe Medlin Caywood and Carol J. Lisle, Rogers, AR (Arkansas)

Ashton Area Cookbook, Ashton Area Development Committee, Ashton, ID (Idaho)

Atlantic Highlands Historical Society Cookbook, Atlantic Highlands Historical Society, Atlantic Highlands, NJ (Mid-Atlantic)

Aunty Pua's Keiki Cookbook ©1991 by Ann Kondo Corum, Bess Press, Honolulu, HI (Hawaii)

Authentic Cowboy Cookery Then & Now ©2004 JB Publications, Carol Bardelli & F. E. "Lizzie" Hill, JB Publications, Stagecoach, NV (Nevada)

Back Home Again ©1993 The Junior League of Indianapolis, IN (Indiana)

Basque Cooking and Lore ©1991 by Darcy Williamson, Caxton Press, Caldwell, ID (Idaho)

The Bed & Breakfast Cookbook ©1991 by Martha W. Murphy, Narragansett, RI (New England)

Best Bets ©1993 Nathan Adelson Hospice, Las Vegas, NV (Nevada)

The Best from Libby Hillman's Kitchen ©1993 by Libby Hillman, Countryman Press, Woodstock, VT (New England)

The Best Little Cookbook in the West ©1996 by Loaun Werner Vaad, Chamberlain, SD (Great Plains)

The Best of Amish Cooking ©1988 Good Books, Phyllis Pellman Good, Intercourse, PA (Pennsylvania)

Best-of-Friends, Festive Occasions Cookbook, Darlene Glantz Skees, Farcountry Press, Helena, MT (Big Sky)

The Best of the Sweet Potato Recipes ©1992 by E. B. Dandar, Penndel, PA (Pennsylvania)

The Best of Wheeling ©1994 The Junior League of Wheeling, WV (West Virginia)

Betty Groff's Up-Home Down-Home Cookbook ©1987 by Betty Groff, Pond Press, Mount Joy, PA (Pennsylvania)

Beyond Chicken Soup, Jewish Home of Rochester Auxiliary, Rochester, NY (New York)

Bitterroot Favorites & Montana Memories ©2002 Bitterroot Favorites & Montana Memories, Laurie Green Blount, Hamilton, MT (Big Sky)

Bluegrass Winners ©1985 The Garden Club of Lexington, KY (Kentucky)

Bon Appétit de Las Sandias, Woman's Club of West Mesa, Rio Rancho, NM (New Mexico)

Bountiful Blessings, St. John Lutheran Church, Linthicum, MD (Mid-Atlantic)

Bouquet Garni ©1989 Independence Regional Health Center, Independence, MO (Missouri)

Breakfast and More ©1992 Porch Swing Publications, Carole Eppler, Cheyenne, WY (Big Sky)

Bringing Grand Tastes to Grand Traverse ©1994 Newcomers Club of Grand Traverse, Traverse City, MI (Michigan)

Cakes...Cakes...and more Cakes, Mariwyn McClain Smith, Parsons, WV (West Virginia)

Calf Fries to Caviar ©1983 Jan-Su Publications, Janet Franklin and Sue Vaughn, Lamesa, TX (Texas)

California Gold ©1992 California State Grange, Sacramento, CA (California)

California Sizzles ©1992 The Junior League of Pasadena, Inc., Pasadena, CA (California)

Calypso Café ©1999 Wimmer Companies, Bob Epstein, Memphis, TN (Florida)

Cape Collection-Simply Soup, Association for the Preservation of Cape Cod, Orleans, MA (New England)

A Cause for Applause, Elgin Symphony League, Elgin, IL (Illinois)

Celebrate San Antonio ©1986 San Antonio Junior Forum, San Antonio, TX (Texas II)

Change of Seasons ©1986 Vanderbilt University, Department of Nutrition Services B802, Nashville, TN (Tennessee)

Charleston Receipts ©1950 The Junior League of Charleston, Inc., Charleston, SC (South Carolina)

The Chef's Palate Cookbook ©1992 by Jane Pettit, Quechee, VT (New England)

Chesapeake Bay Country ©1987 by W. C. (Bill) Snyder, The Donning Company Publishers, Virginia Beach, VA (Virginia)

Chips, Dips, & Salsas ©1999 by Judy Walker and Kim MacEachern/Photos by Northland Publishing, Flagstaff, AZ (Arizona)

Chorizos in an Iron Skillet ©2002 by Mary Ancho Davis, University of Nevada Press, Reno, NV (Nevada)

Christmas Memories Cookbook ©1985 Mystic Seaport Museum Stores, Inc., Lois Klee and Connie Colom, Mystic Seaport Stores, Mystic, CT (New England)

The Coastal Cook of West Marin ©1991 Riley and Company, Laura Riley, Bolinas, CA (California)

Coastal Cuisine ©1999 by Connie Correia Fisher, Small Potatoes Press, Collingswood, NJ (Mid-Atlantic)

Coastal Flavors, American Association of University Women, Seaside Branch, Seaside, OR (Oregon)

Collected Recipes ©1995 by Linda D. Channell, Allamuchy, NJ (Mid-Atlantic)

A Collection of Recipes, St. Joseph's Home and School Assn., Stratford, WI (Wisconsin)

Colorado Cache Cookbook ©1978 The Junior League of Denver, Inc., Denver, CO (Colorado)

The Colorado Cookbook ©1981 University of Colorado Norlin Library, Friends of the Libraries/University of Colorado at Boulder, CO (Colorado)

Colorado Foods and More... ©1990 by Judy Barbour, Bandera, TX (Colorado)

Come Savor Swansea ©1992 First Christian Congregational Church, Swansea, MA (New England)

Comida Sabrosa ©1982 by Irene Barraza Sanchez and Gloria Sanchez Yund, University of New Mexico Press, Albuquerque, NM (New Mexico)

Company Fare I, Presbyterian Women First Presbyterian Church, Bartlesville, OK (Oklahoma)

Company's Coming ©1988 The Cookbook Collection, The Junior League of Kansas City, MO (Missouri)

A Complete Guide to Dutch Oven Cooking, Ken and Cheryl Allred, Riverton, UT (Utah)

Connecticut Cooks II ©1985 American Cancer Society, CT Division, Wallingford, CT (New England)

The Conner Prairie Cookbook ©1990 Conner Prairie Press, edited by Margaret A. Hoffman, Conner Prairie Press, Noblesville, IN (Indiana)

Cook 'em Up Kaua'i ©1993 Kaua'i Historical Society, Lihue, HI (Hawaii)

A Cook's Tour of Alaska ©1995 A Cook's Tour of Alaska, Gwen Stetson, Anchorage, AK (Alaska)

A Cook's Tour of Iowa ©1988 University of Iowa Press, Iowa City, IA (Iowa)

Cookbook 25 Years, Madison County Farm Bureau Women's Committee, Edwardsville, IL (Illinois)

Cookin' in the Keys ©1985, 2003 by William Flagg, Palm Island Press, Key West, FL (New Florida)

The Cooking Book ©1978 The Junior League of Louisville, Inc., Louisville, KY (Kentucky)

Cooking on the Coast ©1994 by Rose Annette O'Keefe, Cooking on the Coast, Inc., Ocean Springs, MS (Mississippi)

Cooking on the Road, Montana Whitfield, Steele, MO (Missouri)

Cooking with Iola, Iola Egle, McCook, NE (Great Plains)

Cooking with Pride, Pridefest Celebration Committee, Milwaukee, WI (Wisconsin)

Cooking with the Allenhurst Garden Club, The Allenhurst Garden Club, Allenhurst, NJ (Mid-Atlantic)

The Cool Mountain Cookbook ©2001 by Gwen Ashley Walters, Pen & Fork Communications, Carefree, AZ (Big Sky)

Corazón Contento ©1999 Texas Tech University Press, Madeline Gallego Thorpe and Mary Tate Engels, Lubbock, TX (Arizona)

Coronado's Favorite Trail Mix ©1995 Community Food Book, Inc. of Tucson, Tucson, AZ (Arizona)

Country Cookbook, Marilla Historical Society, Copemish, MI (Michigan)

Country Cupboard Cookbook, Panora Church of the Brethern Women, Panora, IA (Iowa)

Country Inns and Back Roads Cookbook ©Berkshire Traveller Press, Berkshire House Publishers, Lee, MA (New England)

The Courier-Journal Kentucky Cookbook ©1985 The Courier-Journal and Louisville Times Co., Louisville, KY (Kentucky)

Court Clerk's Bar and Grill, Tulsa County Court Clerk's Office, Tulsa, OK (Oklahoma)

A Cowboy Cookin' Every Night ©2004 JB Publications, Stagecoach, NV (Nevada)

Crossett Cook Book, Presidents' Council and Executive Board of Adopt-A-School, Crossett, AR (Arkansas)

The Cubs 'R Cookin' ©1994 Cubs' Wives for Family Rescue, Chicago, IL (Illinois)

Culinary Contentment ©1984 Virginia Tech Faculty Women's Club, Blacksburg, VA (Virginia)

Culinary Creations ©1998 Bnos Zion of Bobov, Brooklyn, NY (New York)

The Dairy Hollow House Cookbook ©1986 Crescent Dragonwagon, Cato and Martin Publishers, Eureka Springs, AR (Arkansas)

'Dat Little New Orleans Creole Cookbook ©1994 Relco Publishing, Chef Remy Laterrade C.E.C., Lafayette, LA (Louisiana II)

Dd's Table Talk, Deirdre Keiko Todd, Booklines Hawaii, Ltd., Mililani, HI (Hawaii)

Decades of Mason Cooking ©1992 Riata Service Organization, Mason, TX (Texas II)

Deke's BBQ Hush Yer Mouth! This is It!, David Baskin, Oxford, MS (Mississippi)

The Dexter Cider Mill Apple Cookbook ©1995 by Katherine Merkel Koziski, Chelsea, MI (Michigan)

Dining on Deck ©1986 by Linda Vail, Williamson Publishing, Charlotte, VT (New England)

The Durango Cookbook, Jan Fleming, Durango, CO (Colorado)

Dutch Pantry Cookin', Dutch Pantry Family Restaurant, Williamstown, WV (West Virginia)

Dutch Touches ©1996 Penfield Press, Iowa City, IA (Iowa)

Easy Does It Cookbook ©1982 Woman Time Management, Liz Miller and Carol Burns, TX (Texas)

The Enlightened Titan ©1988 Trinity Patrons Association, The Patrons Association of Trinity Episcopal School, Richmond, VA (Virginia)

Eskimo Cookbook, Students of Shishmaref Day School, On the Wall Productions, St. Louis, MO (Alaska)

Ethnic Foods of Hawai'i ©2000 by Ann Kondo Corum, Bess Press, Honolulu, HI (Hawaii)

Even More Special ©1986 The Junior League of Durham and Orange Counties, Inc., Durham, NC (North Carolina)

Fair's Fair, Del Mar Fair, Del Mar, CA (California)

Family & Company ©1992 Junior League of Binghamton, NY (New York)

A Family Tradition, Wicomico County Fair, Salisbury, MD (Mid-Atlantic)

Famous Florida Recipes: 300 Years of Good Eating ©1972 by Lowis Carlton, St. Petersburg, FL (Florida)

The Farmer's Daughters ©1987 S-M-L, Inc, Flora Sisemore, Martha Merritt and Mary Mayfield, DeWitt, AR (Arkansas)

Favorite Recipes from Our Best Cooks, St. John Vianney Altar Society, Spokane, WA (Washington)

Favorite Recipes from Utah Farm Bureau Women ©2000 Horizon Publishers & Distributors, Inc., Utah Farm Bureau Women's Committee, Sandy, UT (Utah)

Festival Foods and Family Favorites ©1995 by Sara Anne Corrigan, Evansville, IN (Indiana)

Fillies Flavours ©1984 The Fillies, Inc., Louisville, KY (Kentucky)

Finn Creek Museum Cookbook, Minnesota Finnish American Historical Society Chapter 13, New York Mills, MN (Minnesota)

Flavors of Cape Henlopen, Patty Derrick, Rehoboth Beach, DE (Mid-Atlantic)

Foxy Ladies ©1981 by Ellen Kort, Appleton, WI (Wisconsin)

Frederica Fare ©The Parents Association of Frederica Academy, St. Simons Island, GA (Georgia)

Fresh-Water Fish Cookbook, Dave Hopfer, Turner, OR (Oregon)

From Amish and Mennonite Kitchens ©1984 Good Books, Intercourse, PA (Pennsylvania)

From Generation to Generation ©1989 B'nia Amoona Woman's League, St. Louis, MO (Missouri)

From Minnesota...More Than a Cookbook ©1985 Gluesing and Gluesing, Inc., Laurie and Debra Gluesing, Shoreview, MN (Minnesota)

From Our Kitchen to Yours, Jewell and Jeanette, Vader, WA (Washington)

From the Apple Orchard ©1984 by Leona N. Jackson, Maryville, MO (Missouri)

From the High Country of Wyoming, Flying A Guest Ranch, Pinedale, WY (Big Sky)

From the Inn's Kitchen © by Deedy Marble, Chef, The Governor's Inn, Ludlow, VT (New England)

Garden of Eatin', Book Club of Sorrento East, Nokomis, FL (Florida)

Gazebo I Christmas Cookbook ©1984 by Rex Barrington, Auburn, AL (Alabama)

Get Your Buns in Here ©1999 by Laurel A. Wicks, Jackson, WY (Big Sky)

The Give Mom a Rest (She's on Vacation) Cookbook ©1998 by Rita Hewson, Larned, KS (Great Plains)

Going Wild in Mississippi ©1995 Mississippi Telephone Pioneers, BellSouth Pioneers, Jackson, MS (Mississippi)

Golden Isles Cuisine ©1978 Dot Gibson Publications, Waycross, GA (Georgia)

Golden Moments ©1996 by Arlene Giesel Koehn, Golden Moments Publishing, West Point, MS (Mississippi)

Good Food From Michigan ©1995 by Laurie Woody, Grawn, MI (Michigan)

Good Morning, Goldie!, Goldie Veitch, Meeker, CO (Colorado)

Good Sam Celebrates 15 Years of Love, Socorro Good Samaritan Village, Socorro, NM (New Mexico)

Goodness Grows in North Carolina ©1989 North Carolina Department of Agriculture, Raleigh, NC (North Carolina)

Gottlieb's Bakery 100 Years of Recipes ©1983 Gottlieb's Bakery, Isser Gottlieb, Savannah, GA (Georgia)

Grand Tour Collection ©1981 The Tennessee Chapter, American Society of Interior Designers, Germantown, TN (Tennessee)

Grannie Annie's Cookin' on the Wood Stove, Ann Berg, Nikiski, AK (Alaska)

Great American Recipes from Southern 'n' Cajun Cook'n, James S. Gwaltney, Sr., Florence, MS (Mississippi)

The Great Entertainer Cookbook ©1992, 2002 Buffalo Bill Historical Center, Cody, WY (Big Sky)

Great Flavors of Texas ©1992 Southern Flavors, Inc., Pine Bluff, AR (Texas II)

Great Island Cook Book ©1965 New Castle Congregational Church, New Castle Island Church Guild, New Castle, NH (New England)

Great Lake Effects ©1997 Junior League of Buffalo, Inc., Buffalo, NY (New York)

The Great Nevada Cookbook ©1993 Nevada Magazine, Carson City, NV (Nevada)

A Great Taste of Arkansas ©1986 Southern Flavors, Inc., Pine Bluff, AR (Arkansas)

Great Taste of Virginia Seafood ©1984 material by Mary Reid Barrow, cover and interior photography by Public Relations Institute, Inc., Mary Reid Barrow with Robin Browder, The Donning Company Publishers, Atglen, PA (Virginia)

Grits 'n Greens and Mississippi Things ©2002 Parlance Publishing, Sylvia Higginbotham, Columbus, MS (Mississippi)

Hall's Potato Harvest Cookbook ©1993 by The Hall Family, Alamo, ND (Great Plains)

Halvorson-Johnson Family Reunion Cookbook, Halvorson-Johnson Family, Kaleva, MI (Michigan)

Hancock Community Collection, The Guild, Hancock, NH (New England)

Happy Times with Home Cooking ©1960–90 by Barbara Easter, Mt. Airy, NC (Virginia)

The Happy Cooker 3, Sisterhood Beth Ohr, Old Bridge, NJ (Mid-Atlantic)

Hasbro Children's Hospital Cookbook, Hasbro Children's Hospital Nursing Staff, Providence, RI (New England)

Hawaii's Best Tropical Food & Drinks, Hawaiian Service, Inc., a division of Booklines Hawaii, Ltd., Mililani, HI (Hawaii)

Hawai'i's Spam Cookbook ©1987 by Ann Kondo Corum, Bess Press, Honolulu, HI (Hawaii)

Head Table Cooks ©1982 American Camellia Society, Inc., Fort Valley, GA (Georgia)

Heartland ©1991 by Marcia Adams, Heartland, Westminster, MD (Ohio)

Heavenly Delights, Sacred Heart Altar Society, Nelson, NE (Great Plains)

Heavenly Recipes, Milnor Lutheran Church WELCA, Milnor, ND (Great Plains)

Home at/on the Range with Wyoming BILS, Wyoming/PEO Sisterhood, Chapter Y, Casper, WY (Big Sky)

Home at the Range II and III, Chapter E. X. P. E. O., Oakley, KS (Great Plains)

Homespun Cookery, Marie Carter Durant, Boscawen, NH (New England)

Honest to Goodness ©1990 The Junior League of Springfield, Inc., Springfield, IL (Illinois)

Honolulu Hawaii Cooking ©1991 by Betty Evans, Hermosa Beach, HI (Hawaii)

Hopewell's Hoosier Harvest II, Hopewell Presbyterian Church, Franklin, IN (Indiana)

Horse Prairie Favorites, Grant Volunteer Fire Department, Gran-Dillon, MT (Big Sky)

How to Enjoy Zucchini ©1983 Josie's Kitchen, Josie Carlsen, Carlsen Printing, Ogden, UT (Utah)

Huckleberries and Crabmeat, Carol Cate, C.R. Bears, Winchester, OR (Oregon)

Hudson Valley German-American Society Cookbook, Hudson Valley German-American Society, Kingston, NY (New York)

Hudson's Cookbook ©1982 by Brian and Gloria Carmines, Hilton Head Island, SC (South Carolina)

Huntsville Entertains ©1983 Historic Huntsville Foundation, Huntsville, AL (Alabama)

Idaho's Wild 100! ©1990 Idaho Department of Fish and Game, Boise, ID (Idaho)

If It Tastes Good, Who Cares? II ©1992 Spiritseekers Publishing, Pam Girard, Bismarck, ND (Great Plains)

In the Kitchen with Kendi ©1999 by Kendi O'Neill, Diversions Publications, Frederick, MD (Mid-Atlantic)

Iowa Granges Celebrating 125 Years of Cooking, Iowa State Grange, Cedar Rapids, IA (Iowa)

The Island Cookbook ©1993 by Barbara Sherman Stetson, North Scituate, RI (New England)

Jan Townsend Going Home ©1996 by Janice Lynn Townsend, Auburn, CA (California)

Just Plain Country, Alice Lantz, Glady, WV (West Virginia)

A Kaleidoscope of Creative Healthy Cooking ©1990 by Janet M. Boyce, R.N., Little Rock, AR (Arkansas)

Kansas City Barbeque Society Cookbook ©1998 Kansas City Barbeque Society, Kansas City, MO (Great Plains)

Kansas City BBQ ©1989 Pig Out Publications, Inc., Kansas City, MO (Missouri)

Kay Ewing's Cooking School Cookbook ©1004 by Kay Ewing, Baton Rouge, LA (Louisiana II)

The Kearney 125th Anniversary Community Cookbook ©1998 Morris Press, Kearney, NE (Great Plains)

The Kentucky Derby Museum Cookbook ©1986 Kentucky Derby Museum Corp., Louisville, KY (Kentucky)

Ketchum Cooks ©1995 by Dee Dee McCuskey, Graphic Arts Center, Boise, ID (Idaho)

Kitchen Klatter Keepsakes, Kiwash Electric Cooperative, Inc., Cordell, OK (Oklahoma)

Kona on My Plate ©2002 Kona Outdoor Circle Foundation, Kailua-Kona, HI (Hawaii)

Korner's Folly Cookbook ©1977 by Beth Tartan and Fran Parker, TarPar, Ltd., Kernersville, NC (North Carolina)

Kountry Kooking ©1974 by Phila Hach, Clarksville, TN (Tennessee)

Kum' Ona' Granny's Table, Senior Citizens Retirement Facility, Montgomery, AL (Alabama)

La Cucina Casalinga, Italian American Association of the Township of Ocean, Interlakes, NJ (Mid-Atlantic)

LaConner Palates ©1988 by Patricia Flynn and Patricia McClane, Bookends Publishing, Oak Harbor, WA (Washington)

Lafayette Collection ©1995 Lafayette Arts and Science Foundation, Lafayette, CA (California)

Lake Reflections ©1968–1987 Circulation Services, Wayne County Extension Homemakers, Monticello, KY (Kentucky)

Las Vegas Glitter to Gourmet, Junior League of Las Vegas, NV (Nevada)

Laurels to the Cook ©1988 Laurels to the Cook, Talus Rock Girl Scout Council, Inc., Johnstown, PA (Pennsylvania)

Lavender and Lace, Arlington United Methodist Women, Bridgeton, MO (Missouri)

The Loaf and Ladle Cook Book ©1979, 1983 by Joan S. Harlow, Down East Books, Camden, ME (New England)

The Louisiana Crawfish Cookbook ©1984 Louisiana Crawfish Cookbook, Inc., Lettsworth, LA (Louisiana)

Love Cookin', St. Joseph's Holy Family Hall, Rockville, IN (Indiana)

The Lymes' Heritage Cookbook ©1991 The Lyme Historical Society, Florence Griswold Museum, Old Lyme, CT (New England)

Maine's Jubilee Cookbook ©1969 Courier-Gazette, Inc., Edited by Loana Shibles and Annie Rogers, Down East Books, Camden, ME (New England)

The Marlborough Meetinghouse Cookbook, Congregational Church of Marlborough, CT (New England)

Marquette University High School Mother's Guild Cookbook, MUHS Mother's Guild, Milwaukee, WI (Wisconsin)

Maryland's Way ©1963 Hammond-Harwood House Association, Annapolis, MD (Mid-Atlantic)

A Matter of Taste ©1989 The Junior League of Morristown, Inc., Morristown, NJ (Mid-Atlantic)

MDA Favorite Recipes, Maple Dale Elementary School, Cincinnati, OH (Ohio)

Memories from Brownie's Kitchen ©1989 Bangor Publishing Co., Mildred "Brownie" Schrumpf, Magazines, Inc., Bangor, ME (New England)

Merrymeeting Merry Eating ©Regional Memorial Hospital, Mid Coast Hospital, Brunswick Auxiliary, Brunswick, ME (New England)

Mincemeat and Memories ©1980 Xi Chapter of Kappa, Kappa, Kappa, Inc., Tri Kappas of Anderson, IN (Indiana)

Minnesota Heritage Cookbook I ©1979 American Cancer Society, Minnesota Division, Inc., Minneapolis, MN (Minnesota)

The Mississippi Cookbook ©1972 University Press of Mississippi, Home Economics Division of the Mississippi Cooperative Extension Service, Jackson, MS (Mississippi)

Mom-Mom's Cookbook ©2001 by Marilyn Hudson, Monterville, WV (West Virginia)

The Mongo Mango Cookbook ©2001 by Cynthia Thuma, Pineapple Press, Sarasota, FL (Florida)

Monterey's Cookin' Pisto Style ©1994 by John Pisto, Monterey, CA (California)

Moose Racks, Bear Tracks and Other Alaska Kidsnacks ©1999 by Alice Bugni, Sasquatch Books, Kodiak, AK (Alaska)

More Favorites from the Melting Pot, Church of Saint Athanasius, Baltimore, MD (Mid-Atlantic)

More Fiddling with Food, First Baptist Church of Mobile, AL (Alabama)

More Tastes & Tales ©1987 by Peg Hein, Heinco, Inc., Austin, TX (Texas II)

More than Beans and Cornbread ©1993 by Barbara McCallum, Charleston, WV (West Virginia)

A Mormon Cookbook ©2002 by Erin A. Delfoe, Apricot Press, American Fork, UT (Utah)

The Mormon Trail Cookbook ©1997 Morris Press, Kearney, NE (Great Plains)

Mountain Brook's Wacky Wonders of the Woods ©1995 Mountain Brook Ladies Club, Kalispell, MT (Big Sky)

Moveable Feasts Cookbook ©1992 Mystic Seaport Museum Stores, Inc., Ginger Smyle, Mystic Seaport Stores, Mystic, CT (New England)

Mrs. Boone's Wild Game Cookbook, Momentum Books, Troy, MI (Michigan)

My Old Kentucky Homes Cookbook, A Taste of Kentucky, Louisville, KY (Kentucky)

My Own Cookbook ©1982 Parnassus Imprints, Gladys Taber, Martons Mill, MA (New England)

Neighboring on the Air ©1991 University of Iowa Press, Iowa City, IA (Iowa)

Nibbles Ooo La La ©1984 by Suzie Stephens, Fayetteville, AR (Arkansas)

Norman Lutheran Church 125th Anniversary Cookbook, Norman Lutheran Church WELCA, Kindred, ND (Great Plains)

North Carolina and Old Salem Cookery ©1955 by Elizabeth Hedgecock Sparks, TarPar Ltd., Kernersville, NC (North Carolina)

North Dakota...Where Food is Love ©1994 by Marcella Richman, Tower City, ND (Great Plains)

Of Tide & Thyme ©1995 The Junior League of Annapolis, MA (Mid-Atlantic)

Off the Hook ©1988 Junior League of Stamford-Norwalk, Darien, CT (New England)

Old-Fashioned Dutch Oven Cookbook ©1969 by Donald R. Holm, Caxton Press, Caldwell, ID (Idaho)

125 Years of Cookin' with the Lord, Trinity Lutheran Church (ELCA), Topeka, KS (Great Plains)

100 Years of Cooking, Oologah United Methodist Church, Oologah, OK (Oklahoma)

Oregon Farmers' Markets Cookbook and Guide @1998 Kris Wetherbee, Maverick Publications, Inc.

Oakland, OR (Oregon)The Oregon Trail Cookbook ©1993 Morris Press, Kearney, NE (Great Plains)

The Original Tennessee Homecoming Cookbook ©1985 Rutledge Hill Press, Edited by Daisy King, Nashville, TN (Tennessee)

Our Best Cookbook 2 ©1995 Wisconsin Restaurant Assn. Education Foundation, Amherst Press, Amherst, WI (Wisconsin)

Our Best Home Cooking, Pearl Luttman, Red Bud, IL (Illinois)

Our Best Home Cooking, Vienna Baptist Church, Vienna, WV (West Virginia)

Our Favorite Recipes, Elliott Prairie Community Church, Woodburn, OR (Oregon)

Our Favorite Recipes II, English Wesleyan Women's Missionary Society, English, IN (Indiana)

Outdoor Cooking: From Backyard to Backpack ©1991 Department of Transportation, State of Arizona, Phoenix, AZ (Arizona)

Padre Kino's Favorite Meatloaf, Community Food Bank, Inc., Tucson, AZ (Arizona)

Parties & Pleasures ©1985 by Wilma Taylor Sowell, Columbia, TN (Tennessee)

Party Potpourri, Junior League of Memphis, TN (Tennessee)

Pass the Plate ©1984 Pass the Plate, Inc., Alice G. Underhill and Barbara S. Stewart, New Bern, NC (North Carolina)

Peachtree Bouquet ©1987 The Junior League of DeKalb County, Georgia, Inc., Decatur, GA (Georgia)

Peanut Palate Pleasers from Portales, Portales Woman's Club, Portales, NM (New Mexico)

Peter Christian's Favorites ©1987 by Shirley Edes, Julia Philipson, and Murray Washburn, Down East Books, Camden, ME (New England)

Philadelphia Homestyle Cookbook ©1984 Norwood-Fontbonne Home and School Assn., Norwood-Fontbonne Academy, Philadelphia, PA (Pennsylvania)

Picnics on the Square ©1994 Wisconsin Chamber Orchestra, Inc., Madison, WI (Wisconsin)

Pinch of Salt Lake ©1986 Junior League of Salt Lake City, Inc., Salt Lake City, UT (Utah)

Pioneer Family Recipes ©1983 by Danielle Stevens, Kingman, AZ (Arizona)

The Plantation Cookbook ©1972 Junior League of New Orleans, LA (Louisiana II)

Potluck Volume II, MN Catholic Daughters of the Americas, Medford, MN (Minnesota)

Potlucks & Petticoats ©1986 by Jerry and Becky Cope, Dillard, GA (Georgia)

Presentations ©1993 Friends of Lied, Lied Center for Performing Arts, Lincoln, NE (Great Plains)

Quail Country ©1983 The Junior League of Albany, Georgia, Inc., Albany, GA (Georgia)

Rainbow's Roundup of Recipes, Rainbow Bible Ranch, Sturgis, SD (Great Plains)

Recipe Jubilee! ©1964 The Junior League of Mobile, Inc., Mobile, AL (Alabama)

Recipes & Remembrances, Covenant Women of Courtland Kansas, Courtland, KS (Great Plains)

Recipes & Remembrances, Dotson Family, Lima, OH (Ohio)

Recipes and Remembering, Dorothy J. O'Neal, Eugene, OR (Oregon)

Recipes for Rain or Shine, First Christian Church, Artesia, NM (New Mexico)

Recipes for Roughing It Easy ©2001 by Dain Thomas, Holladay, UT (Utah)

Recipes from Our Friends ©2001 Friends of Whitman County Library, Colfax, WA (Washington)

Recipes Logged from the Woods of North Idaho ©1999 Friends of the West Bonner Library, Priest River, ID (Idaho)

Recipes Thru Time, Tooele County Daughters of Utah Pioneers, Stansbury Park, UT (Utah)

The Red Lion Inn Cookbook ©1992 Berkshire House Publishers, Suzi Forbes Chase, Lee, MA (New England)

Red River Valley Potato Growers Auxiliary Cookbook, R.R.V.P.G. Auxiliary, East Grand Forks, MN (Great Plains)

Red, White & Blue Favorites, American Legion Auxiliary Unit 81, Lake Havasu City, AZ (Arizona)

River Brethren Recipes, Sonlight River Brethren School, Mount Joy, PA (Pennsylvania)

Roger's Cajun Cookbook ©1987 by Vernon Roger, Baton Rouge, LA (Louisiana II)

The Route 66 Cookbook ©1993 by Marian Clark, Council Oak Books, Tulsa, OK (Oklahoma)

San Angelo Junior League Cookbook ©1977 Junior League of San Angelo, Inc., San Angelo, TX (Texas)

San Juan Classics II Cookbook ©1988 by Dawn Ashbach and Janice Veal, Northwest Island Associates, Anacortes, WA (Washington)

Sandy Hook Volunteer Fire Company Ladies Auxiliary Cookbook, Sandy Hook Volunteer Fire & Rescue Ladies Auxiliary, Sandy Hook, CT (New England)

Sassy Southwest Cooking ©1997 by Clyde W. Casey, Roswell, NM (New Mexico)

Savannah Style ©1980 The Junior League of Savannah, Inc., Savannah, GA (Georgia)

Savoring the Southwest Again ©1983 Roswell Symphony Guild Publications, Roswell, NM (New Mexico)

Sea Island Seasons ©1980 Beaufort County Open Land Trust, Beaufort, SC (South Carolina)

Seafood Expressions ©1991 by Norman Leclair/Dome Publishing, North Kingston, RI (New England)

Seafood Secrets Cookbook ©1990 Mystic Newport Museum Stores, Ainslie Turner, Mystic Seaport Stores, Mystic, CT (New England)

Seasoned with Love, Faith United Methodist Women, Woodward, OK (Oklahoma)

Secrets of the Original Don's Seafood & Steakhouse ©1996 Don's Seafood & Steakhouse of Louisiana, Inc., Lafayette, LA (Louisiana II)

SEP Junior Women's Club 25th Anniversary Cookbook, SEP Junior Women's Club, Mitchellville, IA (Iowa)

Settings ©1990 The Junior League of Philadelphia, Inc., Philadelphia, PA (Pennsylvania)

The 7 Day Cookbook ©1997 by Nadine Nemechek and Sharon Nemechek Gerardi, Clovis, CA (California)

Sharing Our Best, Bergen Lutheran Church, Montevideo, MN (Minnesota)

Sharing Our Best, St. Paul's Lutheran Church, Saratoga Springs, NY (New York)

Sharing Our Best to Help the Rest, Independent School District 196 and United Way of the Saint Paul Area, St. Paul, MN (Minnesota)

Ship to Shore I ©1983 Ship to Shore, Inc., Jan Robinson, Charlotte, NC (North Carolina)

Simply Colorado ©1989 Colorado Dietetic, Colorado Dietetic Association, Denver, CO (Colorado)

Simply...The Best ©2000 by Kathleen Ledingham, Lake George, NY (New York)

Simply the Best Recipes, Mantanuska Telephone Association, Inc., Palmer, AK (Alaska)

Simply Whidbey ©1991 by Laura Moore and Deborah Skinner, Saratoga Publishers, Oak Harbor, WA (Washington)

Sing for Your Supper, Venetian Harmony Chorus, Englewood, FL (Florida)

Sisters Two II, Nancy Barth and Sue Gergert, Ashland, KS (Great Plains)

A Slice of Paradise ©1996 The Junior League of the Palm Beaches, Inc., West Palm Beach, FL (Florida)

Sooner Sampler ©1987 Junior League of Norman, Inc., Norman, OK (Oklahoma)

Soupçon II ©1974 The Junior League of Chicago, Inc., Chicago, IL (Illinois)

South Carolina's Historic Restaurants ©1984 by Dawn O'Brien and Karen Mulford, John F. Blair, Publisher, Winston-Salem, NC (South Carolina)

South Coastal Cuisine, Friends of the South Coastal Library, Bethany Beach, DE (Mid-Atlantic)

South Dakota Sunrise ©1997 by Tracy Winters, Bed & Breakfast Innkeepers of South Dakota, Greensburg, IN (Great Plains)

Southeastern Wildlife Cookbook ©1989 University of South Carolina Press, Columbia, SC (South Carolina)

Southern Secrets, University School of Jackson Mother's Club, Jackson, TN (Tennessee)

Spitfire Anniversary Cookbook, Quimby Spitfire Ladies Auxiliary, Quimby, IA (Iowa)

Spragg Family Cookbook, Karen Spragg, Ashton, ID (Idaho)

Contributors

St. Joseph's Table, St. Joseph's Catholic Church, Spearfish, SD (Great Plains)

St. Paul Cooks ©1986 Cookbook Publishers, Inc., St. Paul Christian Academy, Nashville, TN (Tennessee)

St. Philomena School 125th Anniversary, St. Philomena Home & School Association, Labadieville, LA (Louisiana II)

Stir Crazy! ©1986 Junior Welfare League of Florence, SC (South Carolina)

Stir Ups © Junior Welfare League of Enid, OK (Oklahoma)

Stirring Performances ©1988 The Junior League of Winston-Salem, Inc., Winston-Salem, NC (North Carolina)

Take Two & Butter 'Em While They're Hot! ©1998 Native Ground Music, Barbara Swell, Asheville, NC (West Virginia)

A Taste from Back Home ©1983 by Barbara Wortham, Marathon International Book Company, Louisville, KY (Kentucky)

A Taste of Christ Lutheran, Christ Lutheran WELCA, Sharon, WI (Wisconsin)

A Taste of Hallowell, Alice Arlen, Hallowell, ME (New England)

A Taste of Montana ©1999 by Tracy Winters, Montana Bed & Breakfast Association, Winters Publishing, Greensburg, IN (Big Sky)

A Taste of New England ©1990 Junior League of Worcester, Inc., Worcester, MA (New England)

A Taste of Newport, Shank Painter Publishing Co., Provincetown, MA (New England)

A Taste of Salt Air & Island Kitchens, Ladies Auxiliary of the Block Island Volunteer Fire Department, Block Island, RI (New England)

A Taste of Tradition, Sandra Nagler, Georgetown, DE (Mid-Atlantic)

Taste the Good Life! Nebraska Cookbook, Morris Press, Kearney, NE (Great Plains)

Tastefully Oregon ©1996 Oregon Dietetic Association, Portland, OR (Oregon)

Tasty Temptations, The Ladies Auxiliary of Knights of Columbus, Fremont, CA (California)

Tasty Temptations from the Village by the Sea, Holy Redeemer Guild, West Chatham, MA (New England)

Texas Barbecue ©1994 Pig Out Publications, Paris Parmenter and John Bigley, Kansas City, MO (Texas II)

Think Healthy, Fairfax County Department of Extension, Fairfax, VA (Virginia)

Thomas Jefferson's Cook Book ©1976 The Rector and Visitors of the University of Virginia, Marie Kimball, The University Press of Virginia, Charlottesville, VA (Virginia)

Tidewater on the Half Shell ©1985 Junior League of Norfolk-Virginia Beach, Inc., Norfolk, VA (Virginia)

To Market, To Market ©1984 The Junior League of Owensboro, Inc., Owensboro, KY (Kentucky)

Tony Chachere's Cajun Country Cookbook, Tony Chachere, Opelousas, LA (Louisiana)

Tony Clark's New Blueberry Hill Cookbook ©1990 by Arlyn Patricia Hertz and Anthony Clark, Edited by Arlyn Patricia Hertz, Down East Books, Camden, ME (New England)

Treasured Alabama Recipes ©1967 by Kathryn Tucker Windham, Selma, AL (Alabama)

Try Me ©1984 Arthritis Volunteer Action Committee, Arthritis Foundation, Mobile, AL (Alabama)

Tumm Yummies, Y-Wives, Tiffin, OH (Ohio)

Two Hundred Years of Charleston Cooking ©1976 University of South Carolina, Columbia, SC (South Carolina)

Uptown Down South ©1986 Greenville Junior League Publications, Greenville, SC (South Carolina)

Vermont Kitchens Revisited ©1990 Vermont Kitchen Publications, Burlington, VT (New England)

Village Royale: Our Favorite Recipes, Nancy Carden, Boynton Beach, FL (Florida)

Visions of Home Cook Book, York Hospital, York, ME (New England)

Vistoso Vittles II, Sun City Vistoso, Oro Valley, AZ (Arizona)

Wandering & Feasting ©1996 Board of Regents of Washington State University, Mary Houser Caditz, Washington State University Press, Pullman, WA (Washington)

Wannaska Centennial, Riverside Lutheran Church, Wannaska, MN (Minnesota)

Washington Cook Book ©1994 Golden West Publishers, Janet Walker, Phoenix, AZ (Washington)

Washington Street Eatery Cook Book ©1993 Washington Street Eatery Cookbook, Kathleen Tolagian and Lu-Ann Paquette Neff, Greenland, NH (New England)

The Way Pocahontas County Cooks ©1996 Pocahontas Communications Cooperative Corporation, Dunmore, WV (West Virginia)

West of the Rockies ©1994 The Grand Junction Junior Service League, Grand Junction, CO (Colorado)

THE What in the World are we Going to Have For Dinner? COOKBOOK ©1987 by Sarah E. Drummond, Richmond, VA (Virginia)

What's Cookin', Jeanne E. Briggs, Rockford, MI (Michigan)

What's Cookin' in Melon Country, Rocky Ford Chamber of Commerce, Rocky Ford, CO (Colorado)

What's Cooking "Down Home" ©1992 by Eileen Mears, Greenfield, IL (Illinois)

What's Cooking Inn Arizona ©1996 by Tracy M. Winters and Phyllis Y. Winters, Winters Publishing, Greensburg, IN (Arizona)

Why Not for Breakfast? ©1993 by Nancy J. Hawkins, Cape May, NJ (Mid-Atlantic)

Wild Alaska Seafood—Twice a Week ©2003 by Evie Hansen, National Seafood Education, Richmond Beach, WA (Alaska)

Winterthur's Culinary Collection ©1983 The Henry Francis duPont Winterthur Museum, Inc., Winterthur, DE (Mid-Atlantic)

With Lots of Love ©2002 by Taydie Drummond, A. Drummond Ranch B & B, Cheyenne, WY (Big Sky)

With Special Distinction ©1993 Mississippi College Cookbook, Mississippi College, Clinton, MS (Mississippi)

Wolf Point, Montana 75th Jubilee Cookbook, Jubilee Cookbook Committee, Wolf Point, MT (Big Sky)

Worth Savoring ©1997 The Union County Historical Society, New Albany, MS (Mississippi)

Wyoming Cook Book ©1998 Golden West Publishers, Phoenix, AZ (Big Sky)

Y Cook? ©1994 The Fargo-Moorhead YWCA, Fargo, ND (Great Plains)

Yaak Cookbook, The Yaak Women's Club, Troy, MT (Big Sky)

You're Hot Stuff, Flo! ©1995 STAMPEDE, Inc., Jerry Palen, The Saratoga Publishing Group, Inc., Saratoga, WY (Big Sky)

Index

Index

Index

Index

State Cookbook Series

All cookbooks are 6x9 inches, ringbound, contain photographs, illustrations, index, and 300–500 recipes. See "We Did It!" section for how all these recipes were collected.

Best of the Best from
ALABAMA
288 pages

Best of the Best from
ALASKA
288 pages

Best of the Best from
ARIZONA
288 pages

Best of the Best from
ARKANSAS
288 pages

Best of the Best from
BIG SKY
Montana and Wyoming
288 pages

Best of the Best from
CALIFORNIA
384 pages

Best of the Best from
COLORADO
288 pages

Best of the Best from
FLORIDA
288 pages

Best of the Best from
GEORGIA
336 pages

Best of the Best from the
GREAT PLAINS
North and South Dakota, Nebraska, and Kansas
288 pages

Best of the Best from
HAWAI‘I
288 pages

Best of the Best from
IDAHO
288 pages

Best of the Best from
ILLINOIS
288 pages

Best of the Best from
INDIANA
288 pages

Best of the Best from
IOWA
288 pages

Best of the Best from
KENTUCKY
288 pages

Best of the Best from
LOUISIANA
288 pages

Best of the Best from
LOUISIANA II
288 pages

Best of the Best from
MICHIGAN
288 pages

Best of the Best from the
MID-ATLANTIC
Maryland, Delaware, New Jersey, and Washington, D.C.
288 pages

Best of the Best from
MINNESOTA
288 pages

Best of the Best from
MISSISSIPPI
288 pages

Best of the Best from
MISSOURI
304 pages

Best of the Best from
NEVADA
288 pages

Best of the Best from
NEW ENGLAND
Rhode Island, Connecticut, Massachusetts, Vermont, New Hampshire, and Maine
368 pages

Best of the Best from
NEW MEXICO
288 pages

Best of the Best from
NEW YORK
288 pages

Best of the Best from
NO. CAROLINA
288 pages

Best of the Best from
OHIO
352 pages

Best of the Best from
OKLAHOMA
288 pages

Best of the Best from
OREGON
288 pages

Best of the Best from
PENNSYLVANIA
320 pages

Best of the Best from
SO. CAROLINA
288 pages

Best of the Best from
TENNESSEE
288 pages

Best of the Best from
TEXAS
352 pages

Best of the Best from
TEXAS II
352 pages

Best of the Best from
UTAH
288 pages

Best of the Best from
VIRGINIA
320 pages

Best of the Best from
WASHINGTON
288 pages

Best of the Best from
WEST VIRGINIA
288 pages

Best of the Best from
WISCONSIN
288 pages

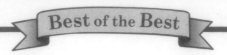

Recipe Hall of Fame Cookbook Collection

   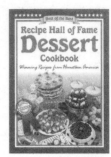

The extensive recipe database of Quail Ridge Press' acclaimed BEST OF THE BEST STATE COOKBOOK SERIES is the inspiration behind the RECIPE HALL OF FAME COOKBOOK COLLECTION. These HALL OF FAME recipes have achieved extra distinction for consistently producing superb dishes. Appetizers to desserts, quick dishes to masterpiece presentations, the recipes in this collection are the **Best** of the BEST OF THE BEST.

The Recipe Hall of Fame Cookbook
Features over 400 choice dishes for a variety of meals.
304 pages • Paperbound • 7x10 • Illustrations • Index

Recipe Hall of Fame Dessert Cookbook
Consists entirely of more than 300 extraordinary desserts.
240 pages • Paperbound • 7x10 • Illustrations • Index

Recipe Hall of Fame Quick & Easy Cookbook
Contains over 500 recipes that require minimum effort but produce maximum enjoyment.
304 pages • Paperbound • 7x10 • Illustrations • Index

The Recipe Hall of Fame Cookbook II
Brings you more of the family favorites you've come to expect with over 400 all-new, easy-to-follow recipes.
304 pages • Paperbound • 7x10 • Illustrations • Index